D1595917

The Fall of Afghanistan

Pergamon Titles of Related Interest

Alsudairy FIVE WAR ZONES: THE VIEWS OF LOCAL
MILITARY LEADERS

Deibel & Gaddis CONTAINING THE SOVIET UNION:
A CRITIQUE OF U.S. POLICY

Eliot & Pfaltzgraff THE RED ARMY ON PAKISTAN'S BORDER:
POLICY IMPLICATIONS FOR THE UNITED
STATES

Joes FROM THE BARREL OF A GUN: ARMIES AND
REVOLUTIONS

Whelan & Dixon THE SOVIET UNION IN THE THIRD WORLD:
THREAT TO WORLD PEACE?

Related Journal

(Free specimen copy available upon request)

Defense Analysis

The Fall of Afghanistan

An Insider's Account

ABDUL SAMAD GHAUS
Former Deputy Foreign Minister of Afghanistan

PERGAMON-BRASSEY'S
INTERNATIONAL DEFENSE PUBLISHERS
(a member of the Pergamon Group)

WASHINGTON · NEW YORK · LONDON · OXFORD
BEIJING · FRANKFURT · SÃO PAULO · SYDNEY · TOKYO · TORONTO

U.S.A. (Editorial)	Pergamon-Brassey's International Defense Publishers, 8000 Westpark Drive, Fourth Floor, McLean, Virginia 22102, U.S.A.
(Orders)	Pergamon Press, Maxwell House, Fairview Park, Elmsford, New York 10523, U.S.A.
U.K. (Editorial)	Brassey's Defence Publishers, 24 Gray's Inn Road, London WC1X 8HR
(Orders)	Brassey's Defence Publishers, Headington Hill Hall, Oxford OX3 0BW, England
PEOPLE'S REPUBLIC OF CHINA	Pergamon Press, Room 4037, Qianmen Hotel, Beijing, People's Republic of China
FEDERAL REPUBLIC OF GERMANY	Pergamon Press, Hammerweg 6, D-6242 Kronberg, Federal Republic of Germany
BRAZIL	Pergamon Editora, Rua Eça de Queiros, 346, CEP 04011, Paraiso, São Paulo, Brazil
AUSTRALIA	Pergamon-Brassey's Defence Publishers, P.O. Box 544, Potts Point, N.S.W. 2011, Australia
JAPAN	Pergamon Press, 8th Floor, Matsuoka Central Building, 1-7-1 Nishishinjuku, Shinjuku-ku, Tokyo 160, Japan
CANADA	Pergamon Press Canada, Suite No. 271, 253 College Street, Toronto, Ontario, Canada M5T 1R5

Copyright ©1988 Pergamon-Brassey's International Defense Publishers, Inc.

First edition 1988

Library of Congress Cataloging in Publication Data
Ghaus, Abdul Samad.
The fall of Afghanistan.
Bibliography: p.
1. Afghanistan—Foreign relations.   I. Title.
DS357.5.G42   1987   327.581   86-30548

British Library Cataloguing in Publication Data
Ghaus, Abdul Samad
The fall of Afghanistan: an insider's account.
1. Afghanistan — Foreign relations
I. Title
327.581   DS357.5
ISBN 0-08-034701-0

Reproduced, printed and bound in Great Britain by Hazell Watson & Viney Limited Member of BPCC plc Aylesbury Bucks

This book is dedicated to the memory of those Afghan martyrs who fell to the Communist onslaught in the early hours of April 28, 1978.

Contents

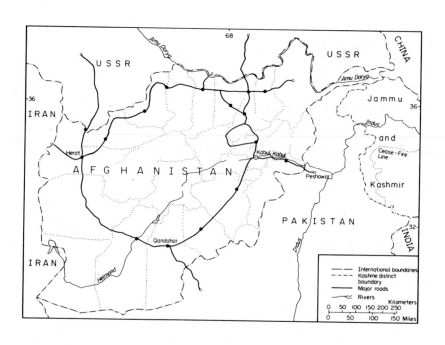

Preface

This book is of special significance for at least two reasons. First, it tells the story of Afghanistan's foreign policy and how that policy in the end failed to preserve Afghanistan's independence from its imperialist northern neighbor, the Soviet Union. In unfolding this tale, the book focuses on the period of the first Afghan Republic, which was inaugurated in 1973 with high hopes but was brought down in 1978 by Soviet-backed Communist insurgents. This story is one of great importance for what it teaches us about a small country whose freedom depends on its relationship with a superpower with which it shares a border.

Second, the author of this book, Abdul Samad Ghaus, is an experienced Afghan diplomat; in fact, he is the most senior official of the Afghan Foreign Ministry to survive the Communist *coup d'état* of April 1978. Particularly in the five years preceding that event, he was intimately involved in all major aspects of Afghan foreign policy, including top-level talks with the Soviet Union, the United States, and Pakistan. As an eyewitness to the tragic failure of Afghan policy, he is uniquely qualified to analyze the history and events that led to the downfall of independent Afghanistan. To my knowledge, this is the first such comprehensive history of Afghan foreign policy ever written by an Afghan, and it is the first such analysis of the republican period in particular.

There are two basic themes in this book. One is the Afghan effort to maintain independence from its imperialist neighbors. In the nineteenth and early twentieth centuries, Afghanistan pursued this goal while sandwiched between the expanding Russian and British empires. During this period it was able to survive by balancing the interests of the two superpowers against one another. Following the British withdrawal from India in 1947, the Afghans sought the help of other powers, especially the United States, to continue to offset the influence of the Russians. Samad Ghaus provides considerable insight into the failure of American policy, which aimed to preserve Afghan independence but had neither the will nor the means to achieve that aim.

The other major theme, which has received far too little attention in studies of international relations, is the situation of the Pashtun people, who, as a consequence of British imperialism, have been split between Afghanistan and Pakistan. Because the leaders of Afghanistan have themselves been Pashtuns and Pashtun territory in Pakistan was once part of Afghanistan, the fate of the

Pashtuns outside Afghanistan has long troubled Afghanistan's relations with, first, Great Britain and, since 1947, Pakistan. Whatever the merits of the dispute, it is a fact that it played a major part in creating opportunities for the Soviet Union in Afghanistan. Should the Soviets succeed in establishing their control over Afghanistan in the months and years to come, a revival of this as yet unresolved dispute could serve as a pretext for further Soviet aggression, against Pakistan.

For Americans and for all who are interested in limiting Soviet imperialism, this is therefore an important book. The Afghan freedom fighters are today fighting our battle. If they fail, the Soviets will be one step closer to the warm-water ports and oil resources they and their czarist predecessors have so long coveted.

I have known Abdul Samad Ghaus since shortly before I arrived in Afghanistan to serve as United States ambassador in November 1973. At that time, he was director of the United Nations and International Conferences Department of the Afghan Foreign Ministry. In 1976 he became director general of political affairs, and early in 1977 he was promoted to deputy foreign minister. He was the last Afghan official I had contact with as Communist tanks rolled into Kabul on April 27, 1978. Following the Communist coup, he was placed under house arrest. In 1980, he was imprisoned. He was finally able to reach the United States in March 1981. President Mohammad Daoud, his brother and foreign policy advisor Mohammad Naim, and the minister in charge of foreign affairs, Waheed Abdullah, were all executed by the Communists; thus, Ghaus is the most senior survivor of Daoud's foreign policy team.

During the course of our friendship, I have known Samad as an Afghan patriot, an accomplished diplomat, and a man of integrity. It was a happy moment when we agreed that he should undertake the writing of this book. It has not been an easy task for him because he was unable to bring any files with him from Afghanistan. He has had to rely on his memory, checking it against published sources, where available, and the memories of other participants, in those few instances where others also survive. For Americans and for all who are interested in limiting Soviet imperialism, I repeat, this is therefore an important book.

I want to thank the Asia, Earhart Hearst, and A. W. Mellon Foundations; the Institute for Foreign Policy Analysis; and a number of private individuals for their support of this project. The Fletcher School of Law and Diplomacy, of which I was then the dean, gave Ghaus a Research Associateship to enable him to write this book.

THEODORE L. ELIOT, JR.

Acknowledgments

My friend Theodore L. Eliot, the former United States Ambassador to Kabul, suggested that I write a book about the diplomatic history of my country, Afghanistan, that would encompass, in particular, the foreign relations of the first Afghan Republic, with which I was closely associated. I confess that the idea had crossed my mind and that, to prepare the groundwork for such an eventuality, I had busied myself since leaving Afghanistan with putting on paper all that I still vividly remembered of Mohammad Daoud and other Afghan leaders' reflections, conversations, exchanges, and speeches and the proceedings of some of the talks between Afghan high officials and representatives of other countries. But I really did not know when I would actually start writing this book. Ted's suggestion had the merit of focusing my attention on the timeliness of such an undertaking and besides made me realize that at least one other person whose opinion I highly prized, Ted Eliot, believed in its usefulness. To me that was sufficient encouragement. I readily accepted what he had suggested. Secretarial and other logistical help for the project on which we had agreed was provided by him within the framework of The Fletcher School of Law and Diplomacy, of which he was then dean.

Now that this book has finally been written, my most cordial acknowledgments must go to Ted Eliot, without whose unfailing encouragement and support it is doubtful whether this project would ever have materialized and been brought to a satisfactory conclusion.

My wife Zulikha typed the first draft of the manuscript. This was a welcome contribution to the progress of my work, of which she had always been affectionately supportive. Ms. Alberta Langley of The Fletcher School typed the final draft, and, after completion of editorial work on the manuscript, Ms. Hedwig Drake, also of Fletcher, incorporated my final changes and corrections into the text and ran the whole book through the word processor. I wish to warmly thank the two ladies for their help and cooperation.

I wish also to thank those staff members of The Fletcher School with whom I came in contact during my work on the book for their kindness and assistance. Finally I want to convey my gratitude to the institutions and individuals who extended their support to this project.

1

The Evolution of a Buffer State

The possession of India has always held a strange fascination for the great Asian and European empire builders. To those conquerors who succeeded in incorporating India or parts of it into their dominions, the securing of these lands against other foreign intruders became a prime consideration, almost an end in itself. Of the alien occupiers of India, perhaps none was more sensitive to this outside threat than the British. As British rule in the nineteenth century expanded into northwestern India, its defense increasingly occupied the minds of the British rulers. In fact, their concern for the defense of India began to determine the formulation of their eastern policies, if not their foreign policy altogether. British sensitivity in this regard grew rapidly with the emergence of czarist Russia as a dynamic imperial power in central Asia and its seemingly inexorable southward move.

By the mid-nineteenth century Russia's threat to the subcontinent and its desire to reach the warm waters of the Indian Ocean were generally accepted as realities in Britain and India. With the exception of short intervals during World War I and World War II, this British perception of czarist danger to India and later of the Soviet menace to that country remained constant until 1947, when Britain's rule in India came to an abrupt end.

Thus, as soon as the two European empires, Russia and Britain, began facing each other in central Asia, although still from a respectable distance, fear of a Russian advance into India prompted the British rulers to turn their most serious attention to the regions that lay between the areas that Britain had reached in northern India and the shifting frontiers of the czarist empire. In fact the British realized, as the previous rulers of India had known, that "the safety of India depends on the degree of control which the rulers of India can exert on the mountains of Hindu Kush and the Oxus Valley beyond, for only thus can the 'barbarian' be kept at arm's length."[1]*

On the basis of this consideration, the British sought to maintain outposts and adequate influence in the peripheral regions, with a view to monitoring

_____

* Superscript numbers refer to Notes at end of chapters

1

Russia's movements and eventually forestalling its advance. These preoccupations led the British to interfere openly in the internal affairs of the states and principalities situated between Russia and them, often to the detriment of those areas' independence. Afghanistan, which lay directly in the path of an eventual Russian advance from the northwest and whose strategic significance in relation to the Russian Asian empire was becoming increasingly clear, came to be particularly affected by these British preoccupations. The British interfered extensively in the internal affairs of Afghanistan and twice during the nineteenth century occupied it militarily.

The British push toward Afghanistan and occupation of advanced positions there came to be called *forward policy*. This policy was at times discontinued in favor of a more restrained *masterly inactivity*, but it was clear that the latter attitude merely meant the forswearance of *military* intervention and occupation and not the total cessation of *political* interference. Then, for the sake of the defense of India, a time came when the British were ready to test the merits of a third formula: the establishment of Afghanistan as a buffer state between the Russian empire and India. This scheme will be dealt with in more detail later in this chapter.

The forward policy was first evidenced in British preparations for invading Afghanistan in 1838. The events leading up to the invasion actually began in 1837, when the Persians, who had fallen under the overwhelming influence of czarist Russia after the Treaty of Turkmanchoi, moved to capture the Afghan city of Herat at the western end of the Hindu Kush. British strategists, who had come to consider Herat as one of the bastions of the defense of India, believed that the Persian move was encouraged by the czarist government. But when, in December of 1838, British forces were finally ordered to march against Afghanistan, the unsuccessful Persian siege of Herat had already been lifted. The fact that the invasion took place when the Persians were no longer in the vicinity of Herat demonstrates that it was mainly motivated by considerations of forward policy and one of its requirements of the moment, namely the substitution of the ruler of Afghanistan, Amir Dost Mohammad Khan, whom the British had come to consider hostile to them and friendly to the Russians, with a more docile potentate who would facilitate the establishment of British dominance in Afghanistan.

That the amir had grown disenchanted with the British and was seeking a rapprochement with the Russians could not be denied. However, this shift in his attitude had occurred when the British responded negatively to his request for support in the recovery of the Afghan lands on the west bank of the Indus, including the city of Peshawar, which had recently been lost by the Afghans to the Sikhs.

At the end of April 1839 the British occupied Kandahar and, at the beginning of August, the city of Kabul. Amir Dost Mohammad Khan surrendered and was exiled by the British to India. This first invasion of Afghanistan, however, ended disastrously for the British when, in 1842,

William H. Macnaghten, the British Resident in Kabul, was killed. The British puppet Shah Shuja, whom the British had brought with them from exile in India and installed on the Afghan throne, was killed by the people of Kabul.[2] The turmoil created by the British invasion subsided only when the British rulers of India agreed to Amir Dost Mohammad Khan's return to Kabul. Dost ascended the Afghan throne once again in early 1843.

During the second period of his reign, apart from a brief campaign against a British army in the Punjab undertaken in association with his former enemies, the Sikhs, no major conflict occurred between Dost Mohammad and the government of India. The amir was by this time more experienced in British imperial ways and more aware of the geopolitically sensitive position of Afghanistan. He had undoubtedly concluded that it was in the best interest of his rule to refrain from any dealings with Russia and to desist, for the time being, from any endeavor aimed at regaining the Afghan territories on the west bank of the Indus, especially now that those territories had been taken from the Sikhs by the mighty British and incorporated into their empire. But the Afghan claim to those lands inhabited by the Pashtuns, kith and kin of the Afghans, was never given up by subsequent Afghan rulers. This claim became the Afghan irredentism that, over the years, profoundly influenced the direction of Afghanistan's foreign policy.

Meanwhile, Russia's advance into central Asia was continuing unabated. The British sought an explanation on several occasions from the czarist government as to where it finally intended to stop. Prince Gorchakov, the imperial Russian chancellor, issued a memorandum in 1864 in which he explained the motives for the Russian advance and assured the other powers that the line reached at that time was considered by the czarist government to be the outer limits of the empire. Gorchakov's memorandum was a typical nineteenth-century imperial document, attempting to convey the impression that the whole of central Asia was populated by half-savage tribes and that Russian territorial expansion was only accidental, its main purposes being the security of the people inside the Russian frontiers and the propagation of Western civilization.

However, whether the Asians were willing to accept Western civilization in return for their freedom was not discussed in the memorandum. According to the Russian rationalization, the wandering Asiatic tribes would start raiding and pillaging the people inside Russian territory. This state of affairs would compel the government to punish them and, for the sake of security, to annex their territory. After a while, the newly acquired territory would become exposed to the aggression of more distant tribes. The state would be obliged once again to defend the population by mounting a new expedition and punishing those who committed aggression. Thus the cycle of punishment and annexation continued and so did the expansion of Russian territory. It was evident that Gorchakov, by circulating his memorandum, was asking for understanding and even appreciation of Russian expansionist policies in Asia.

The greatest difficulty, according to the memorandum, was "in knowing when to stop." The memorandum went on to announce that the actual line reached, just short of the community of Khokand, was the limit of Russian expansion in Asia.[3] However, the ink on Gorchakov's memorandum had hardly dried when the Russians invaded Khokand and occupied it.

Thus, the Gorchakov memorandum lacked any validity. One author has written that this extraordinary document either was a masterpiece of deception or St. Petersburg was totally unable to control its commanders on the frontiers. The British government renewed its efforts to extract from the Russians some formal assurances as to their ultimate goal. At the same time, the British attempted to induce the Russians to accept the maintenance of a "neutral zone" or "belt of independent states" between the two empires in Asia as a means of preserving them from potentially antagonistic contact.

This idea of a neutral zone or belt of independent states, precursor of the buffer arrangements of later years, had been occasionally aired by prominent British statesmen. In 1869, the British foreign secretary recommended to the Russian ambassador in London "the recognition of some territory as neutral between the possessions of England and Russia."[4] Lord Mayo, the viceroy of India, suggested in 1870 that

[A]s it is for the interests of both countries that a wide border of independent states should exist between the British frontier and the Russian boundary, it would be desirable that Russia should be invited to adopt the policy with regard to Khiva and other kindred States (Bokhara and Khokand) that we are willing to pledge ourselves to adopt towards Kalat, Afghanistan and the districts around Yarkent. A pledge of mutual non-interference of this kind, unratified by treaty, would be alike honourable to both nations, and would be better suited to the position in which civilized powers must ever stand towards wild and savage tribes than any specific treaty engagements could ever be.[5]

As the British probing of St. Petersburg's intentions continued, it became apparent that, in a settlement, the czarist government wanted the rich northern plains of Afghanistan, including the region of Badakhshan, to be included in its domains. If that were not feasible, the Russians felt it should be recognized that they had the right to extend their control at least to the ill-defined northern Afghan border. The British realized that, sooner or later, the inclusion of the trans-Oxus lands in the czarist empire would become a fait accompli. That being Russia's goal, it obviously could not be expected to accept the establishment of a neutral zone or belt of independent states that would extend beyond the northern borders of Afghanistan. The British therefore understood that their most urgent task in their dealings with the Russians was to obtain at least the maintenance of Afghanistan's integrity, even if that meant Russian occupation of the whole area north of the Oxus.

This trend in British thinking created a favorable impression in St. Petersburg. As the subject of a proposed neutral zone or belt of independent states (which, in the British view included, besides Afghanistan, some of the trans-Oxus lands) dropped from Russo–British exchanges, the Russian government agreed that Afghanistan was outside its sphere of influence and that it could constitute a distinct entity between the two empires. By adhering to that position, moreover, the Russians implicitly conceded that the northern border of Afghanistan would be the limit of their territorial expansion in central Asia. That position freed the Russians from any scruples they might have entertained concerning the extension of their dominion to the banks of the Oxus.

After protracted negotiations and the exchange of voluminous correspondence, the two powers signed the Russo–British Agreement on Afghanistan in 1873. This was the first major agreement between the two powers concerning Afghanistan, and it came to be known as the Clarendon–Gorchakov Agreement. In it Russia accepted the exclusion of Afghanistan from its zone of influence and recognized a frontier between Afghanistan and its own future annexations in central Asia. British Prime Minister Gladstone had this to say in the House of Commons about the 1873 agreement: "The engagement referred solely to the moral influence possessed by England and Russia in the East; Russia engaging to abstain from an attempt to exercise it in Afghanistan and England engaging to exercise it for a pacific purpose."[6] In fact, a bargain had been struck. In return for British acquiescence to Russian subjugation of the lands beyond Afghanistan's northern border, the Russians recognized that country as falling outside their sphere of influence and within that of the British.

It is ironic to note that the agreement of 1873 did not provide the British with the peace of mind they were seeking, because it did not allay their fears as to the ultimate goal of Russian expansionism. Consequently, the British were still interested in Russian moves in central Asia, and every new Russian advance aroused British concern over India.

By 1878 the Russians had absorbed or vassalized most of the independent or semi-independent principalities and khanates of central Asia, and their influence extended to the Oxus River, the northern frontier of Afghanistan. As a result of the outbreak of hostilities between Russia and Turkey in 1877, an Anglo–Russian war in the Balkans seemed imminent. Because of the emergence of this new crisis in Anglo–Russian relations, the Russians undoubtedly wished to secure the friendship of the Afghan ruler Amir Sher Ali Khan (a son of Dost Mohammad Khan) as part of their diplomatic offensive against Britain. Consequently, in the summer of 1878, a Russian diplomatic mission was sent to Afghanistan to make to the Afghan amir "certain important communications with reference to the then existing relations between Russia and Britain and their bearing on the position of Afghanistan."[7] Although, thanks to the efforts exerted by the Congress of Berlin, the danger of war in Europe had passed before the mission met with the Afghan amir in Kabul, no attempt was made by the czarist authorities to stop the mission or to recall it. The presence of the Russian mission in Kabul, the capital of the country, which by then, in the British view, formed an integral part of the defense of

India, provided high officials in Calcutta with an excellent opportunity to punish Amir Sher Ali Khan, whom they suspected of conniving with the Russians against British interests.

Thus, in the fall of 1878, British armies invaded Afghanistan a second time, in another surge of forward policy, occupying Jalalabad and Kandahar. The imperatives of the defense of India had warranted abandonment of the policy of masterly inactivity that had been followed with regard to Afghanistan since the second part of Amir Dost Mohammad Khan's reign. It can reasonably be assumed that the government of India's objective this time was threefold: (1) to remove an independent-minded monarch, (2) to establish a "scientific frontier" for India along the Hindu Kush range, and (3) to achieve a more permanent solution to the Afghan problem.

The British invasion prompted Amir Sher Ali Khan to request military assistance from the Russians. But his request was turned down; he then left Kabul with the departing Russian mission. Sher Ali died in February 1879 in Mazar-i-Sharif, a city in the northern part of Afghanistan.

The British found in the amir's son, Yaqub Khan, a more docile and malleable monarch. In May 1879 they concluded the Treaty of Gandomak with him, by which he agreed that the British would retain control of the Khyber Pass and of the districts of Kurram, Pishin, and Sibi. From the British standpoint, perhaps the most important clause of the treaty was the amir's acceptance of a permanent British representative of English descent in Kabul and of other British agents elsewhere in Afghanistan as determined by the government of India. Since the end of the first Anglo–Afghan war, this British demand had always been resolutely opposed by Afghan rulers. The treaty also contained a provision that committed the amir to conduct his relations with foreign states through the government of India. At the conclusion of the treaty, the British agreed to pay Amir Yaqub Khan an annual monetary subsidy.

In accordance with the provisions of the Treaty of Gandomak, a British mission headed by Louis Cavagnari established itself in Kabul. After a few weeks of relative calm, the Afghans once again reacted to the invasion of their country and to the presence of the English mission, whose leader acted as the de facto ruler of Afghanistan. In the ensuing revolt, Cavagnari and the members of his mission were massacred. British armies then marched and reoccupied the cities of Jalalabad and Kandahar, which had been evacuated after the signing of the treaty. They also occupied Kabul. Amir Yaqub Khan, who was bitterly despised by the Afghan people, abdicated and fled to India.

The British then took great advantage of the resulting gap in Afghan leadership. In the absence of a legitimate Afghan ruler, most of Afghanistan south of the Hindu Kush came under direct British military rule. In this manner, then, British power had finally reached the great Hindu Kush barrier, considered by many prominent people in England and in India to be the "scientific frontier" of their Indian empire. There is no doubt that British statesmen at this point seriously believed in the dismemberment of Afghanistan as a means of better controlling the country. Kandahar was to be given to a Sadozai chief under British suzerainty. Herat and Seistan were to be annexed by Persia, which by then had been wrested from the Russian grip. Central and eastern Afghanistan were to be administered directly by the British until an Afghan ruler acceptable to both the Afghans and them could be found. As such a person was apparently difficult to find, the consensus was that the British would be in charge of those areas for a long time. From what is known of the official thinking of the period, it can be reasonably assumed that the eventual annexation of the central and eastern regions of Afghanistan by British India was seriously considered. Lord Lytton, the viceroy of India at that time, was even in favor of creating a western Afghan kingdom that would eventually include Herat, Balkh, Merv, and Kandahar and that would be ruled by an Afghan under direct British supervision. Thus, the Hindu Kush mountains, Herat and Kandahar, considered by the British to be bastions of the defense of India, would have been secured and the forward policy would have drawn to its logical conclusion.

While British statesmen in Calcutta and London were deliberating the strategic advantages of the "frontier on the Hindu Kush," they were assuredly aware that their selection of that option would amount to nothing less than an open invitation to the Russians to push their frontier southward, down to the great mountain range of central Afghanistan. Perhaps the grave consequences of the potential Russian presence on the Hindu Kush, coupled with increasing unrest among the Afghan people, the enormous financial burden of the occupation, and the reluctance of the Persians to accept the city of Herat and all of Seistan had a sobering effect on the British. In a curious policy reversal, the British decided to evacuate Afghanistan, with the exception of Kandahar, and to let the Afghans retain the province of Herat. The efforts to find an Afghan ruler to whom the destinies of Afghanistan could be entrusted were suddenly redoubled.

In March 1880, Sardar Abdul Rahman Khan, son of Mohammad Afzal Khan (a half brother of Sher Ali Khan, who had briefly occupied the throne at the death of his father, Amir Dost Mohammad Khan), crossed from Russian Turkestan into Afghanistan in a bid for the Afghan throne. Although the British did not know the sardar well and entertained some doubts as to his allegiances, they were quick to open negotiations with him. Abdul Rahman Khan was informed by the British at the outset that, while he was free to extend his authority over the whole of Afghanistan, including Herat, the province of Kandahar was excluded from among its possessions. It was also made clear to him that control of his foreign relations would remain in British hands, in return for which the British pledged to defend him against unprovoked aggression. The matter of stationing British agents in Kabul and elsewhere in Afghanistan was dropped, and it was left to Abdul Rahman Khan's discretion whether to accept a British envoy of Islamic faith at a future date. The negotiations culminated in acceptance by the sardar of the conditions put forward by the British and led to an alliance embodied in an agreement that came to be called the Anglo–Afghan Agreement of 1880. This agreement consisted of three letters exchanged between Lepel H. Griffin, the foreign secretary of India, and Sardar Abdul Rahman Khan. In July 1880, Abdul Rahman Khan, to whom the British had already pledged their support, proclaimed himself amir and was recognized as such by the government of India. The people of Afghanistan reluctantly acquiesced in that proclamation. The British armies were promptly withdrawn from Kabul and Jalalabad.

At about the same time, a British force was defeated near Maiwand in the Kandahar region by Sardar Mohammad Ayub Khan, a son of Amir Sher Ali Khan. Although the city of Kandahar was not occupied by Ayub Khan, the Afghan victory demonstrated British vulnerability. Probably this event, and the rising opposition in London to the retention of Kandahar, moved the British government to rescind its decision to rule the province through a Sadozai proxy. Shortly afterward, Kandahar was evacuated by the British. The Khyber Pass, the Kurram Valley, the districts of Pishin and Sibi, all part and parcel of the Afghan homeland, were retained by Britain as ceded to it by the Treaty of Gandomak. The defense of India fell back on the fortress mountains of Suleiman and Safed Koh. Amir Abdul Rahman Khan occupied Kandahar and, later, Herat. To strengthen the amir's position, the government of India agreed in 1882 to pay him an annual subsidy.

While the British viewed the Russian southward drive with alarm, the Russians were likewise quite suspicious of the British northward advance. The two invasions of Afghanistan in particular had strengthened the Russian belief that Britain was determined to establish itself along the Hindu Kush and that it would eventually push the northwestern border of India to Herat, and perhaps up to Merv. From the Russian standpoint, the advent of such a situation would be detrimental to the safety of Russian possessions and to Russia's favorable position in the commercial markets of central Asia. In this light, although Russia's expansion toward the warm waters of the south was essentially motivated by the resolve to follow its manifest destiny, some of its conquests in central Asia, or at least their timing, could have been defensive reactions to episodes of British forward policy. The Second Afghan War "and the strong probability that the British would shortly push their administered frontiers forward to Herat and the Hindu Kush stimulated the Russians in their advance to the Arkhal oasis [in June 1879]. They reached it while the British were still in Qandahar."[8] One other interesting aspect of Russia's southward advance can be ascertained from the following passage from the instructions issued to the Baron de Stael by the Russian Foreign Office when he was appointed ambassador to London in 1884:

Great historical lessons have taught us that we cannot count on the friendship of England, and that she can strike at us by means of continental alliances while we cannot reach her anywhere. No great nation can accept such a position. In order to escape from it the Emperor Alexander II of everlasting memory ordered our expansion in Central Asia, leading us to occupy today in Turkestan and the Turkestan steppes a military position strong enough to keep England in check by the threat of intervention in India.[9]

It is difficult to determine the extent to which the Russian Arkhal expedition was one of the factors that prompted the British to evacuate Afghanistan. But that southward move most probably consolidated the thinking of some influential statesmen in Britain and India who wanted to keep the greatest possible distance between the czar's central Asian possessions and the northwestern border of India.

The 1873 agreement had strengthened the idea of transforming Afghanistan into a buffer state in central Asia between the British and Russian empires. When Britain evacuated Afghanistan in 1880 and entrusted its destinies to the new monarch, Amir Abdul Rahman Khan, that concept, as the British understood it, was ready for implementation.

The buffer formula, which, for all practical purposes, did not preclude control of Afghan affairs by the British, was a middle course between military occupation of Afghanistan and stoically waiting for Russian armies to enter the subcontinent. It also implied that the British northwestern push had, for a variety of reasons, finally come to an end and that Britain was now interested solely in defending its Indian possessions behind the shield of a buffer state. This implication of the buffer concept was one of its significant drawbacks. It was bound to convey a sense of retreat, and retreat for a first-class power could not be devoid of danger. But the British hoped that a combination of various elements, of which the assertive role of the Afghan ruler was not the least important, would preserve the viability of the buffer state and consequently the security of India.

The Russian Arkhal expedition had stopped short of the oasis of Merv, its logical objective in that expansionary episode, when the Russians learned that the British were evacuating the whole of Afghanistan. However, three years later, in 1884, Russia annexed Merv, despite all previous assurances to the contrary. At the time this event occurred, British forces had long since left Afghanistan, and there existed no direct British threat to Russia's central Asian possessions.

The British, to say the least, were uneasy about Russia's conquest of Merv, which they considered a threat to Herat, little more than two hundred flat and easily traversable miles to the south. Judging the Russians by their past performance, the British government believed that Russia would not stop at Merv and would sooner or later invade Herat. It was therefore essential to forestall Russia's further advance. The British government, basing its position on the relevant provisions of the 1873 agreement between Russia and Britain concerning the northern frontier of Afghanistan, wanted Russia to formally recognize a demarcated northern Afghan frontier, the western part of which was to constitute a clearly defined line between Herat and Merv. After months of stalling, the Russians agreed to negotiate.

While negotiations were underway in London and in St. Petersburg, the czarist empire once again moved southward. In March of 1885, Russia seized Panjdeh, an integral part of Afghanistan. Panjdeh was a district of Badghis, which in turn was part of the province of Herat. The Russian aim in capturing Panjdeh was quite clear. In doing so they were laying the groundwork for a move on Herat. They were also testing British determination, to ascertain whether Britain would categorically deny them any further territorial acquisitions in the region.

While an enthusiastic Russian press was exhorting the government not to stop and to push on to Herat, the British government and people reacted with a rare intensity to the fall of Panjdeh. Two army corps were mobilized in India. The House of Commons was asked to vote substantial war credits. British army engineers were dispatched to Herat to assist the Afghans in fortifying the city.

Taking stock of the seriousness of British preparations, the Russian government realized that Britain was determined not to allow it any further encroachment on Afghan territory and that another advance toward Herat would certainly mean war between the two empires. That unambiguous British attitude, and perhaps the rise of Germany in Europe as a formidable rival to both the czarist empire and Britain, prompted the Russians to adopt a conciliatory position. Russia halted its southward advance, waiting for more favorable times and conditions to resume it.

Boundary negotiations were reactivated. The line of the Russo–Afghan frontier, beginning at Zulfiquar in the west, running eastward between Merv and the province of Herat to the Oxus, and following that river to Lake Victoria and the Chinese frontier in the northeast, was formally agreed upon and demarcated in stages. The Russians retained Panjdeh in the process. During the protracted negotiations between Britain and Russia that led to the Frontier Agreement, the amir of Afghanistan was never more than a distant observer. In the end he had to accept what had been agreed upon in his absence.

When the northern border of Afghanistan was formally agreed upon in 1895, in the view of the British, two of the most important elements of a viable buffer state were at last in place. First, Amir Abdul Rahman Khan, a strong monarch whose foreign policy remained firmly under British control and who in all likelihood would prevent the spread of Russian influence, had been installed in Afghanistan. Second, the buffer state's formally recognized northern border, the violation of which would constitute a breach of international law, had become a reality. A third important element of the functional buffer, although abstract in nature, was finally locked into place when the British apparently perceived that their manifest determination not to allow Russia any further advance into Afghanistan was well understood in St. Petersburg and that, consequently, their unambiguous attitude in this regard would force the czarist government to honor its often reiterated 1873 pledge concerning Afghanistan's integrity.

The British defensive posture inherent in the decision to erect Afghanistan as a buffer, and Russia's desire at the time to keep Britain away from its Asian frontiers, had brought about a kind of strategic stability through mutual vulnerability. The effectiveness of Afghanistan as a buffer depended on Russian compliance with that buffer arrangement, and the British cautiously hoped that Russia understood the advantages accruing to the czarist empire from such an arrangement. The geopolitical situation of Afghanistan destined it to become a buffer par excellence. However, it could perform that role only so long as the two empires wanted it to function as such and so long as the Afghan rulers managed to preserve its independent identity by keeping a balance between the two European rivals.

The evolution of Afghanistan as a buffer between Russia and India had been a long and tenuous process. But in the early 1880s the British could look at the results with some satisfaction: the Indian empire seemed secure behind the formidable barrier of the buffer, a fluid situation had been stabilized, and, in all likelihood, the "Great Game" in central Asia had finally come to an end. So far as Afghanistan was concerned, with the acquisition of the status of a buffer, it slipped slowly into oblivion.

As a British protectorate, Afghanistan was kept economically weak and politically isolated. On various occasions the British professed that they wanted Afghanistan to be strong and independent. But a strong and independent Afghanistan meant one thing to them and quite another to the Afghan rulers and people. The Afghan rulers, during the heydey of British colonialism, were constantly reminded that their existence depended on the will and the tolerance of the British and that the fate of their country could even be decided in concert by London and St. Petersburg without consulting them. Consequently, the Afghan kings were so preoccupied with the preservation of their throne and Afghanistan's territorial integrity that not enough time, money, or energy could be devoted to development of the country.

While the British determination to keep foreign intruders away from India may have saved Afghanistan from being absorbed by the Russians in the nineteenth century, the defense of India nevertheless left deep and long-lasting scars on Afghanistan and its people. The two Anglo–Afghan wars, in addition to causing substantial loss of life and property, brought to the surface xenophobic sentiments that lingered for many years and proved powerful deterrents to Western-style reforms and innovations undertaken by Afghan rulers decades later. The high-handed and aggressive attitude of the British had convinced the population that they would not rest until Afghanistan, the last independent Islamic country of central Asia, was wiped off the map. This state of mind created resentment of the British, of Europeans, and of everything foreign.

Further, as a result of British and Russian incursions, Afghanistan lost territory to Russia in the north and to Britain in the east and southeast. In addition to the eastern Pashtun lands (which, in the not so distant past, had belonged to Afghanistan and whose inhabitants ethnically, religiously, and culturally were the same as Afghanistan's Pashtuns), Khyber, Kurram, Pishin, and Sibi were also incorporated into British India, and the so-called tribal area was erected as a buffer between India and Afghanistan. The Afghan claim to the eastern Pashtun lands was never taken seriously by the British. Despite Britain's reputation for having great knowledge of the East and its people, it never understood the reality and the depth of Afghan sentiment on this issue. By not attempting to settle the problem, which was an outgrowth of policies related to the defense of India, the British, perhaps inadvertently, sowed the seeds of discord between Afghanistan and the future state of Pakistan. The friction between the two countries brought about by the lingering existence of that colonial legacy helped pave the way for future Russian inroads into Afghanistan.

A Foreign Policy of Balance: The Mechanics of Survival

Amir Abdul Rahman Khan fully understood the precarious geographical situation of his country. The amir and his court generally believed that the policies of czarist Russia were offensive and aimed at the ultimate conquest of India and, thus, naturally, the occupation and destruction of Afghanistan. Because of this belief, the amir may have "feared Russia more than Great Britain, for he saw that the Russian advance was one of accretion and incorporation—in the manner of an elephant, as he put it, 'who examines a spot thoroughly before he places his foot down upon it, and when he once places his foot there, there is no going back.'"[10]

Some influential members of the court were of the opinion that British northwestern expansion had run its course and that, consequently, the English rulers did not feel any compulsion to annex parts of Afghanistan. This passive British posture, however, did not mean that the Afghans, including the amir, felt assured that Britain would never again violate Afghanistan's national territory. Past history bore testimony to the fact that, whenever the British felt a resumption of forward policy would best address a particular threat to India, considerations about the preservation of Afghanistan's territorial integrity never deterred them from moving into that country.

Afghanistan's geopolitical situation necessarily determined the Afghan ruler's foreign policy. His policy could be nothing other than the preservation of an independent Afghanistan as a buffer between the two rival empires. "Abdul Rahman knew that the powers that agreed to a buffer between their territories could also agree to divide the country; the existence of an independent buffer was desirable at that time, but not vital to his neighbors."[11]

To ensure the survival of Afghanistan as an independent entity, the amir embarked on a foreign policy aimed at keeping a certain balance between his two mighty neighbors. The cardinal requisite for the maintenance of that equilibrium was, in the amir's view, adherence to strict isolationism, in order to keep British and Russian influence out of the country. The British were to be convinced that they could count on Afghan friendship and that Afghanistan and India were complementary in the defense of India against Russia, the common enemy. They were to be made aware that Britain's too close ties with Afghanistan and its greater influence in that country would render Russia suspicious and might provoke it into aggression. On the other hand, the Russians were to be given no reason to doubt the amir's determination to preserve Afghanistan as an independent entity. They were to be given no opportunity to believe that Afghanistan would willingly open its territory to an invasion of Russian central Asia by Britain.

As a corollary to this policy of balance, it was important for the amir to demonstrate that the buffer was stable and indivisible and that its stability served to maintain peace and tranquility on the borders of Russia and India. Certainly one of the aims of the amir's internal consolidation of power was to achieve the kind of stability that would render the perpetuation of the buffer attractive to its neighbors. Undoubtedly the stability of Abdul Rahman Khan's Afghanistan contributed to the realization that the buffer was useful and to the advantage of the two empires. Yet the isolationism that the amir advocated to help safeguard his independence displeased the British, who wished to be treated as an ally and not kept at bay like the Russians.

The Anglo–Afghan Agreement of 1880 tilted the balance toward Britain. It was taken for granted that the Anglo–Russian Agreement of 1873 had made that tilt acceptable to the Russians. The Afghan ruler knew that the pro-British inclination had to be subtle and carefully monitored. The Afghan people were not to be given the slightest inkling that the British had assisted the amir in his accession to the throne, since that would certainly undermine his authority. It was likely that the amir's unequal alliance with Britain would bring about a situation whereby the strong could peacefully penetrate the weak, resulting eventually in complete integration. Great vigilance was therefore needed to ensure that British indirect control of Afghanistan did not exceed certain limits. These limits were determined by the amir himself. It was in this spirit that the amir, to the displeasure of the British, successfully opposed their demands for the extension of telegraph lines and a railway from India to locations in Afghanistan. Likewise, he never agreed to the stationing of British military advisers in his country. Although, a year after his accession to the throne, Amir Abdul Rahman reluctantly agreed to the appointment of a British envoy of Islamic faith, he never permitted him to properly discharge his duties, and he kept him isolated from the court and the Afghan people.

The amir also protested the extension of the British railroad to New Chaman (Baluchistan), and, when it was completed, he ordered his subjects not to use it. That boycott reduced the anticipated economic gains from the railroad. The British were extremely angry over the amir's stubborn stand on this matter. But the amir never reversed his decision because he knew that the real purpose of the railroad was to penetrate territories hitherto in dispute.

When Russia occupied Panjdeh in 1885, the amir and his people expected

Britain to come to their assistance. The ultimate British acceptance of the fait accompli angered the Afghans and opened to question Britain's determination to defend Afghanistan's territorial integrity. Although Amir Abdul Rahman Khan swallowed the bitter pill of Panjdeh, it can reasonably be assumed that his resentment of Britain greatly increased.

The amir also felt that his alliance with Britain obligated the latter to assist him with arms and military equipment. The reluctance of the British to respond satisfactorily to his requests for military hardware profoundly embittered him. The British feared that a substantial portion of the weapons furnished to Afghanistan would find its way to the tribal areas of the Frontier, as the area between Afghanistan and India was called. In the British view, this flow of arms from the amir to the Frontier Pashtuns would not only increase his prestige in the tribal areas but also provide impetus for Afghan irredentism and make the pacification of those regions much more difficult.

As time passed, relations between the amir and the British grew more strained. The major issue between them was, of course, the fate of the Frontier, or the eastern Pashtuns, whom the amir considered part of the Afghan nation. The amir felt that he was free to have open intercourse with them, and most of the eastern Pashtuns considered him, if not their sovereign, at least their spiritual leader. He provided them with guns and money, and, in return, they almost always heeded his call for jihad (holy war). Like all other Afghan rulers, Abdul Rahman Khan considered the Pashtun tribes one of the bulwarks of Afghanistan. He often used the tribes to pressure the British or to relieve pressure from them. In so doing he also indirectly demonstrated to the Russians the leverage that he could use in his dealings with Britain and his ascendancy in that sensitive region. Britain wanted the amir to desist from aiding and abetting the tribes in their anti-British activities and to recognize British sovereignty in the tribal areas. But, to their great disenchantment, the amir, while paying lip service to the British, never changed his basic attitude with respect to the Pashtun tribes.

A break in relations between Afghanistan and Britain seemed imminent in the second half of 1883, when Abdul Rahman Khan was asked by the government of India to receive a British representative empowered to conduct negotiations with a view to delimiting the frontier between Afghanistan and India. For some time, the British had been steadily escalating their military operations against the independent tribes in order to extend their influence over them. Meanwhile, resistance by the tribes was becoming increasingly effective. The British suspected that the amir had a hand in the concerted tribal response to their new forward policy. British Viceroy Lord Lansdowne, a proponent of the forward policy on the Frontier, was of the opinion that a majority of the problems related to disturbances in the tribal area could be solved by delimiting the frontier. In his view, the delimitation would, first, solve the issue of disputed territories and, second, enable the British more easily to disarm and control the tribes under their jurisdiction. Third, it would make it difficult for Afghan agents and weapons to reach the eastern Pashtuns.

Amir Abdul Rahman Khan refused to receive the British representative to discuss delimitation of the frontier. Lord Lansdowne reacted by ordering an embargo on all shipments of arms and metal to Afghanistan and, when the amir still did not change his mind, threatened him with military intervention. Thereupon, war preparations started in India. The amir, knowing full well how his country had suffered in the past from the consequences of British forward policy, adopted a more conciliatory attitude. He informed the government of India that it could send its representative.

In September 1893, Sir Mortimer Durand, the government of India's foreign secretary, arrived in Kabul carrying with him concrete British demands for a well-defined buffer zone between Afghanistan and India. The amir was horrified when he became acquainted with the nature and extent of those demands, according to which territories and people who since time immemorial had been considered part of the Afghan homeland and nation were arbitrarily included in British India. Some of the tribes and their lands were dissected, one part remaining attached to Afghanistan and the other given to India. Durand was not prepared to entertain the amir's objections, since the government of India had already decided upon the line that the frontier would follow. The amir soon realized that he was defending a lost cause and that, in fact, he had been confronted with an ultimatum. Disgusted with the heavy-handed, imperialistic handling of the matter by the government of India, he reluctantly agreed to the frontier as set by the British. Only two small districts that were to be given to India in the original British proposals were, in the end, given to Afghanistan.

On November 12, 1893, Abdul Rahman Khan signed, under duress, the frontier agreement known as the Durand Agreement. Thus, by British diktat, one nation and one land were cut in two, separated by an artificial frontier, the notorious Durand Line. The most disastrous effect of the agreement for the Afghans was that, by accepting it, the amir had in fact officially sanctioned British annexation of the lands east and south of the line, lands originally belonging to Afghanistan. Major parts of the line were demarcated on the ground the following year; some of its sections were never demarcated.

It is reasonable to assume that, had the amir not accepted the British demands, the hawks in Delhi would have once again ordered the invasion of Afghanistan. After the signing of the Durand Agreement, the government of India lifted the embargo against Afghanistan and increased the amir's annual subsidy. The amir, though shaken by what had taken place, knew realistically that British friendship was in Afghanistan's best interest. So the difficult alliance with Britain continued.

The Durand Line did not solve British problems in the frontier region, however. Tribal unrest continued, and the situation in those areas became increasingly serious. The tumult subsided only when Lord Curzon, the new viceroy of India, withdrew the British garrisons from those areas and returned the maintenance of law and order to the tribes themselves.

It is ironic that, during the long years of Abdul Rahman Khan's reign, his relations were more often strained with his British ally than with his undeclared Russian enemy. This was because the British would not refrain from trying to control events in Afghanistan, and Afghanistan would not desist from actively aiding and supporting the Pashtun tribes of the Frontier. So far as Russia was concerned, matters were simpler: The amir knew that any unilateral anti-Russian action by him would not be tolerated by the British, and the Russians were well aware that Britain would view with extreme displeasure any move by them against Afghanistan. After the Panjdeh aggression, apart from a few incidents in some northern frontier districts which concerned questions of jurisdiction, no Russian intervention occurred in Afghan territory. Occasionally, the amir caught and hanged a few Russian spies, to which the Russian authorities reacted by looking the other way. On the whole, the tenuous agreement of 1873 seemed to hold.

Although the amir's contractual engagement with Britain barred him from political intercourse with Russia, he did not find it advisable to adopt a hostile attitude toward his northern neighbor. Rather, the amir wished to project a neutral profile with regard to Russia. While he vehemently checked the spread of Russian influence and kept the northern Afghan border closed to Russian subjects, he permitted Afghan merchants to cross regularly into Russian Turkestan to carry on a lucrative business.

For his acceptance of the Durand Line, Amir Abdul Rahman Khan to this day stands accused by the people of Afghanistan, especially the intelligentsia, of betraying the Afghan nation and its vital interests. However, almost a century later, in the mid-1970s, Mohammad Daoud, the president of Afghanistan and one of the most outspoken opponents of the Durand Agreement, shared with me the following observation:

From the safe perspective of years it seems unpardonable that the Amir accepted the so-called Durand Line. But if one tries to imagine the tremendous pressures to which he must have been expose , and the knowledge that he had of British imperial ways, one tends to become more chari· ble and agree that those were really extenuating circumstances. By accepting the Durand Line , the Amir may have saved what remained of the Afghan territory. Thinking of the unenviable position in which the Amir found himself, one has to give him the benefit of the doubt.

Despite the stigma of the Durand Line, the amir succeeded in building a united Afghanistan and in giving the country a strong central power, including an administration, an army, and an embryonic industrial sector. He considered himself the ruler of an independent Afghanistan and allowed no interference by any power in the internal affairs of his country. So far as his foreign ties were concerned, he succeeded in circumventing the letter of the 1880 agreement by maintaining commercial representatives in Meshed, Bukhara, and Peshawar and by sending missions to Islamic countries. During the last years of his reign, the amir was actively seeking the establishment of formal relations with Islamic countries and openly promoting the cause of pan-Islamism. He also became increasingly insistent on having direct relations with London, not through the government of India.

The amir was often accused, as some other Afghan rulers were in later years, of playing off Russia against Britain to secure his survival. Those who voiced such criticisms failed to understand the predicament of a small state sandwiched between two rival giants, a small state that wished only to survive and prosper in peace.

Amir Abdul Rahman Khan, by implementing a foreign policy of balance, succeeded in preserving the integrity of Afghanistan. In treading the fine line between firmness and accommodation, he managed to limit British influence in his country and to prevent the spread of Russian influence. He excelled in the art of diplomacy; he knew what was possible and what was not.

As conditions changed, subsequent Afghan rulers modified the foreign policy of balance to adapt to new circumstances. But the basis of that policy remained essentially as laid down by the Iron Amir. It was a rational, consistent policy dictated by geopolitical realities, the constant of which was the preservation of Afghan independence. Former Afghan rulers had also discerned the necessity of adhering to a foreign policy of balance, but none of them had possessed the amir's strength and agility at formulating it so clearly and implementing it so adroitly.

Having ushered his country into the new century, Amir Abdul Rahman Khan died in Kabul on October 3, 1901. The political testament he left to his successor has not lost its relevance to this day.

Afghanistan is a country that will either rise to be a strong famous kingdom or will be swept altogether from the earth. In its present condition Afghanistan is of no use financially to any foreign government except for military service. In this last it can be of some use in helping a foreign government which may be crossing through Afghanistan to invade or attack another foreign country. But to keep possession of Afghanistan itself would not be a good investment for any foreign government for at least fifty or sixty years. . . . The policy of Afghanistan toward her two strong neighbors should be friendly toward the one which at the time is least aggressive and hostile to the country wishing to pass through her country or to interfere with her independence.[12]

Notes

1. W. K. Fraser-Tytler, *Afghanistan: A Study of Political Developments in Central and Southern Asia*, 3rd ed. (London: Oxford University Press, 1967), 282.
2. Shah Shuja was the last of the Sadozai kings. The first Sadozai monarch, Ahmad Shah Durrani, became king in 1747 and organized Afghanistan into a modern nation state.
3. Fraser-Tytler, *Afghanistan*, Appendix II.
4. Dr. Munawwar Khan, *Anglo–Afghan Relations 1798–1878* (Peshawar: University Book Agency, 1963), 145.
5. Ibid., 132.
6. Ibid, 153.
7. Fraser-Tytler, *Afghanistan*, 144.
8. Ibid., 159.

9. *Cambridge History of India*, vol. VI, p. 408, as quoted by Khan, *Anglo–Afghan Relations*, 104–105.
10. Arnold Fletcher, *Afghanistan: Highway of Conquest* (Ithaca, N.Y.: Cornell University Press, 1965), 157.
11. Ludwig W. Adamec, *Afghanistan 1900–1923: A Diplomatic History* (Berkeley and Los Angeles: University of California Press, 1967), 17.
12. Quoted in Fletcher, *Afghanistan*, 153.

2

World War I:
Afghanistan Remains Neutral

Before the War

After the death of Amir Abdul Rahman, his eldest son Habibullah Khan ascended the Afghan throne. The British hoped that the change of monarch in Kabul would provide them with an opportunity to strengthen their position in Afghanistan. Moreover, a speedy readjustment of Anglo–Afghan relations was made necessary by the fact that Russia was becoming increasingly interested in having direct relations with Afghanistan, since both countries now had a common frontier and the trans-Caspian railway had been completed. To tighten its control over Afghanistan and plug loopholes in the alliance, the government of India informed the new amir that it would be to the advantage of both parties to renew the 1880 agreement in a formal document. The amir replied that he was perfectly satisfied with the terms of the agreements concluded between his father and Britain and was going to honor them "as long as the illustrious British Government firmly adhered to them."[1]

The government of India's request for the renewal of the 1880 agreement partly stemmed from a long-established British practice aimed at preserving Britain's freedom to deal with each new ruler in Kabul afresh, without being bound by previous agreements. The British always insisted that agreements with Afghan rulers were personal and not dynastic or concluded between the two states. For the Afghans, however, a new treaty more often than not led to new concessions. Thus, they were reluctant to heed the British request.

On two occasions, in February and June of 1902, Lord Curzon invited the amir to India to discuss renegotiation of the agreement, and twice the amir demurred. The amir "complained of the Viceroy's insistence and said that since it was not necessary to renew the alliance at the death of Queen Victoria, it was unnecessary to take such action now at the death of his father."[2] Lord Curzon was greatly disappointed with Habibullah Khan's stubbornness and ordered that arms shipments to Afghanistan be stopped. Because the British contended that payment of the annual subsidy was personal, Curzon decided to discontinue the subsidy to Habibullah Khan. The government of India also expressed the view that, until a treaty was concluded with the new amir, he could not claim its protection.

Nonetheless, since Amir Habibullah had expressed his desire for maintenance of the alliance in his replies to the government of India, and had professed his friendship for Britain, it was decided in Delhi to wait before taking any further action against him. It is likely that the reverses suffered by Britain in the Boer War also contributed to this British leniency toward the amir.

This uneasy situation led to incidents and disputes on the Indo–Afghan frontier, some of a rather serious nature. Rumors started to circulate that Afghanistan might soon renounce the British alliance. Which power would take Britain's place in such an event was not difficult to guess.

After some time, an event of major importance occurred in Asia. The Russo–Japanese War in the Far East ended with a resounding defeat for the czarist empire. For the amir of Afghanistan, Russia lost its credibility as a world power. On the other hand, the possibility of Russia's compensating for its defeat in the Far East by initiating a new adventure in central Asia was deemed quite likely. The amir was also becoming increasingly disturbed by the intensification of Russia's efforts to establish direct contact with Afghanistan. Although he profoundly felt the burden and disgrace of the unequal treaties with the British, he was even more apprehensive about Russian intentions.

In a sudden change of attitude, perhaps influenced by these occurrences and perceptions, the amir invited a British mission to Kabul to discuss matters of common interest. The British mission, led by Louis W. Dane, foreign secretary to the government of India, arrived in Kabul in December 1904. Dane was instructed to conclude two treaties with the amir. These treaties, drafted by the government of India, were to be personal and not permanent. The first one was considered the basic treaty, aimed at regulating the rights and obligations of the two partners in the alliance. The second was a subsidiary treaty that covered practical matters related to military cooperation between Afghanistan and Britain.

The proposed treaty was quite similar to the previous arrangement [the Agreement of 1880], except that it permitted the British troops to enter Afghanistan in defense of foreign aggression. The subsidiary treaty also permitted British involvement by institutionalizing the delegation of British officers to assist the Amir in matters of defense. Although the treaty gave the British much less than the Government of India desired, it provided for an increase of British influence in Afghanistan and could have led to a tightening of British control which might have proved fatal to the Amir's independence.[3]

In addition to the conclusion of treaties, Dane was instructed to settle with the amir a series of problems that, over the years, had greatly chagrined the British. Chief among these "grievances" were the

- Necessity of putting a stop to Afghan intercourse with eastern Pashtun tribes

- Delimitation on the ground of the undemarcated portions of the Durand Line
- End of the Afghan boycott of the Chaman railroad
- Acceptance by Afghanistan of a more liberal commercial attitude toward India
- Improvement of the status and treatment of the British agent in Kabul and of the British "newswriters" in Herat and Kandahar
- Appointment of British newswriters in northern Afghanistan at Maymana, Mazar-i-Sharif, and Faizabad
- Cessation of incidents on the Indo-Afghan border.

Dane was also to obtain from the amir a promise not to adopt a hostile stance with regard to construction by the British of railroads up to the Khyber Pass and the Kurram Valley. The British mission was not to mention to the amir the advisability of extending the railroad from India to points within Afghanistan. However, the mission was asked to draw the attention of the amir to the importance of linking Kabul to India by telegraph line and to the benefits that would accrue to Afghanistan from such a linkage.

Very soon after the negotiations started, the well-known difference of opinion with regard to the contractual nature of agreements between Britain and Afghanistan came to the fore. The amir insisted that, if the previous agreements with his father were not agreements between states and thus were no longer in force, the Durand Agreement was also not valid and had to be renegotiated. But the representatives of the Indian government, by resorting to legal acrobatics, tried to explain that, while some agreements concerning territories (like the Durand Agreement) were permanent, the others (like the Agreement of 1880) were not. These arguments did not convince the Afghans, least of all the amir. As a compromise seemed unlikely on this issue, the matter was left unresolved, with each side adhering to its own interpretation.

The contents of the British drafts as explained by Dane did not appeal to the Afghans. The amir reserved his position on the settlement of the Indian government's grievances until agreement was reached on the size and scope of British military and financial assistance. So far as the nature of military assistance was concerned, there existed a fundamental difference of opinion between the amir and the government of India. While the Afghan ruler believed that military assistance should consist only of handsome amounts of military equipment and money, India wanted military assistance to lead to a British military presence in Afghanistan, such as the stationing of British officers in Seistan and on the Russo–Afghan border, the reconnoitering of the country beyond Kabul by British officers, and the training of the amir's troops. The British draft also included a provision that would have conceded to Britain the right to determine unilaterally when to enter Afghanistan in case of foreign aggression. The amir categorically rejected this particular British demand, and Dane hastily shelved it.

As time passed, it appeared that the discussions had reached a stalemate. It was in the middle of this period of frustration that Habibullah Khan put forward his counterproposals, in effect proposing an offensive military alliance between Afghanistan and Britain "to break the back" of recently defeated czarist Russia.[4] Dane was not at all prepared to engage in a discussion of such an alliance. Amir Habibullah seemed greatly disappointed by Dane's refusal to consider his proposed scheme. Most likely the amir's proposals represented a tactical move to blunt the thrust of British demands, but they did little to break the impasse that had been reached in the negotiations.

More lenient than the government of India, London was ready to make concessions, because, in its view, the importance of a treaty with Afghanistan lay not so much in its stringent provisions as in the deterrence that it provided against Russian aggression. The home government held the view that, as long as Amir Habibullah agreed to the cardinal principle that his foreign relations remained firmly in British hands, there was no point in coercing him into accepting the other British proposals. The home government argued that, treaty or no treaty, the British would be obliged to move into Afghanistan and defend it if Russia decided to attack.

Upon instructions from the home government, India asked Dane to renew the Agreement of 1880 and not insist on the Indian government's drafts. The new attitude eased the atmosphere, and an accord along the lines of the 1880 agreement was signed on March 21, 1905, between the amir and Louis W. Dane. The British agreed to an annual subsidy for the amir and lifted the ban on arrears. They likewise removed the ban on the importation of armaments by Afghanistan. The amir promised to give satisfaction to the British with regard to some of their grievances. He did not agree, though, to the appointment of newswriters in the northern cities of Afghanistan. The status of the British resident was improved. The amir gave no clear-cut answer to the British trial balloon regarding their intention to extend the Indian railway to Khyber and the Kurram Valley. The Afghan amir endorsed the Durand Agreement and consented in principle to the demarcation of the undemarcated portions of the Durand Line. (Practical difficulties that emerged later prevented the completion of that project so dear to the British.) So far as the main grievance was concerned, namely, relations between Afghanistan and the transborder Pashtuns, the amir stated that he "would not in the future go beyond the principles of his father."[5] As the principles of his father with regard to that matter were well known to the British, they were to draw their own conclusions from the amir's statement.

From the military point of view, the British gained nothing tangible by the conclusion of the new agreement. But the wise and realistic decision of the home government not to push or embarrass the amir favorably influenced his disposition toward the alliance and consequently gave it new impetus. After all, Britain's chief objective was to have a friendly ruler in Afghanistan who would understand the imperatives of the defense of India and realize that the survival of his country and that of India were complementary. That the British seemed to have achieved.

Meanwhile, Russian pressures on both Afghanistan and Britain for direct relations between Russia and Afghanistan continued. Russian authorities were frequently creating frontier incidents, to force the Afghans to settle them locally with their own representatives. But the amir stayed aloof from these provocations. He informed the Russians that whatever the nature of the problem, he unfortunately had no authority to deal with foreign powers except through Britain. The amir kept the British informed of the incidents and expressed his apprehensions to them.

Because of Russia's defeat in the Far East and the advent of new conditions in Europe, notably, the emergence of Germany as a rival of both empires, Britain was experiencing one of its rare periods of decreased Russophobia. That frame of mind led British officials to accept the fact that some form of direct relations between Afghanistan and Russia was unavoidable. But they felt strongly that those relations should remain strictly regulated and confined to nonpolitical matters. The British government was willing to make such a concession to the Russians only within the framework of an overall settlement of their differences in Asia. In the British view, such a settlement would have to secure for them the areas lying to the west of the Hindu Kush, considered the most vulnerable of the western approaches to India. For this purpose the British already had a bargain in mind: the division of Persia into zones of influence. Under this plan, northern Persia would be placed under Russian protection, and eastern Persia would fall within the British zone of influence.

The czarist empire, hoping to regain its strength after its defeat by Japan, viewing with anxiety the expansion of German power, and suffering internal political agitation, welcomed the opportunity to settle its differences with Britain. Completed in 1907, the Anglo–Russian negotiations produced a three-part convention concerning Tibet, Persia, and Afghanistan. This became known as the Convention of St. Petersburg. No representatives of any of those Asian countries were allowed to take part in the deliberations regarding the status of their homelands. The convention of 1907 was an arrangement between two traditionally hostile colonial powers, who, perceiving that their immediate interests could not be served by confrontation, chose to solve their differences by dividing a vast region of Asia into zones of influence.

By virtue of the provisions of the convention, Russia and Britain recognized Chinese suzerainty over Tibet. With regard to Persia, the convention simply divided the country into three zones. The northern part of Persia was placed under Russian influence, western Persia was left to the Persians, and southeastern and eastern Persia were included in the British zone of influence. Thus, Britain succeeded in finding a way to reinforce the protection of Afghanistan's western border and to close the gap in the outer perimeter of Indian defenses.

In the part of the convention that concerned Afghanistan, Russia had agreed that Afghanistan was outside its sphere of influence, and Britain declared that it had no intention of changing that country's political status. Thus, Afghanistan's British-imposed limited sovereignty was reconfirmed by London and accepted by the Russians in an important treaty regulating the fate of several Asian nations. The British, furthermore, promised neither to take any measures threatening Russia nor to encourage Afghanistan to do so. In Article III, the British conceded that Russia and Afghanistan could establish direct relations with each other for the settlement of local questions of a nonpolitical nature. Article IV permitted equality of Anglo–Afghan and Russo–Afghan trading opportunities and stated that "should the progress of trade establish the necessity for Commercial Agents, the two Governments will agree as to what measure shall be taken, due regard, of course, being had to the Amir's sovereign rights."

But the amir's sovereign rights had already been flouted by the heavy-handed fashion in which the two colonial powers had regulated matters pertaining to Afghanistan without even consulting him. The British disregard to which he had been subjected and the convention's contents infuriated the amir. The much-feared entente between Britain and Russia, which in Afghan thinking of the time meant the eventual partition of Afghanistan and an end to the buffer state, seemed to have at last materialized. Anti-British elements in the Afghan court became restless and started advocating for severance of the alliance with Britain and even the declaration of jihad.

For the part of the convention concerning Afghanistan to come into force it had to be ratified by the amir, but he refused to do so in spite of British pressure. Britain and Russia then agreed that his consent was not needed for its implementation. But without the goodwill and concurrence of the amir, their agreement with regard to Afghanistan had no practical value. Perhaps Britain, in order to get Russia's agreement to other parts of the convention, led it to believe that the acceptance of the amir would be obtained in due time. Be that as it may, until the end of Habibullah Khan's reign, no direct relations were established between Afghanistan and Russia, and nothing of a privileged nature in the field of trade was accorded the Russians. The two colonial powers had grossly underestimated the amir's determination to resist their diktat.

The winner in the conclusion of the Anglo–Russian Convention of 1907 was, of course, Britain, which had realized its essential aim in the negotiations with the partitioning of Persia. Amir Habibullah, in his shrewdness, perceived that the British alliance, even as tenuous as it had become, was better than no alliance. To those who wanted to abandon Britain, he advocated patience. After a time, the tumult created by the convention subsided, and another crisis in the erratic history of Anglo–Afghan relations had passed.

The War Years

The outbreak of World War I, in which Russia and Britain were allied, revived the Afghan fears that such rapprochement always engendered. But it soon became apparent that the two European allies would be satisfied to have the amir stay neutral in the war. The British were fully aware of the Afghan amir's influence among the transborder Pashtuns and of his ability to create trouble for the government of India in those areas. They therefore sought his goodwill to avoid an uprising on the frontier while they were occupied in the European theater. The British also hoped that a neutral amir would not use his influence to encourage Indian revolutionaries to fan the flames of political agitation in India. Although to a lesser degree than in India, the struggle for independence in Russian central Asia was not negligible. Pan-Islamic aspirations, to which the amir enthusiastically adhered, had also spread among those central Asian Muslims who were active in anti-czarist movements. These central Asian Muslims viewed the amir as a natural ally in their struggle for freedom; his neutrality was, therefore, also important to Russia.

In the meantime, powerful anti-British elements in the court, including the amir's son Amanullah and his influential brother Nasrullah, were pressuring the amir to declare his support for the Central Powers, especially when Turkey (the site of the caliphate) entered the war against the Allies. Those elements were urging the amir to demand complete independence from Britain and even the restoration of the Pashtun lands to Afghanistan. If Britain did not accept those demands, it was to be confronted with large-scale tribal rebellion. To the voice of those anti-British elements, that of the Afghan intelligentsia was added.

The amir, who disliked Afghanistan's subservience to Britain in matters of foreign relations and firmly believed in the common destiny of transborder Pashtuns and the people of Afghanistan, must have been tempted to adopt a hard line toward Britain now that the Raj had become more vulnerable to external pressures. However, after weighing the options, he decided that the interests of Afghanistan would be served best by staying neutral, at least for the time being. He undoubtedly believed that the imperatives of survival necessitated the maintenance of a balance and made neutrality the natural choice. The amir, likewise, did not think it advisable to take advantage of British preoccupations and make demands that, if not granted, would adversely affect his prestige. According to an authoritative source, the British, in turn, led the amir to believe (through their resident agent in Kabul, Hafiz Sayfullah Khan) that, if he maintained his neutrality and upheld the alliance, they would recognize Afghanistan's full independence at the end of the war. Moreover, they implied that direct diplomatic relations, to which the amir attached obsessive importance, would also be established between Kabul and the Court of Saint James.[6]

The amir managed to keep the Frontier relatively quiet for the duration of the war. In fact, the tribal areas had never been as quiet as in those years of World War I. He also abstained from encouraging Indian revolutionaries to foment unrest in India; no systematic large-scale upheaval occurred in the subcontinent during this period.

The maintenance of this neutral stance was not easy for the amir, however.

Apart from continued internal pressures, there was the fact that the Central Powers were actively attempting to draw the amir into their camp. They were aware that Afghan influence could be used to destabilize British rule in the subcontinent and wanted to capitalize on that potential. Although some of their agents were crossing into Russian central Asia, using Afghan territory as a conduit, the main thrust of their clandestine activity was aimed at India. Agents of the Central Powers infiltrated the tribal area through Afghanistan and established contact with Indian revolutionaries in Afghanistan and India. Some of the Turkish nationals working in professional jobs in Afghanistan and active in the pan-Islamic movement redoubled their efforts to channel and organize anti-British sentiments in Afghanistan and the tribal areas and to promote the Central Powers' cause in the ongoing war. The community of religion between the Turks and the Afghans and the latter's profound sympathy for Turkey made that task an easy one.

Of the Central Powers' endeavors to win the amir to their side, none was as daring and serious as the dispatch of the Niedermayer–Hentig expedition to Afghanistan. This expedition, initially organized by the German government, but including Turks, Austrians, and Indian revolutionaries, reached Afghanistan in September 1915 after a long and perilous journey. The mission was instructed to encourage the amir to ally himself with the Central Powers against his traditional enemies. His alliance with the Central Powers was to be rewarded by military and financial assistance and, at the end of the war, by the return of the transborder Pashtun lands to Afghanistan. The mission also sought the endorsement by the amir of a proclamation of jihad by the Sultan of Turkey. In spite of British diplomatic maneuvers to remove the mission, Habibullah Khan received it with great courtesy. He was curious to know what it had to offer and whether there were viable alternatives to neutrality. But, most probably, by receiving the mission he wished to demonstrate the extent of Afghanistan's independence from the British and remind them that under prevailing circumstances they needed him more than he needed them.

For months, Habibullah forestalled an agreement while he carefully observed the direction the war was taking. At last, to satisfy the anti-British, pro-Turkish feelings of his people, he initialed a treaty with Niedermayer and von Hentig. But the conditions put forth by the amir for helping the Central Powers in their war effort were so exorbitant that the Germans realized that the Afghans would not act against the Allies on empty promises.[7] The reverses suffered by the Central Powers in the war and the gradual coolness of the amir toward the mission contributed to its disbanding in 1916. Almost all of its European members left Afghanistan. The Turks stayed behind until the end of the war, roaming the tribal areas and spreading their anti-British propaganda. One author has provided interesting insight into the mission's true objectives:

Although the Niedermayer mission was technically a failure, its other, secret purpose was successful. While Niedermayer . . . negotiated with the Shah [Amir Habibullah Khan], other members of the mission were dealing with his subjects and with agents from India. The Indian revolutionaries with the mission had been in touch with the Muslim students on the frontier, and through them, with the tribes and dissident groups in India itself. The formidable, if unrealistic plan in which this activity was to culminate was scheduled for completion in late 1916, when a general uprising of India Muslims was to be coordinated with a similar revolt in Russian Asia. An army was to be raised from among German prisoners in Tashkent. Afghanistan was to be the center of the campaign, and in the event of success Habibullah Khan was to become king of India.[8]

The Niedermayer–Hentig expedition was viewed by some as an opéra-comique episode. It was nothing of the sort. The Germans were convinced that the defenses of India could be breached through Afghanistan and that it was not impractical to launch an offensive against the subcontinent from Afghan territory. In fact, during the early stages of their talks with the amir, they were quite certain that conditions were favorable for such an undertaking.

In the agreement concluded between the amir and the Niedermayer–Hentig mission, Germany officially recognized the complete independence of Afghanistan. It is interesting to note that, contrary to widespread belief, Germany was the first country to recognize Afghan independence, not Soviet Russia in 1919. The Niedermayer–Hentig expedition brought Germany into contact with Afghanistan for the first time. In later years it was to become one of the major contributors to Afghanistan's development efforts.

The British feigned ignorance of the initialing of the treaty between the amir and Germany. What mattered for them was the de facto neutrality of Afghanistan, and the amir, in spite of apparent digressions from that policy, was maintaining it firmly.

The defeat of the Central Powers in 1918 produced great resentment among the Afghan people toward their amir. They believed he had betrayed Turkey (the Ottoman Empire) by not moving to defend Islam against infidels. The amir was also vehemently criticized for not having pressured Britain to recognize Afghananistan's full independence and was openly maligned by influential sardars and members of the intelligentsia for having done nothing to regain the lands formerly belonging to Afghanistan.

The amir had entertained the hope that his pro-British neutrality during the war would be rewarded by full independence, direct diplomatic representation between Kabul and London, and even territorial concessions. He also thought that the Communist takeover in Russia in 1917, which had added a new dimension to the threat from the north, would encourage the British to consolidate their alliance with Afghanistan along the lines he advocated. But the British had no interest in the amir's aspirations once the war was over and, perhaps in part because of the advent of communism in Russia, declined to give up their control of Afghanistan's foreign relations.[9] The only reward the amir had received from the British during the war was a letter from King George V addressing him as "Your Majesty" instead of "Your Highness" and praising him for his neutrality. The amir's decreasing popularity could only have been boosted by a substantial British concession, but they were not prepared to move in that direction.

Habibullah Khan, to strengthen his position internally, wrote to the viceroy of India, Lord Chelmsford, on February 2, 1919, demanding that Afghanistan be represented at the peace conference in Versailles and that the conference proclaim and guarantee his country's independence. Before a reply to that request could be received from India, the amir was assassinated, on February 19, 1919, in Qala Gosh, in the present Laghman province. The assassin or assassins and their motives were never discovered, but undoubtedly the winds of change sweeping the country and the unfulfilled aspirations of Afghan nationalism could no longer tolerate a conservative ruler subservient to a colonial power that had humbled Islamic Turkey and had defaulted on its promises of independence for Afghanistan.

Notes

1. Adamec, *Afghanistan, 1900–1923*, 30.
2. Ibid., 31.
3. Ibid., 49.
4. Ibid., 40.
5. Ibid., 64.
6. Related to me in 1973 by the late Ali Mohammad Khan, who, at the time, was a young courtier close to the amir and later occupied positions of importance including ambassador to London, foreign minister, deputy prime minister, and minister of court.
7. The treaty stipulated, among other things, that the German government would furnish to Afghanistan 100,000 rifles, 300 guns, appropriate munitions, other necessary war materiel, and £10 million sterling. The amir had stated, for the record, that he would not act unless 20,000 to 100,000 German or Turkish soldiers arrived in Afghanistan and not before all of India rose against Britain!
8. Fletcher, *Afghanistan*, 182.
9. Conversation in 1973 with Ali Mohammad Khan.

3

Between the World Wars

By the end of World War I, new conditions had emerged in the principal areas surrounding Afghanistan. Russia had fallen to communism, and the short-lived alliance between Britain and Russia had collapsed. The two countries had once again assumed their mutually hostile stance in Asia. Although momentarily preoccupied with the consolidation of their regime, the new rulers of Russia had already embarked on anti-British activities, inciting the peoples of the East to revolt against Britain. One of their principal goals in Asia was to export, under the guise of nationalism, their revolution to India by aiding and abetting Indian revolutionaries, some of whom had already established close ties with Bolshevik authorities.[1] Many Indians had participated actively in the British war effort, and now that the war had been won, in part due to their sacrifices, they felt entitled to receive the long-coveted reward: independence for their country. The Allies had maintained throughout the war that they were fighting for emancipation, democracy, and self-determination. It was, therefore, natural that, at the war's end, not only the Indian but all colonial peoples of Asia would expect that those noble principles would be implemented by their proponents. "Asia for the Asians" was the slogan of the day.

But imperial Britain was not ready to relinquish its Indian empire. The supreme interests of the British Isles could not be reconciled with the new attitudes and outlooks born of the war. Although the British, under pressure from Gandhi's Congress Party, took a small step toward self-rule by initiating in 1919 the much publicized Montague–Chelmsford reforms, they by no means satisfied the urge for independence that was blowing like a hot wind across the subcontinent.[2]

In fact, those reforms were heavily outweighed by the enactment of laws curtailing civil liberties and pro-independence movements. Indians vehemently protested such measures. Clashes between protesters and the authorities became increasingly frequent. The most tragic event of that period of confrontation was the Amritsar massacre in April 1919, when British soldiers fired on a large group of people observing a religious holiday in defiance of a government order, killing 379 and injuring more than a thousand.[3]

"The outrage [caused by this event] shocked the world and would shortly end [General Reginald] Dyer's career. It also marked the beginning of Gandhi's rise to power and the beginning of the end of the British rule in India."[4]

The harsh peace terms forced on defeated Turkey were another cause of resentment against Britain. The Indian Muslims were particularly bitter about those terms because, as part of the British armies that had vanquished the Central Powers, they felt somewhat responsible for Turkey's defeat and humiliation.

In addition to these problems with which Britain had to cope, the British rulers in India were profoundly disturbed by the communist takeover in Russia and its avowed aim of world revolution. To counter the communist menace, the British participated in the Allied intervention against the Bolsheviks and actively supported the counterrevolution. But Allied intervention failed to remove the Bolshevik government. For a few more years the counter-revolutionaries in central Asia, who were in fact nationalists and were referred to as the Basmachis (the Bandits) by the Bolsheviks, continued their struggle to shed Russian domination, but after some initial successes, they were crushed by the Red Army. Undoubtedly to the great disappointment of the British, by the end of the decade no anti-Soviet resistance of significance was active in the northern regions bordering Afghanistan. So far as tensions between the British and the trans-Durand tribes were concerned, they were again heightened at the end of the war. Tribal raids were on the increase, and British punitive expeditions were once again part of the Frontier routine.

In Afghanistan itself the atmosphere was charged with a surge for independence. The newspaper *Saradj-al-Akhbar*, started during Amir Habibullah's reign and published by Mahmud Tarzi, had a profound impact on the intelligentsia.[5] Afghans became involved in such issues as the fate of the caliphate, of Islam, and of their own nation.[6] Flames of anti-British sentiment were fanned by Afghan perceptions of Britain's default on its promises of independence, the repression in India and on the Frontier, and the dismantling of the Ottoman Empire. Furthermore, there were some influential elements in the court who argued that the collapse of the czarist empire and the consequent weakness of Russia, resulting in a decrease of pressure from the north, had removed the main motive for Afghanistan to remain in the British orbit.

It was in such an environment that the charismatic and independence-minded Amanullah, third son of the late Habibullah, assumed power as the amir of Afghanistan. One of Amanullah's first acts as amir was to proclaim Afghanistan's independence and to request Britain to negotiate a new treaty of friendship on the basis of equality. The government of India was suddenly faced with a dilemma. War-weary Britain was reluctant to risk coercive measures against Amanullah, and yet it was not ready to relinquish its control over Afghan foreign relations. Furthermore, "after maintaining for so long that Anglo–Afghan agreements were made personally with the Amirs, it was difficult to deny that Amanullah had a right to demand a new treaty for

Afghanistan."[7] In his reply to Amanullah, Viceroy of India Lord Chelmsford refrained from making any reference to independence and alluded to the mourning over the death of the late amir as an excuse for not discussing the treaty suggested by Amanullah.[8]

The amir and his entourage were quick to understand that British recognition of Afghanistan's independence necessitated more than polite requests and diplomatic maneuvers. They decided to use the one device the British feared most, a tribal uprising. Soon, the Frontier was alive with calls for jihad. Tribal leaders held *jirgas* (tribal assemblies) in Jalalabad and Kabul, and tribal *lashkars* (irregular tribal armies) were rapidly formed. The amir decided to buttress the impact of the uprising with the dispatch of regular Afghan armies to the Indian border at Dakka (eastern front), at Khost (central front), and at Spinboldak (southern front). The deployment of troops at the Indian border and the tribal revolt were to be coordinated with an anticipated uprising in India.

Amanullah was aware that his belligerent stand against Britain would upset the balance so painstakingly maintained by his predecessors. He nevertheless thought that a divorce with the past was necessary if Afghanistan were to take its place among the free nations of the world. In his view, reform and progress, to which he was so profoundly attached, were not possible for his country under British tutelage. He knew of the dangers involved in shaking off the vestiges of the colonial era, but he was determined to take the risk and not pass up the unique opportunity brought about by the changed situation in and around Afghanistan to reestablish his country's complete independence.[9]

In preparing to confront the British, the amir was readying himself diplomatically. One of his logical options in this regard was to open a bridge to the new regime in Russia. The amir was aware of Communist dangers, but felt that the Bolsheviks, busy as they were with internal problems, did not pose a threat to Afghanistan and that their militant anti-British stance could be used by the amir as leverage against the British. In April 1919, Amanullah and Mahmud Tarzi, his foreign minister, sent messages to Lenin and his commissar for foreign affairs, Chicherin. In these messages they greeted the new regime in Russia and expressed their desire to establish friendly relations with it.[10] In his reply, Lenin warmly welcomed Amanullah's overture and stated that "the Soviet Government from the first day that they received power have heralded to the whole world their desire not merely to recognize the right of self-determination of all people both great and small, but to render assistance to those people who are struggling for their independence."[11] Mohammad Wali Khan, a close adviser to Amanullah, was sent to Moscow, where he was received by Lenin on October 18, 1919. It was the first time since the downfall of Amir Sher Ali Khan that an Afghan ruler had so openly tendered a hand of friendship to the "barbarian" of the North. Would his destiny be the same as that ill-fated amir's?

Meanwhile, a series of local incidents on the eastern front forced the Afghan commander to start hostilities prematurely, which prompted the British to move and capture Dakka. The government of India informed London of the occupation of that locality, situated inside Afghanistan, on May 15, 1919. The third Anglo–Afghan war had thus started. The British quickly occupied Spinboldak, on the southern front on the road to Kandahar. The government of India prepared to advance from Dakka toward Jalalabad. The capture of Kandahar was also seriously considered. But the home government was reluctant to go along with these measures. It warned India "that an attack on one of the few remaining independent Muslim states might have serious consequences elsewhere. The Paris peace negotiations would surely be affected and London wanted to know whether peace could be made with a return to status quo."[12]

While the Afghans did not fare well on the eastern and southern fronts, General Mohammad Nadir Khan, the commander-in-chief of the Afghan army who was in charge of the central front, advanced from Matun near Khost into Waziristan and attacked the important British fortress of Thal. This success, which forced the British to send to Waziristan part of their force gathered on the eastern front, relieved the pressure on Jalalabad. Nadir Khan's penetration into Waziristan roused the tribes, who were already on the warpath.

Although Thal was the immediate Afghan objective, Nadir's advance had its most lasting repercussions in Waziristan. . . . [T]he militia garrison in Wana [constituted of tribal levies] mutinied and seized the fort. . . . Other Waziristan posts fell like ninepins. Scattered militia and Indian Army units could barely hold their own against some 20,000 Wazir and Mahsud tribesmen, many of whom had fought with the British on the Western Front and in East Africa. More than two years would go by before order could be restored in Waziristan.[13]

The home government in Britain, worried by the repercussions of the confrontation with Afghanistan and the spread of the revolt on the Frontier, wanted a quick and peaceful resolution of the conflict. The Indian government accepted this position under pressure from London. Amanullah, disappointed with the performance of his armies on the eastern and southern fronts, did not want to expose them any longer to a militarily disadvantageous position. Moreover, tribal upheavals had a chemistry of their own. They could spring out of control and boomerang, creating serious problems on the Afghan side of the border. The failure of the Indian revolution to materialize was another factor that cooled Amanullah Khan's warlike disposition and prompted him to exploit instead the psychological shock created in Britain and India by David's challenge to Goliath.

Nadir Khan was thus not allowed to exploit his military success in Waziristan. The amir instructed him to withdraw from Thal and let diplomats try their hand at settling the Anglo–Afghan dispute. Thus, the third Anglo–Afghan war, also known as the War of Independence, ended in the beginning of June 1919. A de facto armistice between the regular forces of the two antagonists came into effect, although the British supply lines were frequently attacked by Pashtun tribes. Meanwhile, at the end of May, the independence of Afghanistan had officially been recognized by Soviet Russia.

Afghan and British delegations met for the first time on July 26, 1919, at Rawalpindi, India, for the purpose of making peace. The Afghan delegation was headed by Ali Ahmad Khan, minister of home affairs and the British side by A. H. Grant of the Foreign Secretariat of the Government of India. As Britain's recognition of Afghanistan's complete independence was essential to the amir, the Afghans' principal aim at the Rawalpindi talks was to secure that recognition. Amnesty for the trans-Durand tribes, principally the Wazirs, Mahsuds, Afridis, and Mohmands who had assisted Afghanistan in the war, and the return of certain territories, like Waziristan, to Afghanistan were the other important items on which the agreement of Britain was sought.

Despite Afghanistan's de facto independence, best illustrated by its unhampered dealings with Soviet Russia at the time, it was difficult for the British to accept that fait accompli. Afghanistan for them was still the key to India. So far as territorial concessions to Afghanistan were concerned, the British were categorically opposed to any such arrangements and made their stand on that matter quite clear. Likewise, considerations of sovereignty compelled Britain not to heed the Afghan demands regarding amnesty for the tribes whose fate and future the British believed were no one's business but theirs. The most that the British were prepared to concede at the negotiations was the reestablishment of peace, withdrawal to their own side of the Frontier, and the signing of a friendship treaty after a probationary period of six months "if the Amir were contrite."[14]

Very early in the talks, Grant perceived that the Afghans had gone to war only to get their independence confirmed by the British and that now their delegation would not return home without having it officially recognized. He realized that it would be impossible to deny the Afghans recognition of their independence unless Britain were ready to resume hostilities and face a tribal quagmire on the Frontier. He therefore advised his government to move toward acceptance of Afghanistan's independence. Lord Chelmsford, the Viceroy of India, also "recognized that there were profound changes in the political outlook of the Middle East, which were caused by 'general unrest, awakened national aspirations, the pronouncements of President Wilson, and the Bolshevik catchwords.'"[15] Under the circumstances, the viceroy felt that Afghan independence could no longer be postponed. But he thought that this should not worry the British because "Amanullah would soon be convinced of the impossibility of conducting his affairs single-handed."[16] The viceroy expected that, "if we regain the confidence of Afghanistan and get them to turn voluntarily to us in their difficulty, we shall have secured more than we can do by any 'scrap of paper.'"[17] Among other things, considerations of this Machiavellian nature persuaded the home and Indian governments to reappraise their attitudes with respect to Afghanistan's independence and to make the necessary mental adjustment to accept that eventuality.

Ali Ahmad, in his presentation of the Afghan position, made it clear that Afghanistan wished to have good relations with Britain. He "warned of the danger of Communism, expressing his 'horror' of it and claimed that it was in their joint interest [Afghanistan's and Britain's] to keep the Communists out of Afghanistan."[18] He stressed, however, that Afghanistan's complete internal and external independence was not negotiable. In the mind of the Afghan representative, independence from Britain and close ties with it were not irreconcilable. In connection with the tribal situation he submitted that

. . . the entire tribal territory should be ceded to Afghanistan, who would run it along the lines that would spare the British government all the trouble they had in this matter. The Afghan government should be rewarded half the amount of money spent by the British government on the control of the tribes.[19]

While Grant rejected the Afghan position with respect to the fate of the tribes and territorial concessions, including cession of Waziristan, he hinted that a favorable change in the position of the British rulers had occurred with regard to the restoration of Afghanistan's independence.

The question of expulsion of Indian revolutionaries from Afghanistan was brought up by Grant but was quickly dropped when Ali Ahmad insisted on the return of tribal areas to Afghanistan and clemency for the tribes. The Afghans and their hosts had been attending their somewhat boring meetings for quite some time when the British delegation formally announced its recognition of Afghanistan's independence. It informed the Afghans of the termination of the annual subsidy and the cancellation of the arrears due the late amir. The official British reason for taking this position was that payment of subsidies was not compatible with Afghan independence. But it was clear that, by terminating the annual subsidy and, especially, the nonpayment of arrears, the British wanted to show their displeasure toward Amanullah, since he had committed the affront of rising against them. The British also stated their decision that the transit of arms and ammunition to Afghanistan through India was to be postponed until the conclusion of a treaty of friendship between the two countries.

The Treaty of Peace between the Illustrious British Government and the Independent Afghan Government was concluded at Rawalpindi on August 8, 1919, and signed by the leaders of the two delegations. As its title indicated, this was only a treaty of peace that officially ended the hostilities. Because the treaty was between the two states and not between the amir and the British Government, it was clear that the British had at last abandoned their traditional position, which was to conclude only personal treaties with Afghan rulers. Afghan independence had simply rendered that British stance obsolete. In a letter forming an integral part of the treaty, Grant expressed his assurance to Ali Ahmad that "the said Treaty and this letter leave Afghanistan officially free and independent in its internal and external affairs. Moreover, this war has cancelled all previous treaties."[20] However, Article V of the new treaty stated,

"The Afghan Government accepts the Indo–Afghan frontier accepted by the late Amir." Thus, in spite of their efforts, the Afghans did not succeed in canceling the one treaty they really wished to abrogate, the Durand Agreement.

Article I of the treaty stipulated that, "From the date of signing of the Treaty there shall be peace" between the two governments. Article II announced the withdrawal of the privilege "enjoyed by [the] former Amir of importing arms, ammunition or war-like munitions through India to Afghanistan." Article III proclaimed the confiscation of Amir Habibullah's arrears and the discontinuance of subsidy payments to the new amir. Article IV, which related to the probationary period of six months, stated that the British government was prepared "to receive another Afghan mission after six months for the discussion and settlement of matters of common interests to the two Governments and the reestablishment of the old friendship on a satisfactory basis."

Shortly after the treaty was signed, Dakka and Spinboldak were returned to the Afghans. But a British commission, on the basis of a stipulation in the treaty, unilaterally demarcated a portion of the yet undemarcated section of the Durand Line west of the Khyber in August and September of 1919, resulting in the addition to British territory of an area claimed by the Afghans.

At last the battle for independence had been won. "Although the course of this war did not go as the Afghans anticipated, it was destined to be a great victory, for as a result of it Afghanistan obtained her complete and permanent independence from Britain."[21] An interesting assessment of the British position with regard to the restoration of Afghan independence was given by Fraser-Tytler.

The British Government had no desire whatever to add to their commitments by continuing a fight which would in all probability lead to the disintegration of Afghanistan and the disappearance of the buffer between India and Russia. Once again and for very good reason the British refused to accept the offer fate held out to them. Instead they went to the other extreme. They handed back to an irresponsible hot-headed young man, ruler of a people who had for generations looked on them with hatred, the keys to the defense of India which they had taken from his ancestors. It was once again a remarkable act of statesmanship, an act which could only find justification in the ultimate success of a long-term policy, and which if it failed would have been looked on as a most unjustified gamble in political strategy. But the decision communicated to the Afghan Delegation who came down to Rawalpindi in July, that Afghanistan should be "officially free and independent in its internal and external affairs," was the outcome of a realistic appraisal of a changing world. However valuable the Convention of St. Petersburg may have been as an instrument designed to solidify a fluid situation, the remote control of the foreign relations of another country without the physical presence at any time of the controller or his agents could not continue for very long.[22]

The situation between Afghanistan and Britain became increasingly tense in 1920 when the British renewed their penetration of the Pashtun borderland, moving on an unprecedented scale into the lands primarily inhabited by the Wazirs and the Mahsuds. Tribal resistance to this British advance was fierce.

A military operation in Waziristan always seemed to exceed its predecessor in carnage and the "police action" of 1919–20 was no exception. In one fight for possession of a narrow cleft through some rocks, 5,000 Indian Army regulars and 10,000 Mahsuds went at each other in five consecutive days of hand-to-hand combat that resulted in more than 2,000 British and Indian dead and wounded. It was the highest butcher bill ever by Empire troops in the history of Frontier warfare. But 4,000 Mahsuds also fell in the same brawl. . . .[23]

No Afghan ruler could have remained indifferent to this harsh treatment of the trans-Durand Pashtuns, particularly Amanullah, who had been assisted so gallantly by them in the war for independence. As could have been anticipated, he provided the Pashtuns with moral support and material assistance. Those who fled British repression found a safe haven in Afghanistan.

The resumption by Britain of the policy of pacification and integration in the Frontier, which came to be called the *modified forward policy*, probably was adopted to make up for the "loss" of Afghanistan. It seems reasonable to assume that the British, preoccupied as always with the defense of India, wanted to transform the tribal belt into a controlled buffer zone between India and Afghanistan and position themselves more advantageously in the area, since the "irresponsible" ruler in Kabul had proved himself untrustworthy and hostile to British interests.

The worsening of Anglo–Afghan relations, resulting from the aggressive British Frontier policy and the provisions of the Rawalpindi treaty prohibiting the import of arms from and through India, forced Amanullah to seek closer relations with Soviet Russia and to turn to that country for weapons.[24] Mohammad Wali Khan, after his reception by Lenin, had begun talks with Soviet authorities to explore the possibility of a Russo–Afghan treaty. The Bolsheviks promised military and technical assistance to Afghanistan and urged "the construction of a railroad from Kushk [Soviet Turkestan] to Herat, a request that the Afghans seemed unwilling to grant."[25] But these talks, apart from creating an atmosphere of goodwill among the parties, did not produce anything concrete.

Alexander Bravin, the first Russian emissary to visit Kabul after independence, continued in late 1919 the negotiations started in Moscow. The Bolsheviks were eager to draw Afghanistan away from Britain and gain an ally who would support them in the consolidation of their power in the East.[26] But their promises of assistance to and alliance with Afghanistan were still quite vague. This vagueness, coupled with uncertainties about Soviet Russia's internal situation, made the amir reluctant to conclude a hasty agreement with that country. On the other hand, tenuous Anglo–Afghan relations dissuaded the Afghans from breaking off negotiations with the Russians.

The newly found friendship between Afghanistan and the Soviets did not prevent the Afghans from pursuing their activities in Russian central Asia, which had sped up in the wake of the Communist takeover and the loosening of Russian control in Turkestan. These activities were motivated by considerations of pan-Islamism and the desire to regain the Afghan territories, notably Panjdeh, annexed a few decades earlier by the czarist government. Afghan pan-Islamic activists were advocating the establishment of a confederation of central Asian states with Amanullah at its head and made no secret of their wish to see him appointed caliph by a congregation of Islamic countries. There are no indications that Amanullah disapproved of those pursuits. Initially the Soviets had no quarrel with pan-Islamic propaganda, which they considered to be aimed at British domination of the East. However, when pan-Turanism (the unity of Turkic peoples, an offshoot of pan-Islamism) gained importance, they began to become concerned.

As the probationary period stipulated in the Rawalpindi agreement came to an end, the British, probably in a bid to forestall a Russo–Afghan alliance, invited an Afghan mission to Mussoorie, India, for a new round of talks, with a view to concluding a treaty of friendship. It can be reasonably assumed that in the British view the "Red menace" from the north was important enough to warrant such a conciliatory gesture toward Afghanistan, in spite of their openly professed antipathy toward Amanullah and their disapproval of his continued relations with the tribes and support for Indian revolutionaries. The Afghan delegation, headed by Foreign Minister Mahmud Tarzi arrived at Mussoorie in April 1920. The British delegation was headed by Foreign Secretary Henry Dobbs of the Government of India.

From the outset of the conference, Mahmud Tarzi insisted that settlement of the tribal matters was of the utmost importance if a meaningful treaty were to be concluded. In the Afghan view, this settlement could be reached by Britain's either ceding the tribal areas to Afghanistan or granting them independence. It was during the talks in Mussoorie that the Afghans invoked for the first time the principle of self-determination in their search for a solution to the problem of the Pashtun areas under British domination. This presentation met with complete British intransigence.

Tarzi conveyed to Dobbs the Afghan government's desire to receive financial and technical assistance from Britain in its development efforts. He asked Dobbs that the arms embargo against Afghanistan be ended. The Afghans also expressed their wish to establish direct diplomatic relations between Kabul and London. Since the Afghans were greatly concerned about the caliphate and the plight of Islamic Turkey, Tarzi explained to Dobbs that the Afghans would like to see Turkey treated justly by the Allies. He expressed his belief that such treatment would remove at least one negative element from Anglo–Afghan relations. But Tarzi's advocacy of the Turkish cause did not impress the British. In the councils of Europe the fate of Turkey had already been decided. "In the meantime the peace terms with Turkey were announced and Tarzi complained that it looked like a new holy war was afoot against Islam, especially since Germany was not similarly divided."[27]

Throughout the talks, Dobbs complained about Afghanistan's interference in the tribal areas, its granting of asylum to Indian "dissidents," and its gradual inclination toward Soviet Russia, a country openly hostile to Britain. So far as the tribes were concerned, the Afghans replied that their position needed no clarification. With regard to the Indian revolutionaries living in Afghanistan, Tarzi replied that it was against the laws of Islam and hospitality to expel them from the country and asked Dobbs that the British treat their Indian subjects with greater tolerance and show understanding for Indian nationalism. In response to the apprehensions expressed by the British delegation about the growing closeness between Afghanistan and Russia, the Afghans showed themselves surprisingly accommodating. "If given Waziristan the Afghans declared themselves willing to conclude an alliance with Britain against the Bolsheviks and to extricate the Turkomans, Bukhara and Khiva from Russian influence."[28] But Waziristan was not going to be ceded to Afghanistan. On the contrary, military operations there increased, and the British planned the permanent occupation of Mahsud country.[29]

Since there were so many areas of strong disagreement, both delegations believed that there was no possibility of concluding a treaty. Before the Afghan delegation departed in July 1920, Dobbs gave it a written summary incorporating the elements of a future treaty of friendship between Afghanistan and Britain. One of its essential elements was the requirement that Afghanistan abandon its relations with the transborder tribes and not allow anti-British activities in its territory. If such conditions were accepted by the Afghan government in a legally binding document, Britain would pledge to aid and financially assist Afghanistan in its modernization effort and not prevent the free import of arms by Afghanistan through India. Moreover, Britain would help in the construction of railways and telegraph lines and would accept special concessions concerning the lowering of tax and import duties for trade and transit of goods.[30]

From the sometimes astonishingly explicit pronouncements of the Afghan representatives in Mussoorie, one can draw the conclusion that Amir Amanullah was aware that Afghanistan's security lay to the east and that he preferred to conclude a treaty with the British rather than the Soviets.[31] But there were certain important elements that had to be accepted by Britain in a rapprochement with Afghanistan, which apparently did not mix well with the old imperial ways still adhered to by the British. A partnership of equals, based on geopolitical realities and a balancing of the sensitivities and interests of both parties, was not yet acceptable to Britain.

The Afghans, frustrated in their efforts to conclude a treaty with Britain, sought again to reach an agreement with Soviet Russia. Relations between Afghanistan and the Soviets had deteriorated considerably because of the Soviet overthrow of the amir of Bukhara and the establishment of a Soviet government there.[32] Nonetheless, "the Afghans seemed to feel that without having a treaty with Britain they could not break with the Russians.[33] The Soviets had become increasingly worried by Amanullah's pan-Islamic and pan-Turanic activities. Not only had he assisted the amir of Bukhara in his struggle against the "Young Bukharans" but he was also now giving material, political, moral, and perhaps even financial support to the Basmachis.[34] To lure Amanullah away from those pursuits and attract him into their orbit, the Russians, in spite of their hesitations, presented to the Afghans a series of "concessions" in a proposed treaty that had been under consideration for some time by the Afghans.

The Soviets were then experiencing serious economic difficulties at home that had led to the adoption of the New Economic Policy, and the disagreement with Turkey over the division of Armenia was giving the Bolshevik leadership much cause for concern. These problems probably also played a role in inducing the Soviets to speed up their efforts to reach an agreement with the Afghans. Amanullah Khan agreed that Afghanistan should sign the treaty, perhaps only to impress Britain and pressure it to be more accommodating. The draft of the Russo–Afghan treaty was signed by the Afghans late in September 1920. It was then sent to Moscow for approval. Initially there was opposition to some of the draft treaty's provisions, but, after a lapse of a few months, the Bolshevik leadership finally agreed to it, and it was ratified by the Russians in February of 1921 without any change.

Two Soviet concessions included in the draft treaty were contained in Articles VIII and IX. Article VIII stipulated that "the High Contracting Parties accept the actual independence and freedom of Bukhara and Khiva, whatever may be the form of their government, in accordance with the wishes of their peoples." It is ironic that Soviet Russia was accepting the "actual" independence and freedom of Bukhara and Khiva at a time when it was busy depriving them of those cherished rights. Article IX of the draft treaty stated "Russia agrees to hand over to Afghanistan the frontier districts which belonged to the latter in the last century [mainly the district of Panjdeh], observing the principles of justice and self-determination of the population inhabiting the same. . . ."

Article IX, stipulating that the parties "bind themselves not to enter into any military or political agreement with a third state which might prejudice one of the Contracting Parties," represented a major gain for the Soviets. This arrangement blocked the conclusion of an alliance between Afghanistan and Britain. A supplemental clause to the Russo–Afghan treaty also provided for Afghanistan to receive from Russia "a yearly free subsidy to the extent of one million gold or silver rubles in coin or bullion" and "technical and other specialists."

Likewise, the Russo–Afghan agreement regulated the establishment of legations and consulates of both countries in each other's territories. In addition to a legation in Moscow, the Afghans were allowed to establish consulates in Tashkent, Petrograd, Kazan, Samarkand, Merv, and Krasnovadsk. The Soviets were authorized to open a legation in Kabul and consulates at Herat, Maymana, Mazar-i-Sharif, Kandahar, and Ghazni. The British were quite disturbed that the Afghans had signed the Russo–Afghan draft treaty, and they became alarmed when they learned that it allowed Russia to open consulates so close to India, in Kandahar and Ghazni. They saw the Red menace pushing its way to their door. The British approached the Afghans with their objections and undoubtedly presented their grievances to the Russians too.[35]

The Afghans were concerned about the sovietization of Bukhara, which eliminated a potential buffer between Afghanistan and Soviet Russia and weakened the forces of Islam as a hindrance to Soviet power in central Asia. Amanullah himself did not feel that Afghanistan was secure from Communism's advances because, even if his country were not a prime target, he knew that India certainly was. By that time the Indian *hijrat* movement (holy immigration of Indian Muslims to Afghanistan) had also failed because of the Afghan administration's inability to properly provide for the thousands of Indian Muslims who had emigrated to Afghanistan and were now stranded there, most of them completely destitute. The movement, conceived of as an anti-British operation, had turned out to be a disappointment to many.[36] Indeed, it had become an embarrassment for the amir, who had earlier encouraged the Indian Muslims to immigrate to Afghanistan, *Dar-el-Islam* (the land of Islam), from under the yoke of the *kofr* (infidels) and had declared the doors of Afghanistan open to the Indian *mahajereen* (holy immigrants). Moreover, Amanullah had perceived that the success of his plans for the development of Afghanistan necessitated the goodwill of its neighbors, especially of Britain because of the close interrelationship between India and landlocked Afghanistan. The amir, therefore, stalled the ratification of the Russo–Afghan treaty and invited a British mission to Kabul. The balance, which had tilted too far in Russia's favor, had to be restored.

Amanullah drifted back to the traditional policy of seeking a balance of power in the area. In part he was led to do so by his increasing apprehensions about Soviet intentions, in part by Britain's consolidation in the North West Frontier Province and strong diplomatic protests, even threats, to the Soviet government over Soviet activities (real or not) in Afghanistan against India. This shift in policy meant a rapprochement with Great Britain, an idea that was repugnant to many Afghan traditionalists and some nationalists.[37]

A British mission headed by Indian Foreign Secretary Henry Dobbs arrived in Kabul in January 1921. Mahmud Tarzi was once again leading the Afghan delegation. Discussions between the two delegations were long and protracted, lasting almost a year. Dobbs was instructed to conclude a treaty along the lines of the Mussoorie memorandum, and the Afghans, basing their position on the principle of self-determination, wanted the return of territories lost to Britain or the complete independence of trans-Durand Pashtuns, and, as an immediate step toward that settlement, they requested clemency for them. This core of the Afghan position was met, as usual, with total rejection by the British. Dobbs wanted Afghanistan to refrain from intercourse with the transborder Pashtun tribes and to prohibit the establishment of Russian consulates near the Indian frontier. He repeatedly stressed that the Afghans should follow a good neighborly policy toward Britain. The British also proposed that the treaty between them and the Afghans contain a clause forbidding either party to enter into an agreement with a third power that would affect the mutual interests of Afghanistan and Britain. The Afghans, while professing their friendship for Britain, made it clear that they considered the British demand concerning the exclusion of Russian consulates from eastern and southern Afghanistan interference in their internal affairs and explained that their compliance with the British demand in this respect would greatly irritate Russia. They asked whether, if Afghanistan abrogated the Russo–Afghan treaty, Britain would be in a position to defend it against a Russian attack. So far as the third-country clause was concerned, the Afghans were extremely reluctant to go along with such a provision, which, in their opinion, was damaging to Afghanistan's sovereignty. In the international sphere, the Afghan delegation demanded from the British the revision of the Turkish peace treaty.[38]

The emotional issue of the Pashtun tribes was the most difficult to deal with. "The tribal question threatened several times to lead to a rupture in the negotiations and according to Dobbs, a breakdown was averted only when Britain signed a trade agreement with Russia on March 17, 1921."[39] Obviously, Dobbs believed that the trade agreement made the Afghans aware of the possibility of a broader entente between Russia and Britain that would leave Afghanistan out in the cold and deprive it of the opportunity to play one power off against the other.

As time passed and the negotiations continued, Amanullah seemingly became increasingly interested in having an exclusive treaty with Britain, despite generous offers of assistance by Russia and the latter's expressed readiness to return Panjdeh to Afghanistan.

Amanullah decided that the way to safeguard this new society that he was building was to link its fortunes entirely with Great Britain's. . . . Suritz [the new Russian envoy who had replaced Bravin in Kabul] sent Amanullah a peremptory note demanding that he ratify at once. Instead, Amanullah told Tarzi to meet with Dobbs and offer to break off completely with Russia, on various conditions which included a gift by Britain immediately of munitions which had been promised only in event of an attack by a third power. . . . "If you will accept our proposal," Tarzi told Dobbs, "we will sign at once and inform Suritz that we will have nothing more to do with Russia. We will make a clean cut. But we feel great uneasiness about the British gift of munitions (contingent on an unprovoked Russian invasion) since they will be required for the distant Northern frontier, and if Russia made a sudden attack, the Afghans could not possibly get them to their Northern troops in time to be of any use. . . . We cannot take grave risks of invasion without [an] immediate gift of munitions. The moral effect of this immediate gift will enable us to give Russia this slap in the face with satisfaction. I will force the rupture of relations on Suritz by complaining about the Russian reaction in Bukhara and Khiva without mentioning the consulate position."[40]

The home government "suggested that the Amir be induced to break completely with Russia by giving him liberal grants in arms and money."[41]

It seemed that Amanullah was satisfied with the turn the talks were taking, but he made it known that he wanted the arms and ammunition *in place* on the northern frontier of Afghanistan before making a "clean cut" with the Russians. This new Afghan proviso worried the British, who were suspicious of Amanullah's tactics and motives. A period of vacillation began.

It was at about this time that Suritz informed the Afghans that the Soviets would not insist that Russian consulates be opened in localities near the Indian frontier.[42] The Afghans were probably not aware at the time that the Russians themselves had agreed with the British, in the interest of trade with Britain, not to press for those consulates.

Meanwhile, several incidents occurred that cooled Amanullah's newfound cordiality toward Britain. First, Britain reacted strongly to the news that an Afghan mission traveling in Europe, Asia, and the United States was on the verge of signing a treaty for commercial and consular relations with Italy. In its official protest to the Italian government, Britain declared that it still considered Afghanistan as lying within its sphere of political influence. Nonetheless, the treaty with Italy was concluded, and the unwarranted arrogance the British displayed in their attempt to interfere in Afghan affairs aroused resentment in Kabul. When the mission arrived in the United States, it was received cooly, apparently the result of British interference. Finally, the meeting in London between the head of the mission, Mohammad Wali Khan, and British Foreign Secretary Lord Curzon was abruptly cut off by the latter when the Afghan representative referred to the negotiations in Kabul. It was Curzon's contention that any matter relating to Afghanistan was under the jurisdiction of the India Office and "not his concern." Neither would he listen to Wali Khan's request to be introduced by him to the King. Curzon's reactions implied that he had not accepted Afghanistan's full sovereignty.[43] Once again Kabul reacted angrily to this affront.

These incidents confirmed the Afghans' belief that the British would never be reconciled to the independence of Afghanistan and still wished it to remain within their sphere of influence. All progress toward an Anglo–Afghan treaty stopped, and Amanullah, undoubtedly frustrated by Britain's unfriendly actions, ratified the Russo–Afghan treaty in August 1921. Stewart gave the following explanation for Amanullah's decision:

Afghanistan's encounters with Lord Curzon convinced Amanullah that he could no longer flee to the safety of close ties with Britain without losing his adult status in the world of nations. To the British, he realized, an exclusive treaty with Afghanistan was the apron-string by which a mother binds a child to herself. He had learned a universal truth, "You can't go home." Independence compelled him to balance his two powerful neighbors against one another. So he ratified with Russia.[44]

By that time, the new Russian envoy, Feodor Raskolnikov, had arrived in Kabul, bringing with him 500,000 rubles, the first payment of the annual subsidy of one million. Two airplanes were also delivered by the Russians. But Panjdeh, to which the Afghans were so much attached, was not returned to Afghanistan. Later, the Soviets would announce that the local population had expressed itself in favor of staying with Russia. The Afghans had no alternative but to acquiesce. The clause related to Panjdeh was quietly dropped from subsequent Russo–Afghan agreements. After ratification of the treaty, Afghanistan opened its consulates in Tashkent and Merv, in addition to its legation in Moscow (the first Afghan minister in Moscow was Mirza Mohammed Khan Yaftalli). Russia, which had already opened its legation in Kabul, opened consulates in Herat, Maymana, and Mazar-i-Sharif.

Dobbs, still in Kabul, pushed for a general treaty of neighborly relations between Afghanistan and Britain, to avoid the awkwardness of a diplomatic defeat for Britain. As time passed, the Afghans felt that they also needed some kind of contractual arrangement with Britain that would end the arms embargo and regulate the issues of trade and transit. Furthermore, Amanullah had come to realize that it would be to Afghanistan's advantage to enter into a treaty with Britain in addition to having one with Russia. The two sides, therefore, agreed to reach an agreement. After a relatively short period of time, a draft was made ready by the British and presented to the Afghans.

In general, this draft treaty recognized the internal and external independence of both parties and reaffirmed the Durand Line as the Indo–Afghan border. Direct diplomatic representation was to be established in the capitals of each nation. The treaty also allowed each party to open consulates in specified cities in Afghanistan and India (Jalalabad and Kandhar in Afghanistan; Delhi, Calcutta, Bombay, Karachi, Peshawar, and Quetta in India). Further, permission was given in the treaty for the importation by Afghanistan of arms and ammunitions through and from India. Trade relations between India and Afghanistan and the latter's transit trade through India were also broadly regulated by that treaty. The treaty contained no provision for the payment of a subsidy or of the arrears due the heirs of Habibullah Khan. The Afghans undertook no formal engagement to sever relations with the eastern Pashtuns or to expel the Indian revolutionaries from Afghanistan, nor did they agree to a clause prohibiting relations or contractual engagements with third parties.

Afghanistan's concern for the trans-Durand tribes was dealt with only vaguely in Article XI of the draft, which referred to the parties' "good will" and "benevolent intention towards the tribes residing close to their respective boundaries." The provisions of that article further obligated each party to inform the other of any "military operations of major importance" that were contemplated for the maintenance of order in their respective spheres. Feeling that these platitudes were inadequate, the Afghans insisted on receiving from the British a letter recognizing at least "that the conditions of the frontier tribes of the two Governments are of interest to the Government of Afghanistan" and demanded that the letter be an integral part of the treaty. Once the British acceded to these requests, Mahmud Tarzi and Henry Dobbs signed the Anglo–Afghan treaty on November 22, 1921 (see note 20).

The Amir announced the conclusion of the treaty in the presence of the British delegation. He emphasized the fact that this was not a friendship treaty, but merely one for neighborly relations. The conclusion of a treaty of friendship the Amir made contingent on the generosity which Britain would show towards Turkey and the frontier tribes and the treatment it would give to the inhabitants of India. In his report to the Government of India, Dobbs asserted that "in all but name the treaty is one of friendship, giving us what we had wished far more cheaply than had been contemplated." By not paying a subsidy, the government of India had lost some of its influence, but Dobbs saw that the real hold of Britain over Afghanistan lay in the fact that the latter depended on Britain for its supplies and communication with the outside world.[45]

The treaty of 1921 was to regulate Afghan–British relations until the day Britain relinquished control of the subcontinent. After the treaty was signed, the Afghans opened their legation in London and the British established theirs in Kabul (the first Afghan Minister in London was Abdul Hadi Khan Dawi). Afghan consulates were established in Delhi, Karachi, Bombay, Peshawar, and Quetta and those of the British in Jalalabad and Kandahar. On the basis of relevant provisions of the treaty, a trade convention was signed between the two countries in 1923. In spite of these developments, relations between Britain and Afghanistan did not improve. Amanullah was not averse to better relations with the British, but their lack of trust in him, his nationalistic stance, their perception of his ambitions toward India, and, last but not least, the novelty of Afghan independence, made it difficult for the imperial rulers of the subcontinent to adopt a more constructive and friendly stance toward Afghanistan.

As Anglo–Afghan relations continued on this rocky course and British subsidies vanished, Afghan reliance on Soviet Russia increased. In spite of their internal difficulties, the Russians started to furnish arms and munitions to Afghanistan. They also began helping the amir build an embryonic Afghan air force, which the outraged British referred to as the "Russofication of the Afghan Air Force."[46]

Amanullah was probably certain that, even in the absence of a formal defensive alliance with Britain, the imperatives of the defense of India would compel the British to defend Afghanistan against Russian aggression. Given the military and economic weakness of Russia at that time, it was unlikely that the Soviets would undertake an attack on Afghanistan. However, the eventual spread of Communist ideology into Afghanistan and India undoubtedly rendered easier by closer contact and increased exchanges between the Afghans and the Soviets, was a matter that disturbed both the Indian rulers and Amanullah. Among the Afghan people, still shocked by what had happened in Bukhara and Khiva, there was also a perception of the dangers that this new closeness with Russia could bring. But the amir, snubbed by the British, had no alternative but to turn to the Soviets.

After the conclusion of the Russo–Afghan treaty of 1921, other agreements were signed between the two countries, including a treaty on neutrality and nonaggression in 1926 and an airline agreement in 1927. As the years passed, the Soviets continued to give financial and technical assistance to Afghanistan and to provide it with arms and munitions. Turkish, German, Italian, and French technicians and professionals were rapidly added to the Russians as Afghan relations with those countries expanded during this period. All of them were expected to make their contribution to the speedy modernization of Afghanistan. It was also hoped that the presence of so many foreigners of different nationalities would prevent the influence of one nation from becoming dominant.[47]

By 1924, when rebellion broke out in Khost, a town in the southeast of Afghanistan, Amanullah's internal reforms, begun immediately after his accession to the throne, had achieved a definite momentum. It was believed by many that the rebellion was a reaction by conservative elements to Amanullah's social reforms, particularly public education for girls and greater freedom for women. The general public never entirely subscribed to such theories. Britain was seen as the arch culprit in the affair, manipulating the tribes against Amanullah in an attempt to bring about his downfall.

The rebellion, which at times acquired serious proportions, was put down with difficulty by Amanullah's armies, with the help of aircraft provided by the Soviets and flown by German and Russian pilots. The two rickety planes the British contributed to the effort did little to absolve them in the eyes of the Afghans.

To commemorate the defeat of the Khost Rebellion, Amanullah built a monument on the bank of the Kabul River and called it *Munar-i-Elm-wa-Jahl* (the Pillar of Knowledge and Ignorance), a monument dedicated to the triumph of knowledge over ignorance. For Amanullah, the real struggle was not against Britain or Russia but against the ignorance he saw as the root cause of Afghanistan's backwardness. In his vision of the future, ignorance was bound to be overcome. This belief, symbolized by that marble and granite monument, guided him as a beacon on the road that he had chosen for placing his country among the free and prosperous nations of the world.

In 1927 King Amanullah undertook a grand tour of Europe, Asia, and Africa. Among the countries he visited were Britain and the Soviet Union. In London he had a rather uncomfortable meeting with Sir Austen Chamberlain, the under secretary of state for foreign affairs, to whom he pointed out that the British claim of sovereignty over the lands inhabited by the independent Pashtun tribes of northwest India was disputed by the Afghans and that those lands rightfully belonged to Afghanistan. In Turkey, he met Kamal Ataturk, for whom he held immense admiration. He also visited Iran and was impressed by the progress achieved by that country. Amanullah's trip was most of all a great public relations feat. He succeeded in introducing Afghanistan to the outside world and dramatically brought his country out of isolation.

But when Amanullah returned home in July 1928, the country was not the same as he had left it nine months before. An atmosphere of unrest and apprehension prevailed. However, he persevered in his task of reform and modernization. Impressed by what he had seen in Europe and, especially, Turkey, he accelerated his efforts to narrow the gap between Afghanistan and the more advanced countries he had visited. Amanullah's new program of political and social reforms included the promulgation of a new, liberal constitution, the establishment of a legislative assembly elected by the vote of all literate male Afghan adults, the abolition of hereditary ranks, land reform, and the extension of military service to three years. At a public gathering, the king announced the abolishment of the veil for women and the establishment of compulsory female education. A few days after the announcement, the queen threw off her veil at a civic meeting in Kabul, and her example was quickly followed by many of the women of the city.[48]

Traditional Afghanistan was not ready for this much modernization this quickly. Reactionary elements whipped the endemic unrest into a huge uprising against Amanullah. Abdur-Rahman Pazhwak, Afghan diplomat, historian, and president of the United Nations General Assembly in 1966, asserted, like some other Afghan writers, that "the political maneuverings of outside elements" were actually the cause of the rebellion.[49]

An obscure figure emerged from among the insurgents as the challenger to Amanullah's rule. His name was Habibullah, nicknamed Bacha Sacao (son of water carrier); he was a native of Kohdaman, a region north of Kabul. He was a brigand who had at one time worked at odd jobs in Peshawar and had spent time in British jails in India. Bacha Sacao was destined to end the reign of Amanullah and his enlightened policies.

After a few initial victories, the royal troops were roundly defeated by Bacha's irregulars. Amanullah abdicated in favor of his elder brother Inayatullah Khan and fled the capital. Inayatullah also abdicated and was taken to India in a British airplane. Bacha occupied the capital. Amanullah left the country for Italy on May 22, 1929.

Amanullah's Russian friends did not help him. Toward the end of the insurrection, when it was in any case too late, the Soviets mounted an expeditionary force and sent it to Afghanistan, but it was soon recalled and disbanded. "Later Chicherin, the Commissar for Foreign Affairs, would say that Russia refused aid to Amanullah for fear of starting trouble with England; he never admitted the existence of the expeditionary force."[50]

Amanullah had been overthrown by the forces of ignorance and reaction that he had fought to vanquish throughout his reign. The army, considerably weakened and preoccupied by the ongoing fight against the tribes in the eastern and southern regions, was not in a position to contain Bacha's irregulars, whose rifles were "far better than the weapons of the Afghan troops."[51] Perhaps, if some tribes hitherto not committed to the rebel cause had not been prevented by reactionary elements from coming to Amanullah's assistance, and if the trans-Durand tribes (like the Afridis and Orakzais) friendly to the Afghan king had been allowed to hasten to his side, the debacle might have been avoided. It is a matter of record that the British barred the Afridis and Orakzais from crossing into Afghanistan, and, when the British orders were ignored by these tribes, fighting erupted between Shiite and Sunni Orakzais, disrupting their plans to aid Amanullah.[52]

Bacha Sacao proclaimed himself King. Although the foreign legations in Kabul did not close, no formal recognition was extended by any power to Bacha Sacao as the ruler of Afghanistan. The two most important neighbors of Afghanistan, the British and the Russians, adopted a wait-and-see attitude.

Bacha's bizarre reign lasted nine months. It was terminated by former Afghan Army Commander-in-Chief, and Amanullah's former minister in Paris, General Mohammad Nadir Khan, who returned to Afghanistan from self-imposed exile in France. General Nadir Khan entered Afghanistan through India on March 8, 1929, accompanied by two of his brothers,

Mohammad Hashim Khan and Shah Wali Khan. With the help of tribal levies, mostly Wazirs from the British side of the Durand Line and the Afghan tribes, he defeated Bacha's forces. Kabul was occupied by Nadir Khan's tribal lashkars on October 10, 1929. Bacha Sacao surrendered and was executed on November 3. On October 17, a jirga of tribal lashkars proclaimed Mohammad Nadir Khan King of Afghanistan and a *Loya Jirga* (Grand Assembly) reconfirmed his accession to the throne in September 1930.

During Amanullah's reign, relations between Afghanistan and Britain had remained precarious. Among the British there was evident dislike for the man as well as for his policies. "Some British officials saw a modernizing of Afghanistan as a threat to British rule in India since it offered an example of the kind of progress free Asians could achieve. . . . This was especially true among the British military."[53] It can be assumed that the British rulers did not much regret the disappearance of King Amanullah from the Afghan scene. Afghans in general remain convinced that the elimination of Amanullah was engineered by the British because, in their view, he had become too friendly with the Russians and an obstacle to the furtherance of Britain's interests. To this day "eyewitness" accounts abound in and around Kabul of surreptitious contacts that took place between Sacao and members of the British legation, of canned English food found in Sacao's trenches, and of Lawrence of Arabia, the famous British secret agent T. E. Lawrence, roaming the Afghan countryside posing as a holy man and inciting the tribes to rise against Amanullah.

The fall of King Amanullah brought about the sudden collapse of the somewhat novel Afghan approach to foreign policy. Perhaps it was his unorthodox foreign policy that had undone him in the first place. In any case, it appeared that there existed objective rules determining Afghan foreign policy, independent of the ruler's will, and that Amanullah had committed the inexcusable act of tampering with these rules for too long. Nadir Shah (as he was now called) saw to it that Afghan foreign policy, having wandered from its natural course, was brought back into line. A more traditional foreign policy was adopted. The pendulum, which had gone too far to the left, swung back to the middle.

The Restoration of Balance in Afghan Foreign Policy

Nadir Shah devoted himself to the consolidation of the monarchy and the reconstruction of the country, which had been severely shaken by Bacha Sacao's misrule and civil war. Aware of the reluctance of Afghan society to accept sweeping reforms, he adopted a step-by-step approach to development and established priorities in such a way as to devote the meager Afghan resources to the most needed and urgent projects. The development of Afghanistan slowed but was by no means reversed. The necessity for progress had become inexorable; King Amanullah had initiated a course that neither could nor would be abandoned by subsequent Afghan rulers.

The new Afghan rulers were quite familiar with British imperial ways and believed that the consolidation of the new regime necessitated a degree of disengagement from the Soviet Union and a friendlier stance toward Britain. The early endorsement in May 1930 by the new regime of the Anglo–Afghan treaty of 1921 and the trade convention of 1923 was a demonstration of this belief, although acceptance of the treaty of 1921 meant confirmation of the Durand Line by the new Afghan rulers. Nadir Shah also knew the significance of having good relations with Afghanistan's northern neighbor, not only to placate the latter's territorial and ideological appetites but also to assure it of Afghan neutrality and evenhandedness. The Soviets and some nationalist and modernist elements, both inside Afghanistan and on the frontier, were inclined to believe that Nadir had been helped to the Afghan throne by Britain and had consequently become a tool of British imperialism. Nadir Shah's goodwill toward the Soviet government was in part motivated by his desire to counter that perception.

Afghan rulers, especially in the first years of Nadir Shah's reign, were obsessed with the idea that Amanullah Khan might return to power with the aid of one of Afghanistan's neighbors whose interests might warrant elimination of the new Afghan regime. It seemed unlikely that Amanullah would be brought to Afghanistan by the British, who disliked him profoundly. Amanullah's passage through the tribal areas of Afghanistan, whose inhabitants had risen against him and been instrumental in driving him out of the country, also seemed unlikely. But the thought that a malcontent Russia could help Amanullah regain the Afghan throne was taken seriously. After all, he was on good terms with the Soviets, and they would gain from his return to power. This was an added reason for Nadir Shah to seek good relations with the Russians; he did not wish to give them any pretext to assist Amanullah's comeback. Thus, until the end of his short reign, Nadir Shah strove to maintain a balance in Afghanistan's relations with its two powerful neighbors. It was obviously a return to the foreign policy of Abdul Rahman Khan, minus, of course, its strict isolationism, which had become both untenable and harmful because of changed conditions and shifts in Afghan attitudes.

In the Afghan thinking of the day, the survival of Afghanistan necessitated that both of its mighty neighbors continue to have a stake in preserving its independence. Britain was to consider Afghanistan part of the defense of India and an obstacle to Communist military and ideological aggression; the Soviets were to accept Afghanistan as a buffer against the ever-present threat of British imperialism. Shortly after his ascension to the throne, Nadir Shah appointed his brother, Mohammad Aziz Khan, minister to Moscow, as he had appointed another brother, Shah Wali Khan, minister to the Court of Saint James. These actions were intended by the Afghan government to demonstrate its even-handedness toward Afghanistan's two European neighbors. However, to keep the climate of Afghan relations with both Britain and the Soviet Union immune from tension was not an easy task. It was particularly difficult to do so where

Anglo–Afghan relations were concerned. The reason was simple: The traditional problem of the contentious trans-Durand Pashtun tribes, as always, continued to bedevil relations between Afghanistan and Britain.

In 1930 Britain renewed its forward policy in the Frontier. Translated into colonial practice, the policy meant that the British had decided to push forward their military roads and establish their military outposts as far as possible into the tribal hinterland. The traditionally independent-minded tribes, further influenced by Khudai Khidmatgaran agitation and to some extent by propaganda from India's Congress Party, reacted violently to the renewal of British penetration into the tribal territory.[54] At one time the uprising grew so serious that the city of Peshawar itself was about to fall into tribal hands. The situation was reversed only by British use of massive air power. Throughout the early 1930s, resistance to alien domination remained extremely intense on the Frontier and provided the British with some of the most horrendous episodes of their long-standing confrontation with trans-Durand tribes.

As in past decades, the Pashtun tribes struggling for the maintenance of their independence sought aid and assistance from the Afghan rulers. Shortly after becoming king, Nadir Shah had forcefully reiterated the traditional Afghan stand with respect to the Frontier Pashtuns, stating that "the inhabitants of Afghanistan and the Afghans of the border are one people by virtue of their Islamic religion and nationality."[55] Besides, he well knew the value of the tribal belt for Afghanistan as a buffer against British expansion. But he could not extend to the tribes all the support he wanted to furnish because, due to the extreme vulnerability of the new regime, he could not risk British wrath. Likewise, Nadir Shah adopted a passive stance with respect to the Indian national liberation movement, which had previously found in Amanullah one of its staunchest supporters.

Nadir Shah's putative neutrality in the war between the trans-Durand Pashtuns and the British obviously irritated the tribes on both sides of the Durand Line, but it pleased the British, who provided him with ten thousand rifles and £180,000 in cash in 1931.[56] This was the only assistance that Afghanistan received from foreign sources during Nadir Shah's reign.[57]

Although Nadir did not assist the transborder tribes in their struggle against the British, he nevertheless continued to welcome their leaders whenever they sought refuge in Afghanistan or visited the country. Nadir repeatedly expressed his disappointment to the British about their treatment of the tribes and asked that the campaign against them be stopped. Sporadic unrest, often fanned by pro-Amanullah elements, occurred among some tribes on the Afghan side of the Durand Line, but Nadir Shah's profound knowledge of tribal matters and his willingness to heed tribal grievances usually contained the uprisings and brought them to a speedy conclusion.

The British, to the great disappointment of the Afghan government and the frustration of the tribal people, did not reverse their forward policy on the Frontier. At times it was pursued less vigorously, owing to external or internal pressures, but it was never entirely abandoned. As mentioned earlier, the British interest in consolidating their military presence in tribal areas increased markedly after Afghanistan became independent. In case the buffer state, whose destinies they no longer controlled, collapsed quickly under an onslaught from the north, the British wanted to be in a position to stop the "barbarian" from invading India through the tribal zone.

The tribes were not destroyed, but they were efficiently contained and much of the independent tribal area came under the influence of the government of India. Ironically, the government of India continued its forward policy on the Frontier even after it was clear that India would eventually attain her independence; thus the means towards the end of defending India—or of establishing a "scientific" frontier—had become an end in itself, as a policy was pursued that had lost much of its former significance.[58]

To the Afghans, the expansion of British power in the tribal areas was disconcerting for a number of reasons. It brought untold hardships to the trans-Durand Pashtuns and deprived them of their cherished freedom. It gradually scuttled the buffer behind which Afghanistan felt relatively secure from British overt and covert interventions. It made it increasingly unlikely that Britain might one day yield to Afghan claims with respect to the transborder Pashtuns and their territories. There were, thus, few incentives for the Afghans to overcome their chronic anti-British feelings. It was not surprising that relations between Afghanistan and Britain, despite their apparent serenity, never became cordial.

Meanwhile, in June 1930, a Russian force from Turkestan crossed the Oxus (Amu Darua) into Afghanistan "either with the idea of capturing Ibrahim Beg or perhaps merely in order to compel the Afghan Government to deal with him themselves."[59] This force penetrated as far as forty miles into northern Afghanistan.[60] Ibrahim Beg was one of the last Basmachi leaders and, according to Fraser-Tytler, an adherent of Bacha Sacao.[61] He operated now and then from Afghan territory against the Soviets in Turkestan and also plundered and pillaged villages and settlements inside Afghanistan in the regions of Mazar-i-Sharif, Andkhoy, and Maymana. The Soviets failed to capture Ibrahim Beg and, after strong protests by the Afghans, withdrew to their side of the frontier. The episode, however, further convinced the Afghans of the necessity of building better relations with the Soviet Union, not only to avoid the recurrence of such violations of their territory but also to discourage the Russians from fomenting trouble in the name of "national self-determination and cultural autonomy."[62]

In April 1931 an Afghan force under the command of Shah Mahmud Khan, another of Nadir Shah's brothers, defeated Ibrahim Beg and drove him north across the Oxus. Shortly afterward he was captured by the Russians and executed. This anti-Basmachi operation apparently pleased the Russians, for in 1931 a treaty of friendship and nonaggression was concluded between Afghanistan and the Soviet Union that institutionalized good neighborly relations between them.[63] After the defeat of Ibrahim Beg, Nadir Shah, to demonstrate his continued goodwill toward the Soviets, refused to allow northern Afghanistan to be used as a base for anti-Soviet activities. This policy was strictly enforced by the Afghan rulers who succeeded him, although anti-Soviet sentiments and the urge to harass the Russians remained strong among the thousands of refugees from Soviet persecution scattered through northern Afghanistan. The consolidation of normal relations with the Soviet Union brought about expansion of trade between the two neighbors. Later a postal agreement was signed between Afghanistan and the Soviet Union.[64]

Nadir Shah was eager to develop cordial ties with Turkey and Iran, two countries with which Amanullah had had excellent relations.

Nadir's efforts to reassert good and friendly relations with Turkey and Iran went far beyond the exigencies of normal diplomatic relations; he seems to have made a deliberate effort to preclude the possibility of either Turkey or Iran being made into a base of operation for pro-Amanullah elements, and to dissuade Iran from making any irredentist claim on Herat. In addition, both he and the Afghan modernists seem to have been anxious to prevent any assumption being made that in rejecting Amanullah Afghanistan had also rejected progress. Overt admiration for Turkey and Iran would be helpful in this connection.[65]

Nadir Shah succeeded in developing good relations with Iran and, particularly, Turkey. The latter's role in the training of the Afghan army and in the health sector was strengthened during Nadir Shah's reign. Turkish constitutional experts aided in the drafting of the Constitution of 1931, which remained in force until 1964. Nadir Shah also moved to establish close relations with other Islamic countries, not only to enhance Islamic solidarity but also to satisfy the staunchly Islamic Afghan nation. Thus, in 1932 Afghanistan signed treaties of friendship with Saudi Arabia and Iraq.

Judging from Nadir Shah's actions, he appears to have believed that, to balance the influence of the Soviet Union and Britain in Afghanistan, it was important to bar their nationals from employment in the country and to deny them any participation in the development of the kingdom. These restrictions were rigorously observed. Committed to Afghanistan's development through a process of "selective modernization," Nadir Shah sought the help of "politically disinterested" industrialized nations, primarily Germany, France, Italy, and Japan. While the three European countries responded favorably to Afghan overtures and increased their participation in Afghanistan's modest program of development, Japan did not join the ranks of those helping Afghanistan in its modernization efforts until years later. Over time, Germany's importance in this area grew rapidly. On the eve of World War II, Germany had become the major provider of financial and technical assistance to Afghanistan and one of its most important trading partners.

Nadir Shah also wished to enlist the cooperation of the United States in the development of Afghanistan. That country was particularly appealing to the Afghans for several reasons. It was a rich, far-away country with no imperialistic ambitions in Asia, its private investors were perceived to be bold and imaginative, and the quality of its technical know-how was second to none.

But, in spite of serious efforts, Nadir's administration did not succeed in interesting the United States in Afghanistan and its development. The U.S. government, after having extended de jure recognition to Afghanistan in 1921, had not yet even established formal diplomatic relations with it. It is likely that the country's remoteness and lack of knowledge in the United States about its internal conditions discouraged the American government and American investors from getting involved in Afghanistan.

On November 8, 1933, Nadir Shah was assassinated during a school prize-giving ceremony. The assassin was motivated by personal vengeance. He was the adopted son of Ghulam Nabi Khan Charkhi, a notorious pro-Amanullah sympathizer whom Nadir Shah had executed a year before on charges of fomenting a tribal rebellion in the southern province for Amanullah's benefit. Mohammad Zahir Shah succeeded his father as king of Afghanistan. Mohammad Hashim Khan, another of Nadir Shah's brothers and his prime minister, continued in the same capacity and, in fact, effectively governed the country in Zahir Shah's name until his resignation in May of 1946.

Notes

1. For interesting accounts of the early period of Soviet overt and covert operations against British rule in India and use of the legitimate aspirations of the Asians (notably those of Indian nationalists) by the Bolsheviks to further their anti-British designs, see also Georges Agabekov, *O.G.P.U.: The Russian Secret Terror* (New York: Brentano's, 1931), and Gunther Nollau and Hans Jurgan Wiehe, *Russia's South Flank: Soviet Operations in Iran, Turkey and Afghanistan* (New York: Praeger, 1963).
2. Those reforms did not cover the Pashtun homeland of the North-West Frontier Province.
3. Charles Miller, *Khyber: British India's North West Frontier* (New York: Macmillan Publishing Co., 1977), 314.
4. Ibid.
5. Mahmud Tarzi was an Afghan nationalist and reformer. He was the founder of the newspaper *Saradj-al-Akhbar* during the reign of Habibullah Khan and a prolific writer, poet, and translator of European and Turkish works into Persian. He later became Amir Amanullah's father-in-law and foreign minister.
6. Adamec, *Afghanistan 1900–1923*, 134.
7. Ibid., 110.
8. Ibid., 110–11.
9. The information in this paragraph was gathered by me in conversations with the late King Amanullah in Montreux, Switzerland, in the summer of 1953.
10. Adamec, *Afghanistan 1900–1923*, 142.
11. *The Times* (London), 13 June 1919. Quoted in Fletcher, *Afghanistan*, 197.
12. Adamec, *Afghanistan 1900–1923*, 115.
13. Miller, *Khyber*, 324–25.
14. Adamec, *Afghanistan 1900–1923*, 123.
15. Ibid., 124.
16. Ibid.
17. Ibid., 124–25.
18. Ibid., 127.
19. Ibid., 129.
20. For the Anglo–Afghan treaties of 1919 and 1921 and their annexes, see C. U. Aitchinson, *Treaties, Engagements and Sanads* (Calcutta: 1933), vol. XIII.

21. Adamec, *Afghanistan 1900–1923*, 135.
22. Fraser-Tytler, *Afghanistan*, 196–97.
23. Miller, *Khyber*, 106.
24. Ludwig W. Adamec, *Afghanistan's Foreign Affairs to the Mid-Twentieth Century: Relations with the U.S.S.R, Germany and Britain* (Tucson, Ariz.: University of Arizona Press, 1974), 106.
25. Adamec, *Afghanistan 1900–1923*, 143.
26. Ibid., 147.
27. Ibid., 154.
28. Ibid., 153.
29. Ibid., 154.
30. Ibid., 156.
31. Ghulam Mohammad, a member of the Afghan mission, explained the position to Abdul Kayum, a member of the British delegation, in the following terms (Adamec, *Afghanistan 1900–1923*, 152):

    "We can still make a good bargain with the Bolsheviks; but we prefer to deal with Great Britain, because she is firmly established and an ancient state, and is also wealthier than the Bolsheviks. Moreover, she is our old friend and we would prefer to turn towards her first . . . but we want to know what the British will offer us. If they will not offer us enough, we must turn to the Bolsheviks. There is still time to do so. But also we require Waziristan. . . ."

32. Bukhara, completely vassalized by czarist Russia, was only nominally autonomous. The Bolsheviks did not accept even that much of a facade. The Young Bukharans was a Communist front organization that engineered the overthrow of the amir of Bukhara and, with the assistance of the Red Army, established a Soviet government there. The unfortunate amir fled for his life and settled in Afghanistan. His treasure and personal belongings were plundered by Soviet officials.
33. Adamec, *Afghanistan 1900–1923*, 157.
34. Vartan Gregorian, *The Emergence of Modern Afghanistan* (Stanford, Calif.: Stanford University Press, 1969), 236.
35. The amir, while objecting to the British démarche on the ground that it was an infringement of Afghanistan's sovereignty, responded to British sensitivities by seeing to it that the Soviet consulates did not open in Kandahar and Ghazni. (In 1938 the Afghan consulates in Tashkent and Merv and the Russian consulates in Mazar-i-Sharif, Herat, and Maymana were closed by mutual consent. Twice in 1976 Novokreshchnikov, counselor of the Soviet Embassy in Kabul, asked the Afghan Foreign Ministry to consider reestablishment of at least one Soviet consulate, namely in Mazar-i-Sharif, but the ministry did not accept his request.) For the Russo–Afghan Treaty of 1921, see Adamec, Afghanistan 1900–1923, 188–91.
36. Adamec, *Afghanistan 1900–1923*, 158.
37. Gregorian, *Modern Afghanistan*, 238.
38. Adamec, *Afghanistan 1900–1923*, 160.
39. Ibid., 161.
40. Rhea Tally Stewart, *Fire in Afghanistan 1914–1929* (New York: Doubleday & Co., 1973), 163–64.
41. Adamec, *Afghanistan 1900–1923*, 161.
42. Ibid., 162.
43. Ibid., 163–64.
44. Stewart, *Fire in Afghanistan*, 183.
45. Adamec, *Afghanistan 1900–1923*, 165–66.
46. Adamec, *Afghanistan's Foreign Affairs*, 108.
47. As could be anticipated, the interaction between this new foreign community and the Afghans was not always smooth and uneventful. As an example of these frictions, the Peperno affair, which became a cause célèbre, is worth mentioning. Peperno, an Italian, killed an Afghan policeman. He was found guilty by the Afghan courts and executed. The affair aroused great indignation in Italy and Europe and almost caused the severance of diplomatic relations between Afghanistan and Italy.
48. Fletcher, *Afghanistan*, 215.
49. Abdur-Rahman Pazhwak, quoted in Gregorian, *Emergence of Modern Afghanistan*, 292.
50. Stewart, *Fire in Afghanistan*, 562.
51. Fletcher, *Afghanistan*, 225.

52. Ibid., 223.
53. Leon B. Poullada, *Reform and Rebellion in Afghanistan, 1919–1929* (Ithaca, N.Y.: Cornell University Press, 1973), 251.
54. The Khudai Khidmatgaran (servants of God) movement was founded and led by Abdul Ghafar Khan. Adherents of this movement later became known as the Red Shirts. The Khudai Khidmatgaran was a Pashtun nationalist reformist movement located in trans-Durand areas.
55. Quoted in Adamec, *Afghanistan's Foreign Affairs*, 195.
56. Fraser-Tytler, *Afghanistan*, 231.
57. Ibid.
58. Adamec, *Afghanistan's Foreign Affairs*, 211.
59. Fraser-Tytler, *Afghanistan*, 230.
60. Ibid.
61. Ibid.
62. Gregorian, *Emergence of Modern Afghanistan*, 333.
63. Ibid., 332.
64. Adamec, *Afghanistan's Foreign Affairs*, 203.
65. Gregorian, *Emergence of Modern Afghanistan*, 334.

4

World War II: Neutrality, the Natural Course for the Afghan State

The policies of Mohammad Hashim differed little from those of King Nadir Shah. Internally, Mohammad Hashim's government busied itself with consolidating the Afghan monarchy and strengthening law and order throughout the country. It also took gradual and cautious steps to further the process of modernization. Externally,

The Hashim Government was guided by the same principles as Nadir in foreign policy: correct relations with the Soviet Union and Great Britain; close relations with Turkey, Iran, and other Muslim countries; greater international recognition and wider contacts; and a continued attempt to secure the assistance of distant industrial powers in modernizing the country. Safe and cautious economic development continued to be one of the chief aims of Afghan foreign policy.[1]

Continuous efforts were made by the Afghan government to maintain "correct" relations with both Britain and the Soviet Union. Hashim discouraged the trans-Durand tribes from embarking on hostilities against Britain, and Indian dissidents were not allowed to use Afghanistan as a base for anti-British operations and propaganda. The tribal policies of the Afghan government of that period brought about a sense of alienation among the trans-Durand tribes for which continued Afghan subsidies could not compensate. The perception in most of the tribal area was that the tribes had been let down by Afghanistan. Two decades earlier, most trans-Durand tribes had considered the Afghan king their spiritual leader in the struggle for the preservation of their freedom from Britain, and many had hoped for eventual reunion with Afghanistan. The views of their leaders now were mostly divided between transforming their homeland into an independent Pashtun state and including it in a secular Indian union.[2] This state of affairs also deprived Afghanistan of the powerful leverage that the trans-Durand Pashtuns had provided in its unequal relations with British India.

Likewise, the Basmachi and other anti-Soviet elements in northern Afghanistan were prevented from embarking on anti-Soviet activities.[3] The Russo–Afghan frontier was gradually becoming what the Russians came to call "the frontier of peace." As a reflection of developing relations between the USSR and Afghanistan, an arrangement for cooperation in locust eradication in frontier regions was signed during 1935. The commerce treaty signed in 1936 ensured, among other things, transit rights for Afghanistan across Soviet territory, and in 1936 the Soviet–Afghan Pact was extended until March 1946.[4] In 1938 the two countries agreed by mutual consent to close their respective consulates, largely as a result of the Afghans' fear that the Soviet consulates in northern Afghanistan could be used for subversive purposes.

In 1934, Afghanistan applied for membership to the League of Nations and was elected to it as a full member. Membership in the League not only was an assertion of nationhood and independence but it was also hoped that it could provide protection from aggression for a small country like Afghanistan. But in 1936, the Italians overran and occupied Ethiopia, despite the League's warnings and sanctions. This act of aggression, which marked the beginning of the end of the League of Nations, proved that the system of collective security envisaged by the League's covenant was still unattainable. This tragic event made clear to the Afghans that they would not be able to rely on the League for assistance if threatened by one of their mighty neighbors. However, the League did serve the Afghans as a forum for protesting indiscriminate British bombing of tribal areas, especially of Waziristan in 1937.

Anxious to strengthen its relations with its Islamic neighbors and to improve its international posture, Afghanistan concluded the Pact of Saadabad in 1937 with Iran, Turkey, and Iraq. Although the century-old Iranian–Afghan dispute about the sharing of Hilmand River waters was not yet satisfactorily resolved, the prior settlement of a frontier difference between Afghanistan and Iran over an area called Musa Abad and the demarcation of a hitherto undemarcated sector of the Iranian–Afghan border had eliminated some of the major irritants from Iranian–Afghan relations and had consequently paved the way for the pact. Afghanistan's participation in the Pact of Saadabad, the first regional alliance of its kind to which Afghanistan was a party, seemed to have been determined in part by its desire to stem the eventual revival of an Iranian irredentist claim to Herat and parts of Seistan. Further, the Afghans sought a counterbalance to British and Soviet pressures in the context of expanded Islamic solidarity.

But the collective benefits of the alliance were never enjoyed in practical terms by the signatories. Soon the winds of war were blowing worldwide, and the countries of Saadabad were seeking other, more tangible alternatives for their survival. After World War II, conditions had changed so dramatically that they rendered the Pact of Saadabad totally obsolete. Thus, that admirable experiment in regional security and cooperation among a number of independent Islamic countries never really got off the ground.

In 1935 the United States had appointed the American minister to Iran as the accredited U.S. representative to Afghanistan. This long-overdue establishment of diplomatic relations between the two countries greatly pleased the

Afghans, who were actively seeking U.S. economic and political support. But it was not until 1937 that American business became involved in Afghanistan, when the Hashim government gave the American Inland Exploration Company a 75-year concession for the exploration and exploitation of Afghanistan's oil resources.[5]

However, this project was never brought to fruition. Soon after the Inland Company started its preliminary survey in the northern regions, the Afghan government was informed that the Americans wished to quit. Understandably, the Afghans were annoyed, but, according to the terms of the contract, there was nothing that could be done apart from requiring the payment of a cash penalty by the American company, which it promptly conceded.

Several reasons were given for the Inland Company's unilateral termination of the contract. But all of these problems should have been known or ascertained by a company like Inland before embarking on such a venture. There had been rumors at the time in Kabul that the Russians had had a hand in bringing the Afghan–American oil deal to an abrupt close. I could not find any indications that the Russians had asked the Afghans to terminate Inland's contract in the archives of the Ministry of Foreign Affairs. A former high official of the Foreign Ministry told me, however, that the Soviet Union had directly requested the Americans to end their involvement in the exploration and exploitation of oil in Afghanistan. Perhaps there is no need to search for a dramatic explanation for Inland's withdrawal from Afghanistan.[6] It may well be that the worsening of the international situation presaging war prompted the Americans to cut their losses and withdraw to safer shores.

By 1938 German economic and technical cooperation with Afghanistan, as well as trade between the two countries, had attained significant proportions. The Germans had even become increasingly involved in the modernization of the Afghan army. As German power grew and confrontational attitudes in Europe became more discernible, Germany's political interest in Afghanistan heightened substantially. This interest was motivated mainly by Afghanistan's geopolitical position and its potential as a base for future operations against Britain in India. In August 1939, Germany and Afghanistan concluded an "extensive financial and commercial agreement."[7] Under the terms of this agreement, the German government was to extend long-term credits to Afghanistan for the purchase of German machinery for textile and hydroelectric plants, and Afghanistan was to repay the credits over a period of ten years by providing cotton to Germany.[8] This agreement

was a great triumph for Nazi diplomacy. At a time when Great Britain, the USSR, France, and the United States were either unwilling or unable to make long range financial commitments to Afghanistan, Nazi Germany, for political reasons, was "prepared to accept the risk involved in the provision of long-term credits to a country which could offer little or no tangible security for repayment."[9]

When the war started in Europe in September 1939, Germany's presence was well established in Afghanistan. A considerable number of German experts and technicians were working in the country. Some of the German projects were well under way, and the Germans had managed to win Afghan sympathy through the quality of their work and their generous assistance to Afghanistan. In this propitious environment the Germans and Italians had busied themselves, among other things, with creating difficulties for Britain in the trans-Durand regions. Their agents, sometimes working together, had succeeded in establishing contact with anti-British elements in the tribal areas. Chief among these at the time was Haji Mirza Ali Khan, the famed Fakir of Ipi, who, since 1937, had been engaged in leading anti-British uprisings in Waziristan. The German and Italian legations in Kabul played an active role in this work of subversion on the Frontier by providing logistical and communications support for their agents. Sometimes members of these legations doubled as active agents themselves. All this was known to the inner circles of the Afghan leadership, but they did not take any strong measures to stop the German and Italian intrigues out of a desire not to antagonize Berlin and Rome. Occasionally, Afghan authorities did take action against these clandestine activities when the British government protested the subversive acts of a particular German or Italian agent.[10]

Since 1937, the worsening political situation in Europe had had a disquieting effect on the Afghan government, which realized that the important development projects that were being carried out with Germany's financial aid and technical assistance would be seriously affected if an armed conflict involving Germany erupted in Europe. The Afghan rulers were also following with deep concern the rapprochement between Germany and the Soviet Union, especially after the failure in early 1939 of Anglo–Soviet–French negotiations in Moscow aimed at the conclusion of a pact of mutual assistance against aggression in Europe. The perception in Kabul was that, in the event of an Anglo–German war, the Soviets, if aligned with the Axis, would feel free to invade and annex northern Afghanistan. And a besieged Britain fighting German, Italian, and possibly Japanese armies would not be in a position to forestall such a Russian advance. Some Afghans also feared that the German and Russian armies would attack the British in India through Afghanistan, causing in the process the complete destruction of the country. On the basis of these preoccupations, Prime Minister Hashim and other Afghan high officials were interested in knowing what the British reaction would be to an invasion of Afghanistan from the north.

In October 1938 Aubery Metcalf, foreign secretary of the government of India, visited Afghanistan. Although Frontier matters such as the bizarre episode of Pir Shami[11] and the continuing British campaign in Waziristan against the Fakir of Ipi were discussed, the talks centered mainly on Afghan concerns about an eventual Russian invasion of Afghanistan. The British still considered Afghanistan an integral part of the Indian defense and were weighing the possibility of concluding a mutual assistance agreement in which Britain would help Afghanistan militarily if attacked by Russia.

Understandably the Afghans were extremely cautious about such an agreement with Britain, as it would have alarmed the Soviet Union. This could have been risked only if the British would have undertaken concrete commitments to safeguard Afghanistan's independence and explicitly guarantee Afghanistan's northern borders. As had been the case in the 1921 Anglo–Afghan negotiations, the British were hesistant to undertake such definite obligations. Finally, attempts to negotiate a mutual-assistance agreement were postponed, and though further talks were held, no agreement was ever reached except on a small program of training for Afghan army officers in India.

In August 1939 Germany and the Soviet Union concluded a nonaggression treaty. A few days after the conclusion of the treaty, Germany invaded Poland, and on September 17 the Red Army joined the *Wehrmacht* in the rape and division of Poland, as had been secretly agreed in a protocol to the treaty. Immediately after the German attack on Poland, Britain and France, honoring their solemn pledge, declared war on Germany.

These events increased the uneasy feeling among the Afghans that a Russian invasion of Afghanistan could suddenly become a reality. In the Afghan view, Britain's preoccupation elsewhere and its probable inability to deter Soviet ambitions in Asia added to the gravity of the situation. At the same time, the Afghans were equally concerned about a declaration of war on Russia by Britain, which could have precipitated the invasion of India by the Soviet Union through Afghanistan. After the outbreak of hostilities in Europe, Afghanistan proclaimed its neutrality in the conflict. However, because of combined German and Soviet hostility toward Britain and its possible consequences, the maintenance of neutrality was going to be much more difficult than in 1914–1918, when the two European neighbors of Afghanistan were allies. Afghan neutrality from 1939 to mid-1941 primarily benefited Britain, as it provided the latter with assurance that the Afghan government would refrain from initiating tribal revolt against Britain. A tranquil Frontier undoubtedly contributed to the stability of India and meant that a large number of British troops could be released from service in India and the Frontier and be put to better use elsewhere.

While the British appreciated the value of Afghan neutrality and wished its continuation, the Germans, Italians, and Soviets were actively attempting to attract the Afghans to their side. Even before the war started, the Germans and the Italians had known the value of Afghan territory as a staging area for anti-British activities, especially to foment tribal unrest, and had established contacts with anti-British elements in the trans-Durand areas. Now that the newly found friendship between the Soviet Union and Germany had provided the Germans with better access to Afghan territory, the usefulness of Afghanistan for Germany as an advanced base for operations against the British in India had increased dramatically. There was no doubt that the Germans intended to exploit this favorable situation. They were aware, however, that no large-scale action, such as a serious rebellion on the Frontier, could be undertaken and brought to a successful conclusion without the Afghan government's close cooperation. Germany, suspecting the Hashim government of being biased in favor of the British, initially considered replacement of the Afghan regime with ex-king Amanullah or a member of his family. Begun on the basis of an Italian suggestion, the *Amanullah project* was dropped in 1940 because of the opposition of Alfred Rosenberg, the powerful head of the foreign affairs office of the Nazi party, and the refusal of the Soviet Union to cooperate in the plan.[12] Rosenberg was of the opinion that, instead of bringing in Amanullah, attempts should be made to draw the Hashim government to the Axis side and conclude with it "a mutually advantageous political alliance."[13] The Soviets had little confidence in Amanullah's credibility with the Afghan tribes and feared British attempts to incite the tribes against him if he were put back on the throne.

The Germans then began pressuring the existing Afghan government to relax its neutrality by addressing the emotional subject of Afghan irredentist claims. The German envoy in Kabul in 1940 "confidentially announced to them [the Afghans] that Hitler would be in London by August. He reportedly offered Afghanistan a restoration of the Durrani Empire, proposing that she be given Baluchistan, Sind, Kashmir and the Western Punjab, including the port of Karachi."[14] After the 1940 German invasion of Denmark, Norway, and the Benelux countries and France's spectacular defeat in June of that year, it appeared that the Reich's victory over the British Empire was inevitable. The abandonment of neutrality became increasingly tempting to many Afghans. The majority of Afghan modernists and nationalists inclined toward Germany precisely because of Afghan irredentist claims. They believed that Britain would never restore the lost lands to Afghanistan, while a German victory could make that possible.

There is archival evidence that, until the middle of 1941, some Afghan high officials carried out extensive contacts with German authorities in Kabul and in Berlin to determine what position a victorious Germany would take with regard to Afghanistan's claims to lands situated in trans-Durand areas. Those Afghan officials made it known to the Germans that, if the Afghans could expect that the lands severed from Afghanistan by colonialism would be returned to it, Afghanistan were given free access to the sea, and, Germany could obtain from the Soviets a guarantee of Afghanistan's territorial integrity, Afghanistan would openly side with the Germans and even go to war as an ally of the Axis countries or launch tribal uprisings on the Frontier.[15] Whether these negotiations were undertaken with the full knowledge and acquiescence of Hashim Khan is not known, but they were undeniably serious talks. The failure of Germany to assist the pro-Axis government of Rashid Ali al-Gaillani in Iraq against British forces, which was construed as its inability to take action in the region, cooled the Afghans' desire for political cooperation with Germany.

This period of German–Afghan interaction had clearly alarmed the British, for at one point they promised the Afghans a free port on the Baluchistan coast and a railway link between Chaman and Kandahar, probably to lure them away from seeking closer political ties with Germany. Apparently the offer did not satisfy the Afghans, and the project was shelved.[16]

Another alternative with which the Germans, during their alliance with Russia, hoped to secure Afghanistan as a forward base of operations against India was through military occupation by the Soviet Union. "Brauchitsh, the commander-in-chief of Germany's land forces, revealed in January 1940 that the Reich was intent on channelling Soviet expansion into Afghanistan and India."[17] Since the conclusion of the German–Soviet nonaggression treaty, the Germans had encouraged Russian ambitions to expand southward toward India and the Indian Ocean. During a conversation with Soviet Foreign Minister Molotov in November 1940 in Berlin, German Foreign Minister von Ribbentrop suggested that "the focal point in the territorial aspirations of the Soviet Union would presumably be centered south of the territory of the Soviet Union in the direction of the Indian Ocean."[18] In this particular conversation, Molotov avoided making any direct comments about the subject. His caution was understandable. The Russians must have feared that the German aim was not only to engage Britain in a war in central Asia but also to divert the Soviet Union's attention from Europe and, in the process, weaken its military strength. However, two weeks later, Molotov revealed to the Germans "that the area south of Batum and Baku in the general direction of the Persian Gulf is recognized as the center of the aspirations of the Soviet Union."[19] German pressure on Russia to move southward, however, came to an end when Hitler's armies invaded the Soviet Union on June 22, 1941.

Under these circumstances, the difficulty of maintaining Afghanistan's neutrality could be well appreciated. But Hashim Khan's government did succeed in maintaining stable relations with Britain, the Soviet Union, and the German Reich. In fact, these relations were good enough to prompt the Germans to ship equipment and material to Afghanistan, in transit through Russia, and receive Afghan raw materials the same way, until the eve of the Soviet–German war; to allow Afghanistan and the Soviet Union to conclude a mutually advantageous commercial agreement in July 1940; and to encourage the British to continue to supply Afghanistan with much-needed consumption goods such as textiles, sugar, tires, and gasoline. Moreover, the satisfactory state of Anglo–Afghan relations led the Afghan government to ask the British to assist Afghanistan in its development efforts, when it realized that the war in Europe would not allow the Germans to continue to help Afghanistan for long.[20] Although the British turned down the Afghan request, apparently their refusal to assist Afghanistan did not adversely affect Anglo–Afghan relations. It is interesting to note that the urge to modernize was so great within Afghan ruling circles that, in a significant departure from established policies, they were even ready to allow British involvement in Afghanistan's economic development. They were not yet ready though to ask the Soviet Union to embark on such a venture.

After the German invasion of Russia, Britain and the Soviet Union once again became allies, a development that, although it rekindled some of the old apprehensions, rendered the management of Afghan neutrality easier for the Afghan rulers. As a consequence, the Afghan government began discreetly to distance itself from the Axis powers. Germany was no longer in a position to furnish aid to Afghanistan's economic and industrial development in any case, and trade between the two countries had ceased altogether. It was, therefore, without much debate or risk that such a move could be undertaken. It was at this point that the Afghan Foreign Minister Ali Mohammad Khan informed Pilzer, the German envoy, that

the fact that the USSR and Britain had become allies had radically changed the political situation, Afghanistan could do nothing to provoke either of her neighbors, and in the words of the foreign minister, the "Afghan government was at the time neither pro-German nor pro-English, but only pro-Afghan."[21]

Although the Afghans felt the tension of war in economic, developmental, and commercial fields, its political stresses largely subsided once Afghanistan's two European neighbors became allies against Nazi Germany.

However, the Anglo–Soviet invasion of Iran in September 1941, resulting from the Reza Shah's refusal to accept the Allies' demand to expel Axis subjects from his country, came as a great shock to the Afghans. Although it was clear that the Anglo–Russian ultimatum to Iran was a pretext to occupy the country because the Allies needed Iranian railroads and port facilities for supplying Russia with equipment and weaponry, the assumption that a similar request could be made of the Afghan government was taken seriously, especially since it was well known that the British wanted to put an end to the subversive activities carried out by German and Italian agents on the Frontier using Afghan territory as a staging area.

While the debate was going on inside the government over whether to accept or reject such an eventual request by the Allies, the British and Soviet governments presented simultaneous and identical notes to the Afghans on October 20, 1941, asking them to oust all German and Italian citizens from the country, with the exception of their diplomatic missions. This infringement of Afghanistan's neutrality and interference in its internal affairs infuriated many Afghans, who advocated rejection of the Allies' demand. But those who traditionally feared the partition of Afghanistan whenever its two European neighbors became allies and felt no need for a buffer state between them counseled that there was no other choice for the government but to accept the Anglo–Russian request. As this was a matter of grave consequence, a Loya Jirga was convened by the government, which authorized it to heed the Allies' demand. At the same time, it reaffirmed Afghanistan's strict neutrality and the nation's determination to preserve the country's independence and territorial integrity. The Afghan government made its acceptance of the Anglo–Russian request contingent upon the Allies' agreement that the Axis nationals be accorded safe-conduct through British India and areas under Allied control en route to their countries and be allowed to carry all their personal belongings with them to their final destination. The British and Russian governments readily accepted these provisions. It was in mid-November that the Germans and Italians finally left Kabul.

Afghanistan and the United States established direct diplomatic relations during the war years. Although it was obvious that the United States was motivated by wartime necessities, the measure nevertheless pleased the Afghans, who for many years had sought the establishment of such ties. On June 6, 1942, the American legation opened in Kabul, and the first resident American minister, Cornelius Van H. Engert, came to Kabul "with secret orders to prepare the ground for alternative lend-lease transit routes to Russia and China should German and Japanese offensives interrupt those through Iran and Burma."[22]

When the war ended in victory for the Allies in 1945, there was no doubt that American aid and might had primarily contributed to the realization of that victory. World War II confirmed America's rise as the world's strongest power and conferred upon it, as an attribute of that power, a central role in world affairs. The Afghans had watched the emergence of American might with interest and were thrilled about the role that this noncolonial, non-European power would inevitably be called upon to play in shaping the new postwar world.

All things considered, Afghanistan had not fared badly during the worldwide conflict. To a large extent its neutrality had been respected; its territorial integrity had remained intact; and it had not suffered any great shortages of imported goods and commodities. Of course, all development projects had been halted, but that was a small price to pay compared to the hardships and sacrifices endured by other nations. The Afghans were eager to resume their program of modernization as soon as conditions allowed, and they were hopeful that the United States would make a substantial contribution to help them on the road to progress.

At the close of the war, Afghanistan's relations with the principal Allies were good. In addition to the establishment of direct diplomatic relations with the United States, Afghanistan had exchanged diplomatic missions with China, a partner of the Allies in their anti-Axis coalition. The trans-Durand tribal areas, to the acknowledgment of the British, had been kept quiet during the war, and the Soviets had found no cause for any major complaints.

There was, however, one important matter that greatly concerned the Afghans at that stage: the British decision to leave India. Chief among the questions that this decision raised were the fate of the buffer state in central Asia without the British countervailing force, the kind of regime or regimes that would eventually replace the British Raj in India,[23] and whether Britain would be willing to settle with Afghanistan the problem of the trans-Durand tribes in a satisfactory manner before it left the subcontinent.

Thus, the Afghans crossed the threshold of the postwar era anxious to make speedy progress in the development of their country but also seriously preoccupied with the British decision to leave India. Since the British presence in India had frustrated the Afghans in so many ways and for so long, it was indeed ironic that Britain's departure from India would now cause them so many anxieties. One thing, though, was certain: The central Asian environment would not be the same without the British, and this would eventually necessitate making substantial changes in the Afghan policy of survival.

Notes

1. Gregorian, *Emergence of Modern Afghanistan*, 375.
2. Conversations with Ali Mohammad Khan in Kabul in the early 1970s.
3. Gregorian, *Emergence of Modern Afghanistan*, 375.
4. Ibid., 375–76.
5. Ibid., 381.
6. Adamec, *Afghanistan's Foreign Affairs*, 303 (Note 75), stated that, according to accounts primarily written by Faiz Mohammad (then Afghan foreign minister) that appeared in *Islah* (Kabul's newspaper), the deal was canceled because of British pressures.
7. Gregorian, *Emergence of Modern Afghanistan*, 380.
8. Ibid. Adamec, *Afghanistan's Foreign Affairs*, 239, also stated that the Afghan government intended to buy plants for the production of textiles, cement, sugar, leather, and matches from Germany and to set up several coal mining projects and plants for the generation of electricity, with the cooperation of Germany.
9. Gregorian, *Emergence of Modern Afghanistan*, 380.
10. Conversations with Ali Mohammad Khan.
11. Pir Shami, the Holy Man from Syria, suddenly appeared in Waziristan in the spring of 1938 and declared King Zahir Shah a usurper and ex-king Amanullah the legitimate ruler of Afghanistan. With the apparent intention of reinstating Amanullah on the throne, he managed to rally the Mahsuds and the Wazirs around him and marched on Mattun, a provincial town in southern Afghanistan. For a moment it seemed that he would overrun that outpost and continue on to Kabul. But the British persuaded him to abandon his plans. He accepted a bribe of £25,000 sterling and left India for Iraq. Some observers have seen the German hand, and some the British hand, in Pir Shami's scheme. But, in all likelihood, he embarked on this adventure on his own and, surprisingly, the British services in India, to their dismay, found out about him too late.
12. Gregorian, *Emergence of Modern Afghanistan*, 385–86.
13. Ibid., 385.
14. Ibid., 386.
15. U.S. Department of State, *Documents of German Foreign Policy*, XII, 283, 729, 971–72, Weizsacker to foreign minister, 12 March, 6 May, and 6 June 1946. See also Gregorian, *Emergence of Modern Afghanistan*, 387; Adamec, *Afghanistan's Foreign Affairs*, 245–46.
16. Adamec, *Afghanistan's Foreign Affairs*, 245.
17. Gregorian, *Emergence of Modern Afghanistan*, 386.
18. R. J. Sontag and J. S. Bedle, eds., *Nazi–Soviet Relations 1939–1941: Documents from the Archives of the German Foreign Office* (Washington, D.C.: U.S. Department of State, 1948), 250.
19. Ibid., 259.
20. Adamec, *Afghanistan's Foreign Affairs*, 244.
21. Ibid., 247.
22. Leon B. Poullada, "Afghanistan and the United States: the Crucial Years" *The Middle East Journal* (Spring 1981): 181.
23. The Afghans abhorred the idea of sharing a common frontier with India ruled by a Hindu majority. Afghan distaste in this respect could not have been more adequately described than by what one Afghan official said to Sir Fraser-Tytler: "We know what the Durand Line is, but what about the Gandhi line?" Fraser-Tytler, *Afghanistan*, p. 257.

5

The Postwar Era

A fascinating result of World War II for the Afghans was the emergence of the United States as the world's most powerful economic and military power. This was both novel and promising in a world that apparently would no longer be dominated by Britain. Although victorious, Britain had been badly shaken by the world conflict and obviously could no longer hold its empire together. In addition, somewhere, somehow, Britain had lost the will to keep the empire, and the British were suddenly busy making the mental adjustment to a situation where their country no longer held global responsibilities. Almost immediately after the war, Britain withdrew from the subcontinent of India. The termination of the British Raj in India resulted in the establishment of two new independent countries: the Union of India and the Islamic Republic of Pakistan. The British departure from the neighborhood of Afghanistan brought about conditions that would profoundly affect that country and the orientation of of its policies.

The period of entente between the members of the anti-Axis coalition was destined to be of short duration. The immediate postwar era rapidly degenerated into the cold war, dividing the Allies into two antagonistic camps, one led by the United States and the other by the Soviet Union. Before long, China also turned Communist and, for all intents and purposes, joined the Soviet group. As the cold war deepened, the Afghan rulers realized that the American version of a countervailing force barring Russia from moving into Asia was not entirely what they had hoped for. To contain the Soviet Union, and perhaps China, the United States resorted to the instrumentality of military pacts, which, by a process of encirclement, aimed at countering the Communist threat on a global scale. This was different from the classical approach more familiar to the Afghans for containing Russia that had centered on the defense of India per se. Afghanistan did not become part of these pacts nor did it receive the military assistance that it repeatedly requested from the United States.

The USSR had also been profoundly shaken by the war. Nonetheless, it had emerged from that world conflict as a superpower with half of Europe, including half of Germany, under its direct control, and its imperial rival,

Britain, absent from the Asian scene. In Asia, apart from gaining territories in the Far East, Russia had acquired a portion of northern Iran, Azarbaidzhan, as part of the war booty to which it considered itself entitled. (Later the Soviets were expelled from Azerbaidzhan as a result of American and British pressure.)

As a consequence of the British departure from India and of American indifference, the Afghans began to review their attitude toward the Soviet Union. Obviously merely "correct" relations with that country were no longer sufficient. A more friendly stance that could evolve into better understanding and guarantee a greater degree of security for Afghanistan had to be sought. Soon the imperatives of large-scale economic development and the need to strengthen the armed forces, brought about largely by a dispute between Afghanistan and the newly created state of Pakistan over the trans-Durand Pashtun lands and their inhabitants, drew the Afghans closer to Russia.

Problems with Pakistan over the Pashtun Issue

In 1944, when the Allies' victory seemed assured and the British departure from India appeared inevitable, the Afghan government had informed the government of British India that it hoped to be consulted should a change occur affecting the fate of the Pashtuns living east and south of the Durand Line. In their reply, the British observed that the Durand Line was an international boundary, and, therefore, Afghan interest stopped at that line. However, certain statements made later by Lord Louis Mountbatten, the last viceroy of India, were construed by the Afghans as implying that their views with regard to the future status of the Pashtun areas would be sought when independence was granted to India.

On February 20, 1947, the British government proposed that India be given independence by June 1948. The Congress Party of India and the British viceroy had at last agreed with the Muslim League that independence would be granted to India on the basis of the partition of the subcontinent, guaranteeing the Muslims of India their own separate state. This tripartite agreement was accepted by the British government. The Congress Party decided that India, as the successor state, would be called the Union of India, and the Muslim League, after some trepidation, adopted the name of Pakistan for the new Islamic state. On June 3, 1947, upon proposal by the British government, the tripartite agreement was endorsed by Parliament "with the provision that a plebiscite in British India (but not the princely states) should give the population the choice of joining Hindu India or Moslem Pakistan."[1] The princely, or native, states had three alternatives: (1) join India, (2) join Pakistan, or (3) remain independent for a specified period until a decision could be made to join India or Pakistan.[2]

That parliamentary decision, which came to be called the Partition Agreement, meant that the future status of the British-administered North-West Frontier Province (NWFP) would be determined by a plebiscite enabling it to join one of the new states. The NWFP, situated west of the Indus River and part of the Frontier, was mostly composed of lands formerly belonging to Afghanistan and was essentially inhabited by Pashtuns. The Afghan government "promptly protested, asking that two additional choices be offered to the North-West Frontier Province—union with Afghanistan or the establishment of a separate Pashtun nation. Their request brought a curt refusal; a second request was met with silence."[3]

After August 1946, Muslim–Hindu animosity sprang violently into the open. Mass murder, looting, and rape held sway over all of India.[4] Soon, in the NWFP, Hindus and Sikhs were massacred by the hundreds; some of the fleeing Hindus and Sikhs found refuge across the border in Afghanistan. By the end of June 1947, the violence in India had taken on such frightening proportions that the British decided to relinquish their responsibilities sooner and get out of the subcontinent as fast as possible.

Years later, British diplomats would tell me that Britain could not give due consideration to the Afghan proposals with regard to the plebiscite because of its preoccupation with the turmoil in India and its speedy departure. Nonetheless, the departing colonial power hurriedly organized popular consultations in British-administered provinces to find out which one of the new states they wished to join. Such a plebiscite was held in the NWFP in late July 1947.

A couple of months before the plebiscite, the ministry of the NWFP, controlled by the Congress Party, had voted for the union of the province with India. As this decision did not sit well with the Pashtuns in the NWFP and the Tribal Agencies,[5] the majority of the Pashtun leadership joined in requesting that a third option, independence, also be offered in the proposed plebiscite. Besides, by then the Congress Party of India had grown convinced of the impossibility of holding the Indian subcontinent together and preventing the creation of Pakistan. It was, therefore, absurd that the Frontier Congress should continue to insist on union with India,[6] when in all probability the province would be separated from India by the vast expanse of Pakistani territory. Afghanistan, which had always received extremely cooly the Frontier Congress's support of the NWFP's union with India, backed the Pashtun leaders who requested independence.

The plebiscite was held in the NWFP without the requested addition of independence as an option for the Pashtuns. Pashtun leaders like the venerable Khan Abdul Ghafar Khan, who were requesting independence, asked their followers to boycott the plebiscite. The result of that popular consultation was

289,244 votes for union with Pakistan and 2,074 for union with India. The Afghans, however, were unimpressed by the seeming onesidedness of the result. They pointed out that only 55.5 percent of the eligible voters cast ballots in the plebiscite, whereas 68 percent had voted in the provincial elections of the previous year—an indication that a considerable number had boycotted the polls. The Afghans maintained, furthermore, that any other result would have been impossible in a land that was 98 percent Muslim, and in view of the communal hatred that was sweeping India—especially since the Koran was used to designate the ballot boxes of Pakistan and the Sikh Granth those of India.[7]

The majority of the Pashtun nationalist leaders had already rejected the results of the plebiscite on the same grounds. India and Pakistan became independent in August of 1947. The NWFP became part of Pakistan, on the basis of the plebiscite. After the creation of Pakistan, the British held a series of jirgas with the *khans* (tribal elders) of the Tribal Agencies in November 1947 to ascertain their wishes as to the future political status of the tribal belt, which could be attached to either India or Pakistan. These jirgas were held while Muslim–Hindu violence was at its height and fighting between India and Pakistan had started in Kashmir. Encouraged by the government of Pakistan, thousands of tribesmen were invading Kashmir. There is no doubt that these events had stimulated pro-Pakistani sentiments in the tribal areas.

The tribal elders opted for attachment of the Tribal Agencies to Pakistan. In their written statements, however, they expressed the wish that the tribes "preserve the same relations with Pakistan as they had with the British."[8] As the tribes were autonomous in their relations with Britain, the tribal elders had thus added an important qualification to their decision, autonomy. As a corollary to the preservation of the same relations with Pakistan as "they had with the British," the elders probably also had in mind continuation of the generous annual subsidies that they had been receiving from Britain.

The Afghans, who, because of ethnic, linguistic, and cultural affinities with the trans-Durand Pashtuns, could not remain indifferent to their fate, together with the Pashtun nationalist leadership objected to the outcome of the tribal jirgas on the grounds that these assemblies were organized by British colonial officers and care had been taken that they be attended only by pro-British and pro-Pakistan tribal elders. Moreover, the Afghans and the Pashtuns maintained that, as the tribes had separate agreements with Britain, they should have been considered native or princely states and offered a third alternative, namely, to remain independent for a specified period of time. Because of these objections, Afghanistan declared the NWFP plebiscite and the tribal jirgas null and void, maintaining that the people of those areas emerging from colonial domination were not afforded an opportunity to properly determine their own future. Self-determination for the Pashtuns east and south of the Durand Line became the basic Afghan demand.

Undeniably it was Britain's responsibility to streamline Pakistan's entry into statehood by removing the Pashtun problem from Afghan–Pakistani relations beforehand. Pakistan had inherited tremendous problems from Britain with regard to its relations with India and certainly did not need to also be plagued with the Pashtun issue. But the British chose not to attempt to reach a settlement with Afghanistan before their departure from the subcontinent. The leaders of the Muslim League should have pressed the British to do so, but, probably because of their lack of adequate knowledge about the Pashtuns and the frontier issues, they were inclined to believe that the "ideology of Pakistan" was sufficient to cement together into one country all Muslims hitherto living under the British Raj. They failed to realize that the Pashtun people were not geographically part of the subcontinent and had no affinities, ethnic, linguistic, or cultural, with the races of India. One of the characteristics that had set the Pashtuns apart from other people living under the British raj was their refusal to submit to British domination; they fought British colonialism to the end. Thus, the Pashtun problem became a preoccupation of the new state of Pakistan, which historically had no part in creating that troublesome situation.

Afghanistan officially proclaimed its nonrecognition of the NWFP and the Tribal Agencies as part of Pakistan. It announced that a political difference concerning the future of the Pashtuns opposed it to the government of Pakistan. It further announced that it wished to see the fate of the Pashtuns settled on the basis of self-determination and stated that the Afghan government was committed to a peaceful solution of that difference. Afghanistan justified its backing of the Pashtuns on the ground that they were Afghans' kith and kin, linked to them by ethnic, historical, and cultural ties, and that in their moment of need it was Afghanistan's responsibility to assist them in realizing their aspirations. As relations between Afghanistan and Pakistan deteriorated, Afghan radio broadcasts aimed at Pakistan stressed the illegality of the frontier plebiscite and of the tribal jirgas and, consequently, of the artificiality of Pakistan itself. Now that the British were gone from India, Pakistan had to endure alone the brunt of Afghan anger. The Pakistani media did not lose much time in retaliating. In a crescendo of diatribe, it ridiculed the Afghan position and attacked Afghan institutions, even the monarchy and members of the royal family. The Pakistanis began causing delays in the transit of Afghan goods by refusing to allocate to them sufficient railway wagons and by creating unnecessary administrative red tape. These delays not only resulted in the postponement of some development projects but also caused high demurrage charges that the Afghans had to pay. Pakistani officials, according to Afghan trade agents in Peshawar and Chaman, did little or nothing to prevent the pilfering and damaging of Afghan goods passing through Pakistan or stored in warehouses in Karachi, Peshawar and Chaman.

It was in the midst of the mounting tension in Afghan–Pakistani relations that Pakistan applied for membership to the United Nations, in September 1947. Afghanistan, a member of the UN since September 1946, was the only state that cast a negative vote in this matter. In explaining his vote, the Afghan representative, Abdul Hussein Khan Aziz stated that

Afghanistan heartily shares in the rejoicing of the peoples of Pakistan in their freedom. We have profound respect for Pakistan. May Pakistan prosper. The Afghanistan delegation does not wish to oppose the membership of Pakistan in this great Organization, but it is with the deepest regret that we are unable at this time to vote for Pakistan. This unhappy circumstance is due to the fact that we cannot recognize the North West Frontier as a part of Pakistan so long as the people of the North West Frontier have not been given an opportunity free from any kind of influence—and I repeat, free from any kind of influence—to determine for themselves whether they wish to be independent or to become part of Pakistan. . . .[9]

It will be noted that the Afghan representative did not mention in his statement the illegality of tribal jirgas in the Tribal Agencies, because those jirgas had not yet been held. Although Afghanistan withdrew its negative vote on October 20, 1947, the episode further poisoned the atmosphere of Afghan–Pakistani relations. The reason for the shift in the Afghan position in the United Nations was the diplomatic talks scheduled to be held in November of that year between the two countries in Karachi. The Afghans at the time were inclined to believe that the Pakistanis, faced with both internal and external difficulties, would make a genuine effort to settle the Pashtun problem. At the conclusion of the Karachi talks, it seemed that the government of Pakistan might agree to regional autonomy for the NWFP and hold negotiations with Afghanistan in order to seek means of promoting the welfare of the tribes east and south of the Durand Line and of regulating the future legal links of the two countries with those tribes.

But soon these hopes proved to be unfounded. In June 1948, the government of Pakistan arrested Abdul Ghafar Khan, his brother Dr. Khan Sahib (chief minister of the NWFP at the time the Congress-controlled ministry had voted for union with India), and a score of other Pashtun leaders. They were accused of cooperating with subversive forces on the Frontier and were sentenced to prison terms or house arrest. Further, the Pakistanis began increasing their military power in the Tribal Agencies, where it had been reduced immediately after independence, and started to use their air force against their tribal opponents.[10] Thus, by arresting the Pashtun leaders, the Pakistani authorities demonstrated their unwillingness to heed the Pashtun demands, and, by undertaking extensive military action in the tribal areas, they left no doubt as to their aim of complete integration of those areas into Pakistan.

Although Afghanistan and Pakistan had exchanged ambassadors in February 1948, their relations continued to deteriorate. In view of the arrest of the Pashtun leaders and the intensification of Pakistani military action in the tribal areas, the Afghan government lost hope of reaching a compromise with Pakistan regarding the Pashtun problem. As the Afghans became disillusioned with Pakistan's intentions, they intensified their support of independence for the Pashtun lands that were now claimed by the Pakistanis as being legally part of their country. According to the Afghans, the territories that were to form the independent Pashtun state, or Pashtunistan (the land of the Pashtuns), would consist of the NWFP (occupied Pashtunistan), the Tribal Agencies (free Pashtunistan), and some parts of northwestern Baluchistan (inhabited by a mixed Pashtun–Baluch population.)

In this campaign they [the Afghans] made use of their many contacts among the tribes and all the resources of the Kabul radio and the Afghan press department. Pakistan, all the while stoutly maintaining that the matter was of no consequence, retaliated by increasing tribal subsidies, stepping up police activities in the frontier province, and releasing a barrage of attacks on Afghanistan from its own press and radio.[11]

Thus, in the new situation following World War II, Afghanistan's traditional policy aimed at regaining the lost Pashtun territories evolved into the

Pashtunistan issue, in essence a demand for the constitution of an independent nation, on the basis of the right of self-determination of the Pashtuns living east and south of the Durand Line. As time passed and the Pashtun position shifted, Afghanistan's policy evolved further. It became more centered on the restoration and safeguarding of the rights of the Pashtuns, as defined by the Pashtuns themselves and their leaders. The government of Afghanistan acquiesced to whatever decision the Pashtuns and their leaders reached with regard to their rights and their political future.

Support for the establishment of Pashtunistan was rapidly gaining momentum on the Frontier. Jirgas were held along the tribal belt to express support for Pashtunistan. In July 1949, in an atmosphere of heightened tension brought about by the bombing of Mogholgai, a village inside Afghanistan, by Pakistani aircraft, a Loya Jirga was convened in Kabul to deliberate on the Pashtunistan policy of the government. The jirga gave its full support to Pashtunistan and enjoined the Afghan government to pursue its realization. It also formally abrogated all Afghanistan's treaties with Britain that pertained to the Durand Line or affected the status of the Pashtuns.[12]

On August 12, 1949, a meeting of Afridi and other tribes took place at Tirah Bagh, the center of the Afridi homeland on the east side of the Durand Line. That assembly of tribes proclaimed the establishment of Pashtunistan. A National Assembly of Pashtunistan was also constituted, and a flag was adopted for the new nation. The government of Afghanistan pledged its full support to Pashtunistan as proclaimed by the tribal jirga and decreed that, each year on August 31, Pashtunistan Day would be celebrated as a national day in Afghanistan. On that occasion, a commemorative stamp would be also regularly issued by the Afghan postal service. The view among the general public in Afghanistan was that, if the Pashtun lands were not given back to Afghanistan, they should at least be accorded independence. It was believed that an independent Pashtunistan would naturally evolve toward union with Afghanistan, thus bringing about the voluntary reunion of the Afghan nation.

Besides the official position on Pashtunistan, other more radical claims were advanced by influential quarters in Afghanistan. The protagonists of "Greater Afghanistan," for example, advocated the reunification of all Pashtuns under the Afghan flag and the annexation of their territories by Afghanistan. They called also for the incorporation of Baluchistan, which would have given landlocked Afghanistan an outlet on the Indian Ocean. The importance of free access to the sea for Afghanistan was well understood by the Afghans and their rulers. It was, therefore, unlikely that adherence to views like those of Amir Abdul Rahman Khan was confined to the advocates of Greater Afghanistan alone. The late amir had said, "If Afghanistan had access to the ocean, there is no doubt that the country would soon grow rich and prosperous. . . . If no favorable opportunity occurs in my life time to bring about this purpose my sons and successors must always keep their eyes on this corner, i.e., 'Baluchistan.'"[13] There was also a large segment of the intelligentsia, not necessarily

Pashtun, that was unequivocally against relinquishing the Afghan right over the Pashtun territories severed from Afghanistan by colonialism, no matter what the trans-Durand Pashtuns and their leaders decided. Such positions were usually perceived by the Pakistanis as representing the real standpoint of the Afghan government.

Common historical bonds existed between the Afghans and the Baluchis, but Baluch territories south and southeast of the Durand Line, with the exception of a few small enclaves of mixed Pashtun–Baluch population, had not been part of Afghanistan in recent times. About 90,000 Baluchis lived in southern Afghanistan, forming part of the Afghan nation. The annexation by Pakistan of Kalat and the rest of Baluchistan had taken place in the same arbitrary and high-handed manner as that of the NWFP and the tribal areas. Due to close Afghan–Baluchi ties, Afghan sentiments were aroused by the injustice done to the Baluchis, and those sentiments increasingly found expression in the official pronouncements of the Afghan government. To Afghanistan's support for the rights of the Pashtuns, its support for the rights of the Baluchis was thus added. But, while Afghanistan's support for the people of Pashtunistan stemmed from the fact that the Pashtuns had been part of the Afghan nation, its concern for the people of Baluchistan was more altruistic, afforded a neighbor of long standing. Whenever Baluch nationalists raised the banner of independence, the Afghan government supported them.

On the early maps of Pashtunistan prepared by Afghan services, in addition to Pakistan's NWFP and the Pashtun tribal belt comprising the Tribal Agencies, known also as the Independent Frontier, or *Sarhad-i-Azad*, parts or the whole of Baluchistan were sometimes shown as being included in Pashtunistan. Some western analysts were quick to point to this discrepancy as proof that either the Afghans themselves were not quite sure of what was meant by their Pashtunistan claim or that their territorial appetite was nothing less than imperialistic. In reality this ambiguity, which later considerably increased with the abrogation of the Durand Line that served as the de facto border of Afghanistan with both Pashtunistan and Baluchistan, was intentional. It was viewed as yet another means of political pressure on Pakistan in the early years of that country's inception, when it was still felt in Kabul that the Muslim League, plagued with a variety of difficulties, could be pressured to hold popular consultations at least in the Pashtun lands with regard to the political future of their inhabitants.

As time went by, the calculated vagueness of the Afghan stand concerning the province of Baluchistan increased or decreased according to the evolution of the situation and the attitude of the Pakistani government toward the Pashtuns and the Baluchis. In the early days of the Pashtunistan issue, when the Indians were supporting less unambiguously the demand for an independent Pashtunistan because of their own interest in embarrassing Pakistan, there was also an Indian version of Pashtunistan that was often confused with the official Afghan position. In the Indian version, Pashtunistan consisted of the NWFP, the Tribal Agencies, Kalat, and the whole of Baluchistan, with the Makran Coast on the Arabian Sea and part of Sind province, including the port of Karachi.

The government of Pakistan dismissed Pashtunistan as a figment of the imagination of Afghan rulers bent on detaching territory from Pakistan and annexing it to their domain. It was categorically denying the existence of a political difference between Afghanistan and Pakistan and was consequently refusing to begin talks aimed at finding a peaceful solution to the problem. Pakistani authorities maintained that only a few Pakistani Pashtun dissidents were advocating Afghanistan's "Pashtunistan stunt." Probably assuming that this would embarrass the Afghans, they often asked whether the Afghan Pashtuns west of the Durand Line would also be included in an independent Pashtunistan. In their rhetoric, they glossed over the contention that Pashtunistan was to be constituted through the process of self-determination of a people who, in the Afghan view, had emerged from colonial status without having been afforded an opportunity to freely determine their political future. So far as the Afghan Pashtuns were concerned, the Pakistanis' attention was drawn to the fact that they had never expressed a desire to be part of another country or constitute an independent entity and that, as they were not emerging from colonial status, the applicability of the principle of self-determination to them had no relevance. While the Pakistani Foreign Office busied itself explaining the Afghan–Pakistani conflict to the outside world (particularly the Muslims), emphasizing the fallacy of Afghanistan's claim and the ill will of the latter toward Islamic Pakistan, Pakistani security and military authorities continued arresting pro-Pashtunistan leaders in the NWFP and bombing the houses and properties of those Pashtun leaders, khans and mullahs (religious leaders), suspected of pro-Pashtunistan sympathies. To exert pressure on Afghanistan, in addition to hampering Afghan transit trade, the Pakistanis resorted to inciting the tribes against the Afghan government.

In one of the better-known episodes, the Pakistani authorities found a half-brother of the former King Amanullah, Amin Jan, and introduced him into the tribal belt. Under their aegis, he was quick to assemble a tribal lashkar and made preparations to attack Afghan outposts in the frontier region. This adventure failed, however, when the Fakir of Ipi and his followers decided to chase Amin Jan out of Waziristan. In late 1949 a group of tribesmen bribed by Pakistani agent provocateurs also burned a section of the army barracks in Jalalabad. In 1950, after a Pashtun lashkar crossed the Durand Line "with the avowed intention of planting 'Pashtunistan' flags on the Indus River,"[14] Pakistan completely halted Afghan petroleum imports for almost three months on the grounds that the Afghan tankers did not comply with Pakistani safety requirements. Another incident that brought the two neighbors to the brink of military confrontation was the assassination of Pakistan's Prime Minister Liquat Ali Khan in October 1951 by an Afghan living in exile in Pakistan. Influential Pakistani circles accused Afghanistan of having ordered the assassination. The government of Pakistan finally accepted Afghan denials, and that particular crisis subsided.

As the tension in Afghan–Pakistani relations mounted, with little possibility of accommodation, the Afghans felt that, as a result of the Pashtunistan problem, three matters of importance had to be attended to immediately: (1) securing of alternative transit routes, (2) broadening of international support for Afghanistan's position in its conflict with Pakistan, and (3) strengthening and modernization of the army.

Search for Support

While the breakup of British India was taking place, the Afghan government turned its attention to securing closer relations with the Soviet Union and to continuing the consolidation of Afghanistan's warming friendship with the United States. Closer relations with the USSR were essentially intended to stave off dangers from the north. They could also bring other benefits, like transit facilities, increased trade, and aid. America, on the other hand, held an emotional appeal not only for Afghan rulers but also for Afghan intelligentsia in general. They believed that small, staunchly independent countries like Afghanistan were destined to benefit greatly from American idealism and wealth. The Afghan rulers of that era, in seeking to strengthen Afghan–U.S. relations, hoped not only to involve the United States in Afghanistan's economic development but also, more importantly, to obtain U.S. support for the safeguarding of Afghanistan's political independence.

Although now part of Afghanistan's general policy, the rapprochement with Russia was progressing rather slowly, mainly because Shah Mahmud Khan (who had become prime minister in May of 1946 after the resignation of his brother Hashim Khan) and his close associates, reared in the traditional suspicion of Russia, shied away from taking steps that would bring Afghanistan too close to the Soviet Union. The latter, too, under Joseph Stalin, seemed to be hesitant with regard to greater political and economic involvement in Asia, especially after the reverses it suffered in Turkey and Iran in 1945 and 1946, respectively. Despite this lack of enthusiasm, both Afghanistan and the Soviet Union did manage to make some headway in their relations and to conclude two important agreements, a river boundary agreement in 1946 and a barter and transit treaty in 1950.

In the river boundary agreement, both sides accepted the *thalweg* (middle of the main channel) of the Oxus (Amu Daria) as the river boundary between the two countries. The significant aspect of the barter and transit agreement was that it "provided for duty-free transit of Afghan goods over Soviet territory."[15] In 1957 a frontier regime treaty, regulating all matters pertaining to the boundary between the two nations, was also signed between Afghanistan and the Soviet Union.

The Soviets undertook, in conjunction with the barter and transit agreement, to build large gasoline-storage tanks in several localities. This would decrease Afghan dependence in times of crisis on oil flow through Pakistan. By virtue of that agreement, a new transit outlet was established for Afghan foreign trade, which had become subject to the will and whims of Pakistani rulers. Apparently disturbed by the intent and scope of the barter and transit agreement, Pakistan ceased its blockade of petroleum products and halted its slowdown of Afghan in-transit trade through Pakistani territory.

In spite of considerably warmer relations between Afghanistan and the USSR, the Soviets at times could not resist in interfering in the internal affairs of Afghanistan. They more than once objected to the presence of American and other Western specialists working in Afghanistan on various projects.[16] The presence of Western experts in northern Afghanistan, involved in various activities like a UN oil project, was particularly objectionable to them. Although the Russians were later to say that the Afghan government heeded their request and barred Western nationals from northern Afghanistan, Arnold Fletcher, who was living in Afghanistan at the time, stated that all these Soviet protests "were ignored."[17]

Afghan rulers embarked on the consolidation of Afghanistan's relations with the United States with great enthusiasm. After becoming prime minister, Shah Mahmud stated that he was

. . . convinced that America's championship of the small nations guarantees my country's security against aggression. America's attitude is our salvation. For the first time in our history we are free of the threat of great powers using our mountain passes as pathways to empire. Now we can concentrate our talents and resources on bettering the living conditions of our peoples.[18]

Moved by such exceptionally high expectations, Afghan rulers turned to the United States for economic assistance, political support with regard to Pashtunistan, and military equipment to modernize the army.

In 1946 the Afghans requested U.S. economic assistance to repair old irrigation dams, build new canals, and make other improvements in the Hilmand River Valley in southern Afghanistan. This request was turned down by the Americans, who found it to be "too vague in economic concepts."[19] The Afghans nevertheless began the work with their own funds accumulated in New York banks during the war years and contracted for this purpose with a U.S. firm, the Morrison Knudsen Company of Boise, Idaho.

The initial successes of Morrison Knudsen encouraged the Afghans to envisage enlarging the original aims of the Hilmand project to encompass a multi-purpose venture comprising irrigation, land reclamation, hydroelectric development, and settlement of landless nomads on the newly reclaimed and irrigated land. Soon, however, Afghan funds ran out, and the Afghans asked for financial assistance from the United States to launch an integrated long-range development plan in which further work on the Hilmand project was included. The initial request for $118 million was turned down, but in November 1949 $21 million was loaned to Afghanistan through the U.S. Export–Import Bank, to be spent specifically on the Hilmand project.

Meanwhile, Afghanistan had also begun receiving modest U.S. assistance under Truman's Point Four Program, and later from the U.S. International Cooperation Administration, in certain fields like education and agriculture. The political importance of American aid undoubtedly interested Afghan leaders even more than its economic benefits, as evidenced by Shah Mahmud's comment during a conversation with President Truman regarding the Hilmand loan: "The Afghan government tends to think of the loan as of political as well as of economic importance, possibly increasingly so in the light of manifestations of Soviet interest and offers of assistance to Afghanistan."[20]

While the development of the aid component in Afghan–U.S. relations gave cause for some satisfaction, the American response to Afghan overtures for political support in pursuit of the Pashtunistan issue was negligible, and for military assistance utterly negative. The Americans did not know much about Pashtunistan and its ramifications, and the little they knew had been learned from the British, who held no great sympathy for the Afghan position. Besides, the Americans were impressed by the English-speaking, British-trained, pro-Western Pakistani officials, who, together with Britain, quickly convinced Washington of the value of Pakistan as a bulwark of Western concepts wedged between neutralist, left-leaning India and backward, unfamiliar Afghanistan, that could easily be taken by Russia "whenever its broader objectives would be served."[21]

However, "the U.S. proposed on three occasions to help mediate the dispute, once offering to act as mediator, and subsequently suggesting the offices of Egypt and Turkey."[22] Although each time the Afghans accepted the American proposals and the Pakistanis rejected them on the grounds that the matter was an internal one and therefore not subject to mediation,[23] Afghanistan did not succeed in attracting any American appreciation for its conciliatory stance. In fact, the Americans were miffed by Afghanistan's persistence in pursuing the Pashtunistan issue and interpreted its appeal for understanding and support as a threat "to place themselves under Soviet auspices" if U.S. political backing were not forthcoming.[24] In seeking American support, the Afghans did not expect the United States simply to take Pashtunistan from Pakistan and give it to Afghanistan. What they wanted was for the United States, as a friend of both Afghanistan and Pakistan, to impress upon Pakistan the need to negotiate with Afghanistan until an honorable solution to the dispute could be found. In the Afghan view, only the United States was capable of achieving this because of its prestige and influence in Pakistan.[25]

Afghan efforts to garner American political support floundered entirely when, in mid-1952, during the Korean War, it became clear that the United States had decided to choose Pakistan as one of its trusted partners in its struggle to contain Communist expansion and was going to arm it accordingly.[26] Thus, Afghanistan could not muster any significant support to end its international isolation with respect to the pursuance of the Pashtunistan issue. Even Russia's support at that time was nonexistent. The only support in this regard, though opportunistic, unreliable, and rapidly dwindling, was that of India, whose motivations as an enemy of Pakistan were based purely on self-interest. India's ulterior motives drained that support of any significance.

Toward the end of World War II, the Afghans had inquired of General Patrick J. Hurley, head of an official American mission visiting Afghanistan, about the possibility of receiving U.S. armaments as well as military training for their officers in the United States. Although the Afghans provided him with a list of their arms requirements, their request remained unanswered. After the war, requests for weapons were made to the United States by the Afghan government but were consistently put off. In 1950 the United States embassy in Kabul recommended that the American government accede to the Afghan request for armaments. The reasons prompting the embassy to make such a recommendation were "to exclude Soviet influence, cement Afghan–American friendship, maintain internal security, and promote settlement of differences with Pakistan."[27] Clearly, the American embassy in Kabul had realized the importance of the Pashtunistan issue and the need for its speedy settlement and understood the significance of not upsetting the armament balance in the region too drastically in favor of Pakistan.

During Shah Mahmud's visit to Washington in April 1951, however, President Truman was advised by the State Department to indicate that the United States was unable to furnish military assistance to Afghanistan and that, so far as the latter's security was concerned, it would be well advised to rely on the system of collective security provided by the UN charter.[28] Although, in the years to come, Afghanistan profited handsomely from UN assistance in social and economic fields, it had quickly realized that the system of collective security envisaged by the charter remained as unworkable as the one contained in the Covenant of the League of Nations, especially now that antagonism between the two former allies and permanent members of the UN Security Council, the United States and the Soviet Union, had become a permanent fixture on the international scene.

It was somewhat baffling how the U.S. administration expected the Afghans to entrust the maintenance of their security to the United Nations when the U.S. government itself, having realized the inadequacies of that world organization, was actively seeking to set up its own military alliances for the purposes of containing Soviet expansion. The Afghans undoubtedly did not miss this flaw in the U.S. argument, but their reaction to this somewhat unrealistic American attitude has not been recorded.

Afghanistan did not give up in its attempts to acquire military assistance from the United States. In August 1951, it submitted a formal request for armaments to which a list of arms that it wished to receive was annexed. The United States replied in November that "the arms requested will cost $25 million dollars. They will have to be paid for in cash. Transit through Pakistan will have to be arranged with no help from the United States. The sale will have to be made public, and it would help if the Pashtunistan claim is dropped."[29] As the American terms were unacceptable, Prime Minister Shah Mahmud called it a "political refusal."

It thus became clear to the Afghans that they would not be receiving military aid from the United States without Pakistan's acquiescence, and this would not be forthcoming unless the Pashtunistan issue was abandoned, something that no Afghan government could undertake in the absence of an adequate Pakistani quid pro quo. So far as the relationship between American military assistance to Afghanistan and the Afghan–Pakistani conflict was concerned, Washington had missed the logic of the U.S. embassy's presentation recommending the approval of arms sales to Afghanistan. American policymakers probably visualized military assistance to Afghanistan as an action against Pakistan, a close ally of the United States in Asia. They failed to see it as a possible opportunity to bring about a rapprochement between the two neighbors, who would have reached relative parity in military strength as a result of such assistance to Afghanistan, a parity that could have contributed to neutralizing the two neighbors' antagonistic stances toward each other.

It seemed that Afghanistan had no place under the protective umbrella of the United States, which the Afghans mistakenly believed had acquired responsibility for filling the vacuum left by the departure of the British from India. It was basically hoped in the West that Afghanistan's neutral status as a buffer between two antagonistic blocs would continue to ensure its survival. By indulging in that kind of wishful thinking, however, the Americans ignored the fact, perhaps deliberately, that Afghanistan had only been able to maintain that status because it was backed by British military might, and the Russians had known well the seriousness of the British commitment to preserve Afghanistan's integrity.

During this period, Afghanistan's relations with Islamic countries were generally good. The traditional ties with Turkey remained strong, and the army was still basically trained by Turkish instructors. In 1951 the United States, friendly with both Afghanistan and Iran, suggested that they submit their century-old dispute about the sharing of Hilmand River water in the lower Hilmand delta to a neutral commission for advice that would constitute the basis of an amicable solution to the issue. Both sides accepted the U.S. suggestion, and the neutral commission was established. Under the temporary arrangement proposed by the neutral commission (until precise hydrological data became available), Iran was to get 22 cubic meters of water per second during normal years. Afghanistan accepted this proposal, but the Iranians rejected it. The Afghans then offered to give to Iran 26 cubic meters per second, but even this increase was not accepted by that country. Although the lack of agreement on the distribution of the Hilmand waters caused disappointment, Iranian–Afghan relations did not suffer any major setback.[30]

Afghan relations with western European countries, notably France, were warm, and, as the revival of Germany became more discernible, the Afghans successfully enlisted German contributions to their economic development.

All this, gratifying as it was, obviously did not entirely satisfy the Afghans. It was clear that the policies followed to this point had not achieved all the aims that had been sought since the end of World War II. Afghanistan remained politically isolated in its pursuit of the Pashtunistan issue, it had not been able to modernize its army, and the economic development of the country had not reached desired levels. Therefore, it was necessary to seek other avenues to end this stagnant situation.

It was also at this time that the Afro–Asian countries, inspired by men like Nehru and Nasser, slowly began emerging as a "third world," aspiring to be aligned with neither the West nor the East. This new concept was attractive to the younger generation of the royal family, who thought that nonalignment of the kind envisaged by the Afro–Asians was more in conformity with Afghanistan's interests and aspirations. They believed that, measured against the yardstick of nonalignment, the government had shown a tendency to lean too much, politically and economically, toward the unresponsive West. Therefore, they felt it was advisable that this situation be corrected, without jeopardizing Afghanistan's good relations with the United States and other Western countries. Such a reorientation of Afghanistan's attitude required a change of outlook and undoubtedly a change in leadership. Although these changes would not be made without risk, too much caution had brought about a stalemate that Afghanistan could no longer afford to continue.

Early in September 1953, Shah Mahmud resigned, and on September 20 it was announced that King Zahir Shah had appointed General Mohammad Daoud prime minister. Daoud, 43 years old at the time, was a cousin and brother-in-law of the king and had served the country as minister of defense, minister of the interior, ambassador to Paris, and governor of various provinces. His last post before becoming prime minister had been commander of central forces. Mohammad Daoud was well known to the people, was an ardent nationalist, and had a reputation for hard work and honesty.

Soon after Mohammad Daoud came into power, the Afghan government determined that, in addition to the need for institutional and methodological changes, to accelerate Afghanistan's economic development, substantially more financial and technical assistance had to be procured from foreign sources. Afghanistan's political isolation, which the previous regime had failed to bring to an end, not only restricted the provision of foreign aid but also prevented Afghanistan from attracting support for the Pashtunistan issue and impeded the urgently needed modernization of the army. In view of the West's proven negative attitude toward Afghanistan's problems, Mohammad Daoud's government decided to seek the Soviet Union's assistance and support. However, before embarking on such a shift in Afghan policy, the Afghan government decided to ask the United States for development aid and military equipment one more time. The uselessness of requesting American political support being well understood, the Afghans opted to refrain from raising that matter with the United States at the time.

In November 1953, the Afghans approached the United States for a $36 million loan from the Export–Import Bank to finance a program of integrated economic development. Part of this loan was to be used to pave the streets of Kabul. The bank agreed to loan the Afghans $18.5 million to be used only for the Hilmand project. The rest of the request was rejected. Like the 1949 loan, this one had an amortization period of 18 years and an interest rate of $4\frac{1}{2}\%$.[31] It was clear from this response that the Americans were not yet ready to participate fully in Afghanistan's intensive economic development as envisaged by Mohammad Daoud.

While Afghanistan's request for economic assistance was pending in Washington, Vice President Nixon embarked on a tour of several Asian countries. Nixon arrived in Kabul in December 1953 for a two-day visit and a series of meetings with Afghan leaders. While he promised U.S. economic assistance to Afghanistan, Nixon urged the Afghans to put an end to the pursuit of the Pashtunistan issue, which, according to him, had no justifiable basis and created useless friction with Pakistan. The Afghans were greatly displeased by Nixon's lack of consideration for the depth of Afghan feelings and his superficial knowledge of a matter that constituted one of the underlying factors of their foreign policy. In view of the chilly atmosphere of the talks, the Afghans did not raise the important issue of U.S. military assistance to Afghanistan.[32] Thus, the first high-level contact between Daoud's new Afghan government and the new Eisenhower administration ended in disappointment, and cooled U.S.–Afghan relations considerably.[33]

In October 1954 the Afghans renewed their request for armaments from the United States. Mohammad Daoud sent Mohammad Naim, his brother and foreign minister, to Washington to make a personal appeal to U.S. Secretary of State John Foster Dulles. Two months later, the Afghans, as well as the Pakistani ambassador to Washington, were informed "that after careful consideration, extending military aid to Afghanistan would create problems not offset by the strength it would create. Dulles urged instead that the Pashtunistan dispute be settled."[34] It must have been frustrating for the Afghans that their confidential demarche to the United States was revealed to the Pakistanis and that they were asked to abandon the Pashtunistan issue essentially unilaterally, given Pakistani reluctance even to acknowledge existence of the problem.

There had only been a remote possibility, in any case, that the United States would accept the Afghan arms request at a time when relations between Afghanistan and Pakistan were bad and the latter, chosen by the Americans as their close ally in Asia, was seen as the link between the newly established regional arrangements, the Baghdad Pact (later renamed the Central Treaty Organization [CENTO] after the withdrawal of Iraq) and the Southeast Asia Treaty Organization (SEATO). Pakistan's privileged position militated against any U.S. military assistance to Afghanistan.[35] Not only would such a move have irritated Pakistan, but probably a genuine fear existed in Washington that the arms delivered to Afghanistan might be used in overt or covert operations against America's Pakistani allies. In connection with rejection of the Afghan arms request by the U.S. government, Louis Dupree had this to say:

> The Daoud government officially stated the Americans refused to give Afghanistan military aid because the Afghans would not sign the required Mutual Security Agreement or join the Baghdad Pact. The unofficial American version of Afghanistan's reluctance to join the Baghdad Pact differs somewhat. According to U.S. diplomats on the scene at the time, some in the Afghan military wanted to join the Pact, but demanded assurances that they would be defended by the U.S. if their acceptance of arms aid precipitated a Russian invasion or major subversive efforts inside Afghanistan. For strategic (Afghanistan is not all that important to the defense of the free world), logistical (how to defend Afghanistan given its geographic position), and pragmatic (few believed the Soviets capable of sending the Afghans massive military assistance) reasons, American military planners decided against such assurances.[36]

If what was recounted by Nikita S. Khrushchev in his memoirs is not merely Communist disinformation, it appears that, in fact, an effort was then afoot to attach Afghanistan to the system of Western alliances. He stated that

> At the time of our visit there [December 1955], it was clear to us that the Americans were penetrating Afghanistan with the obvious purpose of setting up a military base. . . .[37]

Be that as it may, the thinking of the time in some influential Afghan quarters was not so much opposed to military pacts per se as to the type of alliance that John Foster Dulles, the American secretary of state, promoted in his Northern Tier concept. Afghans believed that the spread of communism could not be contained by arming intrinsically weak countries in Asia, organizing them into military pacts, establishing a few air force bases on their territories, and then asking *them* to contribute to the containment of the Soviet and Chinese threats while the core of American military might was situated thousands of miles away. They thought instead that a serious military alliance, similar to that of NATO (which had its own forces that included important U.S. contingents permanently stationed in Europe and ready to counter Soviet aggression), would be a more meaningful arrangement than alliances like those established in Asia. They were of the opinion that alliances such as CENTO or SEATO were liabilities rather than assets and would make their Asian participants more vulnerable than they had initially been.

Afghanistan's opposition to military pacts grew rapidly when it realized the extent to which Pakistan was being equipped militarily through them. Moreover, the concept of nonalignment, evolving from the first Afro–Asian conference in 1955 in Bandung (Indonesia), was gaining ascendancy in the Third World. By 1960, when the first nonaligned summit was held in Belgrade (at which Mohammad Daoud represented Afghanistan), the nonaligned movement's opposition to military pacts springing from superpower rivalry was upheld by an overwhelming majority of the participating nations. The Belgrade summit institutionalized the movement's opposition to military pacts as a principle of nonalignment. Henceforth, Afghanistan, as a staunchly nonaligned country, could not but adhere firmly to that fundamental principle.

As the reactivation of economic development on a large scale could no longer be delayed, the Afghans, in a bold bid, turned to their only option, the Soviet Union. Most Afghans were aware of the dangers of Russian involvement in their economic development, but Afghanistan had reached a stage in its history when meaningful progress could no longer be delayed.

They [the Afghan rulers] were aware . . . that failure to do so [bring progress to their country] might prove more dangerous than any agent of the Kremlin. The "revolution of rising expectations" had come to Afghanistan at last; and no people so volatile and energetic could be expected to remain contented if their country lagged behind while its neighbors forged ahead.[38]

The Soviets, always sensitive to Afghanistan's attitudes and now, in the post-Stalin era, more eager to have an effective presence in the country, readily accepted the Afghan overture.

In January 1954, the first Russian loan of $3.5 million was extended to Afghanistan to assist in the construction of two grain silos and flour mills, one in Kabul and the other in Pul-i-Khumri.[39] This initial loan was soon followed by other Russian credits, which, coupled with the extension of their technical assistance, allowed the rapid initiation of a number of important projects. In August 1954, the Russians lent the Afghans $2.1 million to finance the building of an asphalt factory and the paving of Kabul's streets, a project that, as mentioned, had been rejected earlier by the U.S. Import–Export Bank. In the same year, a Czechoslovak loan of $5 million was granted to Afghanistan for the building of three cement factories. This project had also been rejected by the United States. With the increase in economic cooperation between Afghanistan and the USSR, Russo–Afghan relations grew closer. Soviet praise for Afghan neutrality and its expressions of friendship for Afghanistan were followed by occasional, subtly sympathetic appraisals of Afghanistan's stand on Pashtunistan by certain Soviet analysts. The way was being prepared to fill the vacuum created by Western disinterest in Afghanistan's future.

Since Mohammad Daoud's assumption of power, Afghan–Pakistani relations had not improved. Although the Pashtunistan issue was being pursued more vigorously by Afghanistan, no major crises between the two countries had occurred. Early in March 1955, Pakistan, emboldened by its accession to SEATO (it would join the Baghdad Pact a year later) and by American political and military support, announced the fusion of all West Pakistan's three provinces and the Baluchistan States Union into a "one unit" system.[40] Although the Tribal Agencies were not made part of the one unit, the inclusion of the NWFP in a single political, administrative, and legislative unit with the more populous, more advanced, and wealthier Punjab was viewed by the Pashtuns and the Afghans as a major step toward destroying Pashtun identity. They feared that the erosion that would occur in Pashtun culture, language, and national characteristics would ultimately bring about the demise of the Pashtun pro-independence stance. While the Pakistanis may have had various motives for the consolidation of West Pakistan into one unit, the Afghans felt that the destruction of Pashtun identity was their primary goal. The government of Afghanistan submitted an official protest to the government of Pakistan, citing the action as further evidence of Pakistan's determination to suppress the rights and aspirations of the Pashtun people. Pakistan replied that the measure was an internal matter and therefore should be of no concern to Afghanistan.

The formation of one unit caused the eruption of a new wave of violence on the Frontier. Tempers also rose in Afghanistan, where, in March 1955, a mob attacked and damaged the Pakistani embassy in Kabul and burned Pakistan's flag. In a reaction to the so-called "flag incident," Afghan consulates in Peshawar and Quetta were attacked by "government-inspired mobs,"[41] and Afghan flags were also burned. In the wake of the flag incident, Pakistan once again "imposed a blockade on Afghan transit which did grievous harm to the Afghan economy."[42]

Afghanistan then asked the United States for assistance in building a new transit route across Iran to the port of Chahbahar on the Persian Gulf, to alleviate its transit problems. But both Iran and the United States refused the request, finding it economically impractical.[43] It was after this rejection that the Afghans asked the Soviet Union to renew the 1950 barter and transit agreement, which they did in June 1955. Further, in August 1955 the Russians and Afghans signed a "barter protocol on commodity exchange [which] guaranteed [for Afghanistan] petroleum imports, building materials [especially cement], and rolled ferous metals, in exchange for Afghan wool, raw cotton and hides."[44]

Although the flag incident was settled in September 1955 through the good offices of Egypt, Iran, Turkey, and Saudi Arabia, and the Pakistanis ended their economic blockade, Afghan–Pakistani relations remained tense. The possibility of armed conflict between the two countries was ever present. Thus the strengthening of the Afghan army had acquired an urgent character.

In August 1955, $3 million worth of Czechoslovak weapons were ordered and paid for in cash.[45] These weapons began reaching Afghanistan via the Soviet Union in October of that year. However, it was not with such weapon procurements that a modern army could speedily be built. In view of Afghanistan's limited financial resources, the kind of modernization that Mohammad Daoud had in mind for the army could not be undertaken without the help of a superpower like the United States or the Soviet Union, whose interest in the matter would not be purely financial. Since the United States was not interested, Mohammad Daoud decided to ask the USSR for military equipment and training. The idea had been aired with the Russians previously, and they had listened "sympathetically," according to Daoud.

By accepting Soviet military aid and training, Afghanistan realized that it was opening itself to Russia's influence. But was there any alternative? In the American view there was: The Afghan abandonment of the Pashtunistan claim was such an alternative. The abandonment of the Pashtunistan issue, however, was impossible for the Afghans. Besides this lack of alternatives, what facilitated the acceptance of Russian assistance was the belief held by some Afghan leaders that strong disincentives existed for the Soviet Union at that time to seize Afghanistan. Chief among these, in their view, were Afghanistan's position among Islamic and nonaligned nations, Russian sensitivity to being dubbed the usurper of the independence of a small Islamic, nonaligned neighbor, and the ruggedness of Afghanistan's terrain, rendering occupation of the country difficult and costly.

A Loya Jirga convened in November 1955 essentially to ponder the constitution of one unit in Pakistan and its consequences for the Pashtun people unanimously endorsed the Afghan government's stand with regard to the issue of Pashtunistan and demanded that the inhabitants of that territory be accorded the right of self-determination. In approving the government's Pashtunistan policy, the Loya Jirga also authorized the strengthening of the Afghan armed forces through the procurement of military equipment and training from whatever source possible, in light of mounting tension in the area. Future Russo–Afghan military cooperation was thus endorsed by the highest political institution in the land.

As relations between Afghanistan and the USSR had become close, in December 1955 Nikolai Bulganin and Nikita Khrushchev, the leaders of the Soviet government and Soviet Communist Party, paid an official visit to Afghanistan with the aim of further consolidating Russo–Afghan ties. The two Russian leaders offered a $100 million long-term development loan to Afghanistan, to be repaid over a thirty-year period at 2% interest.[46] Several projects that were to be financed with this loan were announced in March 1956, including the construction and improvement of hydroelectric plants, automotive maintenance and repair shops, a road from Qizil Qala (Sher Khan Bandar on the Amu Daria) to Kabul including the three-kilometer Salang tunnel, airports, irrigation dams with canal systems, and a bridge.[47] At the same time, the Afghans launched their first Five-Year Plan (March 1956 to September 1961), based on recommendations from Soviet advisers.

According to Daoud, Soviet military assistance to Afghanistan was also agreed upon during the Kabul talks, although the arms sale agreement was not made public until the middle of 1956. It was decided that, at the beginning of 1956, a Soviet military mission would come to Afghanistan to help assess the equipment and training needs of a modern and enlarged Afghan army. Upon the recommendation of that mission, a special long-term, low-interest loan was extended to Afghanistan for the purchase of Russian armaments including infantry assault rifles, machine guns, tanks, and aircraft. Periodic exchanges of military missions took place to evaluate the continuous requirements of modernizing and strengthening the army. The inevitable next step in this military cooperation, dreaded by many, soon occurred. Scores of Russian military advisers and instructors came to Afghanistan to advise and instruct

Afghan officers in the use of the new equipment, and young Afghan army officers, especially pilots and tank personnel, were sent to the Soviet Union for training.[48]

The Kabul talks between the Russian leaders and Mohammad Daoud had hardly begun when the Soviets responded to earlier solicitations by informing Daoud that the Soviet Union supported Afghanistan's position on the Pashtunistan issue. In his banquet speech in Kabul, on December 16, 1955, Bulganin stated that

We sympathize with Afghanistan's policy on the question of Pashtunistan. The Soviet Union stands for an equitable solution of Pashtunistan problems which cannot be settled without taking into account the vital interests of the peoples of Pashtunistan.[49]

The relevant paragraph of the joint Soviet Union–Afghan statement of December 18, 1955, referred implicitly to the matter.

The government of the USSR and the Royal government of Afghanistan are convinced that the peoples and nations which are still deprived of freedom and national sovereignty have the right, as stipulated in the United Nations Charter, to decide their future without pressure of intimidation from outside.[50]

In his report to the Supreme Soviet in Moscow, on December 29, 1955, Bulganin said,

We think the demands of Afghanistan to give the population of bordering Pashtunistan an opportunity of freely expressing their will are justified and grounded. The people of the region have the same right to national self-determination as any other people. There can be no justification for the stand of those who do not want to reckon and disregard the lawful national interests of the people of Pashtunistan.[51]

Thus, so far as the question of Pashtunistan was concerned, the Afghans were no longer isolated and had succeeded in drawing a superpower to their side. The fact that Afghanistan's rival, Pakistan, had chosen to side with the United States was probably an added factor in Russia's decision to back Afghanistan's Pashtunistan position. Apart from strengthening Afghanistan's posture, the Russian support for Pashtunistan had an immediate and practical benefit, which meant that if Pakistan took the Afghan–Pakistani dispute to the UN Security Council, presenting it as Afghanistan's interference in Pakistan's internal affairs, it would be rebuffed by a Soviet veto. But this rumored Pakistani move never materialized. In reality, it is doubtful whether Pakistan would have brought the matter before the UN, but, on the other hand, Soviet support for Afghanistan certainly did not encourage the Pakistanis to do so.

Thus, in the three areas of economic assistance, military aid, and Pashtunistan, the Russians succeeded in drawing a grateful Afghanistan closer to them than ever. The Russians had sensed that the time was right for them to take advantage of the Afghans' wants and sensitivities. They moved in to fill the existing vacuum and made significant inroads into Afghanistan.

At the Kabul talks, Bulganin and Khrushchev also constantly stressed the great importance the Soviet Union attached to Afghanistan's neutrality and nonalignment. The matter was of such significance to them, they claimed, that the Soviet Union was prepared to provide Afghanistan with every possible assistance to enable it to follow its independent policy. They repeatedly stated that they expected nothing from Afghanistan but the permanency of its present political attitude toward the two superpowers. Mohammad Daoud assured Bulganin and Krushchev that no danger would ever threaten Russia through Afghanistan, provided no attempt of any kind was made to interfere in the internal affairs of Afghanistan. To this direct and unequivocal presentation, the Russian leaders replied that they were only interested in Afghanistan's neutrality and prosperity and not in manipulating its sovereignty.[52] A final act of that memorable Russo–Afghan meeting was the signing of a protocol extending the 1931 treaty of friendship and nonaggression between Afghanistan and the USSR for another ten years. A new phase in Russo–Afghan friendship had begun. The Afghans entered this phase cautiously hopeful that their new constructive relationship with the Soviet Union would act as a deterrent to Russia's compulsion to intervene in Afghanistan's internal affairs.

The unprecedented size of Russian economic assistance to Afghanistan, Soviet support for Pashtunistan, and especially the Russo–Afghan military agreement shocked the West. Many in the West immediately decided that Afghanistan had been lost to communism, and Mohammad Daoud was called the Red Prince by *Time* magazine.[53] But, as the months passed and the initial excitement subsided, it became clear that Afghanistan was still determined to preserve its neutrality.

Undoubtedly prompted in part by cold war competition, the United States "rediscovered" Afghanistan and moved to contribute to the preservation of that neutrality. Thus, five months after the Soviet–Afghan arms deal was made public, the United States National Security Council recommended that the United States attempt "to resolve the Afghan dispute with Pakistan and to encourage Afghanistan to minimize its reliance upon the Communist bloc for military training and equipment, and to look to the United States and other Free World sources for military training and assistance."[54] This recommendation, however, came too late and resulted in only a modest program of military training for Afghan officers in the United States. By 1962 only sixty-eight Afghans were receiving training in American military institutions.[55]

In 1956, the United States' renewed interest in Afghanistan's economic development became more apparent. The U.S. International Cooperation Administration (ICA), subsequently the Agency for International Development (AID), "began helping Afghanistan on a more consciously political basis."[56] This increased economic assistance to Afghanistan was mainly geared toward long-term educational improvements (rural schools, textbooks, university education for Afghan students in the United States, and, later, construction of Kabul University facilities), building hard-surface roads, continuation of the Hilmand Valley project, and construction of airports.[57] The Americans also extended technical assistance for improving the agricultural and civil aviation sectors. In addition, Pan American World Airways bought 49% of the Afghan national airline, Ariana Afghan Airlines, organized it into a modern carrier, trained its personnel, and helped expand its services (the remaining 51% of the stock remained in Afghan hands). Moreover, Washington increasingly helped compensate for Afghanistan's shortfall of wheat crops, *donating* 130,000 tons of wheat from 1956 to 1959, compared with the 20,000 tons that were *sold* to Afghanistan from 1952 to 1954 (before the sharp increase in Soviet aid).[58] In 1958, the U.S. Export–Import Bank also agreed in principle to extend a loan to Afghanistan for the construction of a railroad link between Kandahar and Pakistan's railway terminal in Chaman. This project did not materialize, however, mostly because of Afghan–Pakistani political difficulties.

Thus, in the mid-to-late 1950s, U.S. assistance to Afghanistan increased considerably.[59] This greatly pleased the Afghan government, which believed that, aside from resulting in economic benefits, it would offset Soviet influence in Afghanistan.

More American assistance to Afghanistan naturally resulted in better relations between the two countries. Misunderstandings were gradually resolved, and the Americans were demonstrating increasing interest in Afghanistan's geopolitical situation and the significance of its neutrality. It was in this context that Special Presidential Assistant James P. Richards, on a tour of the Middle East to explain the Eisenhower Doctrine, visited Kabul from March 31 to April 3, 1957.[60] In a communiqué issued at the end of the Richards mission, the United States confirmed its "support for Afghanistan's continued independence."[61] Although the communiqué did not specifically indicate whether or not Afghanistan was protected by the Eisenhower Doctrine, the mere facts that Richards had come to Kabul and the United States had publicly expressed its support for Afghanistan's independence were of considerable political importance.

Improved Afghan–American understanding resulted in the exchange of other high-level visits between the two countries. In June 1959, Mohammad Daoud officially visited the United States. He held talks in Washington with President Eisenhower and John Foster Dulles and conferred with Samuel C. Waugh, president of the Export–Import Bank. Daoud addressed both houses of the U.S. Congress and on June 26, signed an Afghan–American cultural agreement with Dulles.[62] Judging from the contents of the joint Afghan–American statement, it was obvious that the American leaders appreciated Afghanistan's political stance and were desirous of continuing to assist Afghanistan in its development efforts. It seemed that American suspicions about Daoud's leftist leanings had completely vanished. According to a *New York Times* article published at the time of Daoud's visit, Afghanistan "had maintained her independence including what State Department officials call a 'wholesomely leery attitude toward the Soviet Union.'"[63]

In December 1959, President Eisenhower paid an official visit to Kabul. He was enthusiastically welcomed by the people of the city and had cordial exchanges with King Zahir Shah and Mohammad Daoud. President Eisenhower assured the Afghans of continued American interest in assisting Afghanistan in its task of social and economic development. The Americans and the Afghans agreed that the president's visit had further strengthened the warm and friendly relations between the two countries.[64]

Meanwhile, Soviet–Afghan relations had continued to develop further. The exchange of high-level visits between Kabul and Moscow had become characteristic of the excellent relations between Afghanistan and the Soviet Union. Mohammad Daoud visited Moscow in October 1956, in May 1959, and in April 1961. King Zahir Shah made official trips to the USSR in July 1957 and August 1962. During the king's trip to Moscow in 1957, the Russians agreed to a loan of $15 million to Afghanistan for the development of natural gas exports to the Soviet Union.[65] In 1956 the two countries had agreed that the USSR would undertake oil and gas exploration in northern Afghanistan. Khrushchev returned to Kabul in March 1960 and, according to one source, reportedly offered to finance the whole Afghan second five-year plan, provided that Afghanistan accept the presence of Soviet advisers in all of its ministries. Mohammad Daoud rejected that offer.[66]

By the early 1960s a great number of projects financed and assisted by the USSR, the United States, and the Federal Republic of Germany were either completed or under way, and new projects were being constantly considered and assessed. A number of other east and west European countries were also involved in areas of social and economic development. Even India had a modest assistance program in Afghanistan. Likewise, financial and technical assistance provided by UN programs and agencies were put to good use, and some of these projects, like the World Health Organization program to eradicate malaria, were highly successful.

It appeared that the slow-moving Hilmand project, "The American Project," had also begun to move ahead. Morrison Knudsen finished the construction of two dams, roads, irrigation canals, and a hydroelectric system. Its "contractual agreement" in the Hilmand Valley was terminated in 1959.[67] Further implementation of the project was taken up by the Afghans themselves, with financial and technical help provided by the U.S. ICA.[68] The Hilmand Valley development, though plagued with shortcomings in its planning and execution, undoubtedly contributed to Afghanistan's overall progress and to the betterment of the quality of life of the people living in the project areas.

In spite of departures from traditional patterns, Mohammad Daoud appeared to have achieved a balance in Afghanistan's foreign relations, perhaps with a little help from the cold war. Once again the buffer state, neutral but friendly toward both superpowers, had been restored. Of course, the conventional wisdom was still held valid that the buffer existed only so long as the two superpowers wished it to exist, and no one was more aware of that fact than the Afghans themselves.

With the exception of Pakistan, Afghanistan's relations with Islamic countries were very friendly. Exceptionally warm relations between Afghanistan and Iran would develop later, and for now the two countries were definitely moving closer to each other. Trade was rapidly increasing between Afghanistan and Iran, and the dispute over the distribution of water from the Hilmand River was gradually becoming less problematic. After the admission of Turkey to NATO and the beginning of Soviet military assistance to Afghanistan, Turko–Afghan military cooperation was terminated. Since the end of World War II, Turkey had become less active in Afghanistan in other fields, too, but the two countries continued to enjoy good relations.

The 1955 crisis in Afghan–Pakistani relations, which had accelerated Russian military aid to Afghanistan, had been defused, but no real progress had been made in settling the dispute itself. Both sides continued their hostile propaganda against each other, and the unrest on the Frontier had not ended. In view of the continuation of that unwelcome situation, Iran, Turkey, and Saudi Arabia renewed their efforts to bring Afghanistan and Pakistan closer together. Pressed by these friendly countries, the President of Pakistan, General Skander Mirza, and King Zahir Shah exchanged state visits. Upon the invitation of the prime minister of Pakistan, S. Sohrawardi, Mohammad Daoud also officially visited Pakistan. The joint communiqué issued at the conclusion of the visit was deemed a constructive step by the Afghans. It mentioned, among other things, that both sides agreed to solve the issue of Pashtunistan peacefully through negotiations. This was the first time that Pakistanis had officially accepted a document that referred to Pashtunistan by name, although, when the communiqué was published in Pakistan's English-language newspapers, the word Pashtunistan appeared in quotation marks.[69]

During these Afghan–Pakistani contacts, the Afghans were given to understand that the government of Pakistan would work for abolishment of the one unit and for the securing of Pashtun autonomy. But, perhaps because of the alarming internal situation in Pakistan, nothing was undertaken to give substance to those perceived promises. One concrete achievement of this period of relative calm, however, was the signing of a transit agreement between the two countries in 1958. It is not unreasonable to assume that Soviet political support and military assistance to Afghanistan also had a sobering effect on the leadership in Karachi, which rendered it more conciliatory toward the Afghans. In spite of some irritating developments such as the recognition of the Durand Line as the international border between Afghanistan and Pakistan by SEATO in 1956 on Pakistan's insistence, the lull in the Afghan–Pakistani confrontation continued until late 1958.

Further Deterioration of Afghan–Pakistani Relations

In October of that year, General Mohammad Ayub Khan, the Pakistani army's chief of staff, seized power in a successful coup d'état. Wishing to continue the dialogue with Pakistan, Mohammad Daoud sent Foreign Minister Mohammad Naim, his brother, to Pakistan to meet with Ayub Khan. Unfortunately, the new Pakistani leader, instead of listening to the Afghan views, lectured Naim about Pakistan's military might and its ability to take Kabul within a few hours. Mohammad Naim, noting the uselessness of the meeting, left promptly for Kabul. Ayub Khan, a Pashtun himself, proved to be more uncompromising than his predecessors with regard to the Pashtun problem and helped plunge Afghan–Pakistani relations to new depths.

In this supercharged atmosphere, hostile propaganda increased, as did tribal incursions by both sides into the territories of the other. The fakir of Ipi, the venerable Pashtun freedom fighter who had fought both the British and the Pakistanis, died in 1959. Although unrest remained endemic all along the Frontier, after the fakir's death, the Bajaur territory (east of the Durand Line and northwest of Peshawar) became an important area of Pashtun resistance to Pakistan's attempts at tribal integration. Twice, in September 1960 and May 1961, Afghan irregulars and "army troops dressed as tribesmen"[70] crossed into Bajaur to assist pro-Pashtunistan elements resisting Pakistani pressures. Pakistan's role in inciting reactionary elements in Kandahar to revolt against Daoud's government when it abolished the wearing of the veil by women probably contributed to the Afghan decision to allow these incursions. In both Bajaur incursions the Afghans did not fare well, particularly in the second one, mainly because of intensive Pakistani air attacks carried out by American-built, Pakistani-piloted F-86 jet fighter-bombers.[71] Elements of the regular Pakistani army (constituted mostly of Punjabis) sent to the area to fight the Afghans could not, however, maintain their position there. Under pressure from the Pashtun tribes, the government of Pakistan had to promptly withdraw them. The Bajaur incidents further worsened Afghan–Pakistani relations, and once again serious interruptions occurred in Afghan transit trade through Pakistan.

The government of Pakistan announced on August 23, 1961, that it was closing its consulates in Afghanistan (Jalalabad and Kandahar) and requested the Afghan government to close its consulates and trade agencies in Pakistan (Peshawar, Parachinar, Quetta, and Chaman). This unexpected decision was clearly Ayub Khan's way of getting tough with the Daoud government, probably in response to pressure from the Punjab establishment, which wanted to retaliate against Afghanistan for the Bajaur forays. Ayub and his colleagues must have assumed that closure of the Afghan consulates and trade agencies would prompt the Afghans to sever trade and perhaps diplomatic relations with Pakistan. They must have concluded that the emergence of such a situation would generate enough internal and external pressure to force the

Afghan government to desist from actively pursuing the cause of Pashtunistan. The official justification given for Pakistan's decision, however, was something else: The Pakistani consulates could not function normally because of the open hostility of the Afghans toward Pakistani consular officials and constant harassment by the Afghan police; Afghan consulates and trade agencies were no longer desirable in Pakistan because they were indulging in large-scale subversive activities.

On August 30 the Afghan government informed the Pakistanis that, unless they repealed their decision within one week, diplomatic relations between the two countries would be severed. On September 6, having received no reply from the Pakistanis, the Afghans severed diplomatic relations with Pakistan and closed the border to all traffic between the two countries. The Pakistanis decried the unilateral closure of the border to commerce, insisting that they intended to honor the 1958 transit agreement and that the flow of in-transit trade to and from Afghanistan could be maintained without the physical presence of trade agencies in Pakistan. The Afghan government took the position that, so long as the trade agencies were not allowed to function, it was impossible for Afghan in-transit trade through Pakistan to move freely and expeditiously to and from Afghanistan. Furthermore, the presence of the Afghan trade agencies in specific locations in Pakistan and their basic role in facilitating Afghan transit trade had figured prominently in the 1958 agreement. Provisions relating to these matters were integral to the agreement and could in no way be separated from the rest of it. If the Pakistanis wanted to honor the 1958 agreement as they claimed they did, the Afghans maintained that they could not honor it selectively. Moreover, even with the direct involvement of Afghan trade agencies, transit trade through Pakistan was subject to serious interruptions. What the state of Afghan transit trade would be without the active presence of those agencies was not difficult to imagine.

The Pakistani position was obviously a propaganda ploy designed to depict Pakistan as a peace-loving country and to put responsibility for closure of the border squarely on Afghan shoulders. The reopening of the border without Pakistan's acceptance of Afghan trade agencies would have been not only unworkable so far as transit trade was concerned but also tantamount to surrendering to Pakistani pressure. Thus, the border remained closed for almost two years to all traffic in both directions. Diplomatic and consular relations between the two countries also remained severed.

The closure of the Afghan–Pakistani border affected American projects in Afghanistan more severely than any other development projects. The United States could not ship its aid materials via the Soviet Union as the Germans, the UN, and other donors were increasingly doing after a new Afghan–Soviet trade and transit agreement was signed in November. Afghan businessmen were also using this route for trade with Europe. Even Japanese goods were shipped via Siberia to Afghanistan. In early 1962 the Afghans briefly opened the border for the passage of some American heavy equipment that was badly needed for completion of Kandahar–Kabul road and improvements in the Hilmand Valley project. But the bulk of American materials intended for American projects in Afghanistan rotted and rusted in Karachi, Peshawar, and Chaman.

In 1962 a transit agreement signed between Afghanistan and Iran established a new transit route that ran from the port of Khurramshahr on the Persian Gulf by rail to Tehran and Mashad, and from there by truck to Herat. Although this route was arduous and long and Khurramshahr's port facilities were not really adequate to handle the increase in traffic, the United States began dispatching all its assistance to Afghanistan through Iran.[72]

Closure of the Afghan–Pakistani border in 1961 also coincided with the beginning of the yearly export of Afghan grape and melon crops to India and Pakistan. Without the Pakistani market, how to transport these perishable goods to other markets became a serious question. The Russians offered unlimited help, airlifting almost the entire fruit crop to the Soviet Union. The remainder was flown by Ariana Airlines to India. Again in 1962 a massive Soviet airlift saved the day, although Ariana transported more fruit to India than it had in 1961. The United States also provided ten cargo flights to India a week for forty weeks at no cost to the Afghans.[73] The closure of the border had dramatically increased Afghanistan's trade and logistical dependence on the Soviet Union.

An offshoot of the closure of the border, interruption by Pakistani authorities of the seasonal migration of the Afghan nomads to the warm banks of the Indus River, preoccupied the Afghan government in the winter of 1961–1962. This Pakistani move was purely political, although Pakistan claimed that any nomad with a passport, a visa, and health and vaccination certificates (for his family and animals) would be allowed to cross into Pakistan. Of course, no nomad ever had these documents. Although some nomads got through and some fought fierce battles with Pakistani militia, the bulk of the migration was halted. The Afghan government avoided military confrontation with Pakistan and relocated most of the nomads in the warmer areas of southern and eastern Afghanistan. This episode created resentment among the Afghan nomads against the governments of both Afghanistan and Pakistan.

The Afghan economy was not the only one that suffered from the closure of the Afghan–Pakistani border. As time passed, the Pakistanis lost large amounts of money that they usually received from servicing Afghan in-transit trade. Pakistani merchants lost income from their traditional trade with Afghan nomads, and a shortage of manpower occurred in the sugarcane fields of the lower Punjab, where, for part of each year, the migratory nomads had supplemented the local labor force.

Soon after relations between Afghanistan and Pakistan were cut off, efforts to bring about a reconciliation between them were undertaken by some of their friends. Chief among these were the attempts made by the United States and

Iran. Both of these countries were seriously concerned about the growing Soviet influence in Afghan affairs, brought about mostly by the deterioration of Afghan–Pakistani relations.

Pakistan did not have the exclusive regional importance for the new Kennedy administration that it had had for Dulles and Eisenhower. Washington was now interested in better ties with neutral India, and it seemed to be more aware of Afghanistan's geographically sensitive situation in Asia. Furthermore, the futility of American-sponsored military pacts in that continent had been fully realized. Thus, in October 1961, President Kennedy offered America's good offices to Afghanistan and Pakistan to enable them to reestablish relations and eventually settle their dispute. This proposal was received unenthusiastically by Pakistan, whereas the Afghans greeted it very warmly.

Between October 19 and November 17, 1961, President Kennedy's special envoy, Livingston T. Merchant (U.S. ambassador to Canada), commuted between Karachi, Rawalpindi, and Kabul, holding talks with the leaders of the two countries. In spite of Merchant's efforts, his mission failed to convince either party to compromise. The Afghans maintained that, before tackling the dispute itself, the border had to be reopened and this could not be done unless the Pakistanis agreed to the reestablishment of Afghan trade agencies. The Pakistanis were not ready to accept this Afghan demand. The Afghans knew the rigidity of Pakistan's attitude, but they expected that the United States, having assumed the responsibility of reconciling the two countries, would apply pressure on Ayub Khan to allow the reopening of the trade agencies. Although Merchant did not succeed in breaking the Afghan–Pakistani deadlock, his meetings with the Afghans enabled them to explain their dispute with Pakistan, its history and ramifications. It was hoped that these talks would at least result in improved American understanding of Afghanistan's position.

For several years the shah of Iran had also been involved in trying to find a solution to Afghan–Pakistani differences. In 1962 the seriousness of the ongoing crisis over the closure of the Afghan–Pakistani border, which further increased Afghanistan's dependence on the Soviet Union, prompted him to renew these efforts. Both the Afghans and the Pakistanis welcomed his initiative. In the summer of 1962 the shah visited Kabul and Rawalpindi, but the irreconcilable positions of the parties prevented him from making any progress, even on peripheral issues. The shah suspended his efforts until a more auspicious occasion.

In spite of the difficulties with Pakistan, by 1963 Afghanistan had witnessed nearly a decade of unprecented economic development. Mohammad Daoud's vast program of reforms had favorably influenced almost all aspects of Afghan society. Administration, health services, education, and commerce had all improved, and per capita income and the standard of living had increased.

Afghanistan's neutrality had evolved into active nonalignment. Afghanistan enjoyed stronger and better relations with the countries of the East and the West. The armed forces had been modernized and strengthened. They dealt swiftly and successfully with uprisings among the Mangal tribe in eastern Afghanistan, west of the Durand Line, and in Kandahar, in the latter part of 1959. Moreover, there was no doubt that the improved army and air force functioned as an effective deterrent to Pakistan's anti-Afghan designs.

Although Afghan leaders had gained the Soviet Union's support for their Pashtunistan position, no practical progress had been achieved in that area. The extended period of time during which the border had remained closed harmed the Afghan economy and did nothing to advance the Pashtunistan cause. Despite the opening of a new transit route through Iran, closure of the traditional routes through Pakistan to India and to Indian Ocean seaports dangerously shifted the bulk of Afghan in-transit trade and commerce northward. This resulted in increased Afghan dependence on the Soviet Union, a pattern deemed unhealthy by many influential Afghans. Moreover, there was the risk that the continuing nonuse of traditional transit routes through Pakistan might be construed as Afghanistan's voluntarily forfeiting its established right to those routes by default.

Clearly, the Pashtunistan issue had overheated. The Afghan leadership reached the consensus that tensions created by the issue were damaging and that a more serene atmosphere would perhaps be helpful in finding an acceptable solution. The first step in reversing the Afghan–Pakistani confrontation would naturally be the resumption of diplomatic relations and the reopening of the Afghan–Pakistani border, an urgent necessity. Mohammad Daoud subscribed to this view and offered to resign to give a new government the needed latitude for a change of attitude toward Pakistan. King Zahir Shah accepted Daoud's resignation, which was made public on March 9, 1963, together with a series of proposals by the former prime minister for the betterment of Afghan society and the promotion of democracy.

The difficult Afghan–Pakistani relations were not the only factor that led to Daoud's departure, however. Differences of opinion between the king and him with regard to the extent of the liberalization of political life in Afghanistan (to which both men subscribed) had also brought about an environment that militated in favor of Daoud's resignation. Both men believed that the time had come for acceleration of the democratic process. But, whereas Zahir Shah was known to favor more extensive liberalization of Afghanistan's political life, Daoud preferred a more restrained, step-by-step approach.

For example, it has been said that the king viewed favorably the establishment of a multiparty system, so long as the parties were not ideologically at variance with the precepts of Islam and the fundamentals of the constitutional monarchy. Daoud, on the other hand, believed that the people's unfamiliarity with political parties and the parliamentary system necessitated that the democratic process begin with one single political party. Otherwise, he felt that confrontation between the parties might result in chaos, which would in turn jeopardize the process itself. This single party would not only form the government but also have responsibility for the political education of the masses. Once the people became familiar enough with the intricacies of the modern party system to make democracy viable, the political setup would be allowed to evolve into a multiparty system. Granted that, in the absence of an opposition party, the system Daoud proposed was not entirely democratic, but what mattered to him was a smooth and unhampered transition to genuine democracy.

Another major difference between the two leaders related to the participation of members of the royal family in the political life of the country. The king believed that political liberalization and increased popular participation in the affairs of state required that members of the royal family not be allowed to hold certain offices like the prime ministership, cabinet posts, or membership in the parliament. Daoud thought this was a wasteful policy, since 95% of the people were still illiterate, and every bit of talent and experience was needed to further the cause of progress.

Mohammad Daoud's resignation stunned many people, but he understood that the time had come for him to withdraw. He did so gracefully, and, during the next decade, little was heard about or from him.

The "Constitutional Period"

After Mohammad Daoud's resignation, King Zahir Shah took an active and direct part in governing the country. He was assisted in this task by a succession of five prime ministers, none of whom were members of the royal family.[74] All of them were committed to Zahir Shah's new democracy, which came into being on the promulgation of the liberal Constitution of 1964.

Unfortunately, this experiment in democracy did not work satisfactorily, for a variety of reasons that are outside the scope of this analysis. The experiment resulted in almost complete paralysis of the Parliament and an appalling lack of discipline in all branches of the state apparatus. But Zahir Shah's experiment in democracy did provide the Afghans with an opportunity to witness firsthand the complexities involved in the functioning of a parliamentary system, and it made them realize that democracy would flourish only if it were dealt with responsibly by all concerned.

Although the Constitution of 1964 granted Afghans the right to form political parties, it was not until after the parliamentary elections of 1965 that the Parliament adopted the Political Parties Act, a piece of legislation that, contrary to expectations, was never signed into law by King Zahir Shah. Nevertheless, the new constitution had hardly become the law of the land when certain circles, especially in Kabul, formed unofficial political groupings, taking their cue from the tolerance reflected in the constitution and the relaxation of governmental control of freedom of expression and association. Some of these groups began publishing their own newspapers and periodicals after the promulgation of the Press Law in July 1965, which provided for a freer press.

It was during this period of democratic euphoria that Nur Mohammad Taraki, a onetime official of the Afghan Press Department, organized a handful of leftists into a political group with marked Communist leanings. On January 1, 1965, this group formed the People's Democratic Party of Afghanistan (PDPA), and thus the Afghan Communist party formally, but unofficially, came into being.[75] Nur Mohammad Taraki was elected secretary general of the party. Babrak Karmal, a known student agitator, was chosen deputy secretary general. Nur Mohammad Nur, Anahita Ratebzad, and Hafizullah Amin, to name only the most prominent among them, became members of the Central Committee.

Some members of the unofficial PDPA sought election to the *Wolosi Jirga* (the lower house of Parliament) in an election held late in the summer of 1965 within the framework of a new election law based on the new constitution. Of these, Babrak Karmal, Anahita Ratebzad, Nur Mohammad Nur, and Fezanul Haq Fezan were elected to the Parliament. Nur Mohammad Taraki and Hafizullah Amin also ran but were defeated. The PDPA candidates did not run as members of that unofficial party but presented themselves to the electorate as militant reformists.

Early in April 1966, Nur Mohammad Taraki began publishing a newspaper, *Khalq* (Masses). The government, alarmed by the politico-ideological orientation of *Khalq*, which openly espoused Marxism–Leninism and the Soviet line, promptly shut it down and labeled it a subversive journal.[76]

In 1967 the PDPA split into two rival groups, one committed to Taraki and the other to Karmal. While many reasons were cited for this separation, its main cause was undoubtedly long-standing personal antagonism between Taraki and Karmal and their competition to control the Afghan Communist party. Both of these groups claimed to be the legitimate PDPA; each had its own Central Committee and party organization, and both remained equally loyal to the Soviet Union.

From the time that the split occurred until the PDPA's reunification in 1977, the USSR did not excommunicate either of the two factions. It is true that at times the Russians favored one over the other, but both groups continuously enjoyed Moscow's moral and material support.

Babrak Karmal and his followers began publishing their weekly newspaper *Parcham* (Banner) in March 1968 (although Karmal was not its official publisher or editor). *Parcham* was less aggressive than *Khalq* in its anticonstitutional stance and promoted Marxism–Lenism in a more veiled manner. This journal was published until the eve of the 1969 parliamentary elections, when, with a handful of other nongovernmental newspapers, it was banned by the government. The publication of *Parcham* served at least one practical purpose: Babrak and his followers came to be identified as Parchamis, whereas Taraki and his adherents were henceforth called Khalqis.

Only two Communists were elected to the Wolosi Jirga in the 1969 parliamentary elections: Babrak Karmal and Hafizullah Amin. The left had lost ground; people now knew the individuals associated with the PDPA and what they stood for. The left was unable to win a substantial number of seats in a lawful, democratically held election. Therefore, aware of its ineffectiveness in legitimate elections, the left resorted to obstructionist tactics in the Parliament, which were partly responsible for the paralysis of that body during the constitutional period. Likewise, it instigated demonstrations among the students and strikes and walkouts among the workers, to sow the seeds of discord between the people and the government and to sabotage the latter's social and political programs. At one of the student riots organized by Karmal in October 1965, aimed at blocking a vote of confidence by the Parliament for the designated prime minister Mohammad Yusuf and his cabinet, two students and one innocent bystander were killed by members of the security forces after one group of students refused to disband. Karmal and his comrades bear full responsibility for this tragedy, which came to be known as the events of *sowom-e-Aqrab* (the third day of the eighth month of the Afghan calendar). "The student riots were a development that set back the cause of democracy in Afghanistan perhaps more than any single event in the 1960s."[77]

For many observers (including myself) who have closely followed the emergence of Afghanistan's modern political life and have experienced those turbulent years of Zahir Shah's experiment in democracy, no doubt remains that the USSR, sensing compelling conditions, pressed for the formation of the PDPA as a Soviet outlet in Afghanistan. It was also at about that time, according to credible accounts, that the Soviets seriously embarked on subverting the military. After Mohammad Daoud's departure, the Kremlin probably came to perceive the Afghan state as increasingly leaning toward the West. Afghanistan's growing rapprochment with Iran, less emphasis on the Pashtunistan issue, and the promotion of a liberal, Western-style parliamentary system may have strengthened that perception. Undoubtedly the Russians hoped their new tactics would enhance their ability to deal with any further development in Afghanistan that they might view as compromising their long-term interests.

Among all the political groupings that mushroomed in the 1960s, the PDPA came to prominence as an instrument of Russian policy and later played an important part in the Communist takeover of Afghanistan. Several of the PDPA's leaders of the 1960s later presided as Russian proxies over the destruction of nonaligned, Islamic Afghanistan and became its first Communist rulers.

Attempts at Normalization of Relations with Pakistan and Iran

Two developments of importance in Afghanistan's foreign relations occurred during the period that Zahir Shah ruled without Daoud: the improvement of relations with Pakistan and a swift and dramatic rapprochement with Iran.

With Daoud's resignation, the way had been cleared for negotiations with Pakistan. In May 1963, at the invitation of the shah of Iran, Afghanistan and Pakistan sent delegations to Tehran. The Afghans, on Pakistan's insistence, had to agree not to discuss their differences over Pashtunistan, but to address only diplomatic, consular, and trade issues. Afghanistan had, in fact, come to accept the separation of the Pashtunistan issue from the other aspects of its bilateral relations with Pakistan. By avoiding the core of the Afghan–Pakistani dispute, agreement on other matters was reached relatively easily.

On May 29, 1963, it was simultaneously announced in Tehran, Kabul, and Rawalpindi that Afghanistan and Pakistan had agreed to reestablish diplomatic, consular, and trade relations and had consented to abide by all the provisions of the 1958 transit agreement. Both sides agreed to the reopening of embassies in each other's capitals and, whereas Afghanistan reestablished its consular offices and trade agencies immediately in Pakistan, the Pakistanis reserved the right to reopen their consulates in Kandahar and Jalalabad whenever they deemed it necessary.[78] Afghanistan and Pakistan further agreed "to approach all mutual problems in accordance with international law, and 'to continue to create an atmosphere of good understanding, friendship, and mutual trust,' an obvious allusion to hope for Afghan moderation on the 'Pashtunistan' issue."[79]

Although the Pashtunistan issue continued to be stressed forcefully in official Afghan pronouncements, after the Tehran agreement, hostile propaganda was scaled down, and tribal provocations on both sides ceased. In July 1963, King Zahir Shah told an interviewer that "We cannot drop the issue of 'Pashtunistan' but we can and have blunted the point of the sword. . . ."[80] But he also conceded during an official visit to Washington in September 1963 that "it was very difficult to expect a full reconciliation with Pakistan . . . until the troublesome question of Pashtu-speaking tribesmen could be settled between the two countries."[81]

In 1965 Afghanistan observed strict neutrality during the second Kashmir war between India and Pakistan, which apparently pleased the Pakistanis. The situation between Afghanistan and Pakistan further eased when the new Pakistani Constitution of July 1, 1970, abolished the one-unit system and the provinces of West Pakistan, including the North-West Frontier Province, were officially restored as separate units. The Constitution of 1970, negotiated between Yahya Khan, then president of Pakistan, and all political parties, granted a measure of autonomy to the provinces and was accepted by representatives of the Pashtuns and the Baluchis. It was becoming increasingly clear that they were moving away from independence and toward autonomy within Pakistan. The Pashtuns, perhaps more than the Baluchis, were hoping that this approach would lead to power sharing in Islamabad, which could in turn lessen the pressure of the Punjabi-dominated establishment and bring about genuine provincial autonomy.

In 1971, when armed conflict broke out between Pakistan and India, resulting in the secession of Bangladesh from Pakistan, Afghanistan once again remained neutral. (Bangladesh was officially recognized by Afghanistan on February 18, 1973.) It did, however, harbor hundreds of Bengalis who were fleeing persecution in Pakistan and help them to reach Bangladesh through Iran and India. After the secession of Bangladesh, a new constitution, not very different from that of 1970, was adopted for Pakistan in 1973. This document was also signed and accepted by the Pashtun and Baluch leadership, with the exception of Khair Bakhsh Marri, one of the Baluch leaders. In the Pakistan-wide elections held on the basis of the 1970 and 1973 constitutions, the Pashtun and Baluch national leaders were elected en masse in the North-West Frontier Province and Baluchistan. This was a demonstration of the trust that the Pashtun and Baluch electorates had in their leaders.

For some time, relations with Iran had been warming considerably, despite uneasiness in some Afghan circles about Iranian expansionism, which was believed to be implicit in Mohammad Reza Shah's ambitious policies. The success of the shah in defusing the Afghan–Pakistani crisis had contributed to bringing the two countries even closer, as did Iranian endeavors to improve the new Afghan transit route through Iran and Iranian willingness to provide Afghanistan with gasoline and other petroleum products at below-market rates. Trade between the two countries had also grown substantially during recent years.

It was in this atmosphere of friendship that negotiations, which had been dormant since 1951, were renewed in Tehran in June 1972 with a view to settling the Hilmand waters dispute between Afghanistan and Iran. The successive rounds of talks led to the solution of all problems related to this dispute. In May 1973, the Hilmand Water Treaty was signed in Kabul by the prime ministers of Afghanistan and Iran, Mohammad Mussa Shafiq and Amir Abbas Hoveyda, respectively.

The Hilmand Water Treaty's importance lay less in what it had achieved in regulating the Iranian share of water from the Hilmand River than in its significance for the future development of relations between Iran and Afghanistan. The Iranians, by virtue of the treaty, did not receive much more water than the amount the Afghans had proposed in 1951. But the treaty allayed suspicions and removed from Iranian–Afghan relations the emotional irritant of the dispute. This consequently brought about favorable conditions for forging stronger ties and wider cooperation between the two neighbors. Despite obstructions from Communist deputies and their sympathizers, the Afghan Parliament endorsed the Hilmand Water Treaty in early 1973. Likewise, the Iranian *majlis* (parliament) ratified it on July 17, 1973. (Because of the change of regime in Afghanistan (see Chapter 6), which delayed exchange of the instruments of ratification, the Hilmand Water Treaty did not come into force until June 5, 1977.)

Close relations with oil-rich Iran paved the way for that country's financial involvement in Afghanistan's economic development. By the early 1970s, Iran had shown interest in this regard, and, with the Hilmand problem out of the way, both countries moved ahead in that direction. Although Afghanistan was eager to receive Iranian aid, it shunned the idea of joining the Regional Cooperation for Development (RCD), an economic cooperation organization created by Iran, Turkey, and Pakistan. The advisability of Afghanistan's joining that organization was occasionally hinted at by some well-placed Iranians. Afghanistan considered association with RCD (viewed as an offshoot of CENTO) contradictory to its nonalignment and, therefore, inadmissible. It should be noted for the record, however, that the shah of Iran made it quite clear on several occasions that Iranian assistance would never be made contingent on Afghanistan's entry into RCD.

During the constitutional period, economic development slowed down considerably (Iranian aid had not started yet), and economic assistance to Afghanistan from the two superpowers decreased from 1963 to 1973. It seemed that, with the demise of the cold war, the superpowers had lost much of their intererst in competing in Afghanistan. However, despite this negative development, Afghanistan remained on good terms with both the United States and the USSR, although Soviet support for Pashtunistan had become less pronounced and more ambivalent. This was largely due to the Soviet Union's desire to court Pakistan and counter China's influence in that country. (By then the People's Republic of China had left the Russian camp.)

In September 1963 King Zahir Shah and Queen Homaira paid a state visit to the United States as guests of President Kennedy. This highly publicized visit, the first ever made by an Afghan head of state to the United States, lasted two weeks and was considered a success in better acquainting Americans with Afghanistan. The joint communiqué issued at the end of the Washington portion of the royal visit reiterated U.S. readiness to assist Afghanistan in its economic development. Further,

It was noted that Afghanistan's traditional policy is the safeguarding of its national independence through non-alignment, friendship and cooperation with all countries. The United States for its part places great importance on Afghanistan's continued independence and national integrity.[82]

On the American side, Vice President Spiro Agnew officially visited Afghanistan in 1969. Although a few stones and rotten eggs were thrown at his motorcade by some onlookers and shouts of "U.S. imperialists out of Vietnam" were heard among the throng, Agnew's visit on the whole went smoothly. Afghanistan's position regarding the Vietnam War (not very different from that of the majority of nonaligned nations—withdrawal of American troops and self-determination for the Vietnamese) was explained to him and, at the end of the visit, the same general elements of U.S.–Afghan relations were again endorsed by both sides.

The Afghan policy of friendship and cooperation with all countries also included the People's Republic of China (PRC), an important neighbor. Afghanistan had had diplomatic ties with the PRC since its inception. During all the years that the PRC was denied membership in the United Nations, Afghanistan insisted, along with the majority of the nonaligned countries, that China's seat in that organization lawfully belonged to the PRC. Despite the deepening rift between the Soviet Union and the PRC, the PRC's invasion of India, and flourishing Sino–Pakistani relations, all sensitive matters to which Afghanistan had to pay due attention, the Afghans continued to develop their ties with the PRC. King Zahir Shah and the Chinese head of state Lu Chao Chi exchanged state visits, and, in the late 1960s, the short but rugged Sino–Afghan frontier high in the Pamirs was demarcated on the basis of a mutually satisfactory agreement.

Toward the mid-1960s, the Chinese began contributing to Afghanistan's developmental efforts. The main Chinese project was the Parwan irrigation project, about forty miles north of Kabul, for which a loan of $8.4 million had been earmarked.[83] By 1969 other Chinese projects were underway, including a carp fishery, an experimental sericulture project, an experimental tea plantation, a lapis lazuli workshop, and a textile plant.[84] Although Chinese assistance was modest, its political usefulness in balancing Russia's overwhelming presence did not escape the Afghans.

The Federal Republic of Germany's relations with Afghanistan had grown steadily stronger since the two countries had reestablished diplomatic, cultural, and trade ties. Although West Germany no longer had political interests per se in Afghanistan, its economic interests there were considerable. It rapidly occupied the third position among providers of foreign assistance to Afghanistan, following the USSR and the United States. West German funds were spent mainly for the overall development of Paktya Province, the Mahipar power station (near Kabul), the expansion of telecommunications, and advisory and training programs.[85]

As the fourth decade of Zahir Shah's reign was drawing to its end, Afghanistan's relations with the two superpowers had stabilized. The excitement of the immediate postwar years was long gone from its relations with the United States, as was the euphoria of its sudden closeness with the USSR in the 1950s. Although Afghanistan still believed that its survival necessitated a degree of involvement by the two superpowers and that, therefore, their interest in Afghanistan as an independent entity should not wane, it was clear that other sources of economic assistance had to be found if rapid advancement were to be achieved.

The warmth of relations with Iran was certainly a solution to some of these preoccupations, and, perhaps in due course, oil-rich Arab countries would also come forward to offer their assistance. In this respect, regional cooperation made sense to the Afghans, and their leaders increasingly pondered its prospects. It was obvious that, for the promotion of meaningful regional cooperation, certain prerequisites had to be fulfilled. Among these the reconciliation with Pakistan could not be overlooked. It was also important to thoroughly assess whether, under prevailing conditions, Afghanistan's commitment to a kind of institutionalized regional cooperation to which Iran, Pakistan, Turkey, and possibly other Middle Eastern countries would belong (an "Asian Common Market," undoubtedly under the aegis of oil-rich, pro-Western Iran) would be a positive or disrupting factor in its struggle for survival. Furthermore, the tendency of regional economic cooperation to evolve toward political collaboration had to be given due consideration.

While this kind of debate was going on among the ruling elite, the monarchy abruptly but peacefully came to an end. It would be the responsibility of the leadership of the new regime to seek answers to these complex questions.

Notes

1. Fletcher, *Afghanistan*, 249.
2. Louis Dupree, *Afghanistan*, (Princeton, N.J.: Princeton University Press, 1973, 489.
3. Fletcher, *Afghanistan*, 249.
4. Ibid., 252.
5. There were five Tribal Agencies with 100% Pashtun inhabitants: Khyber, Malakand, Northern Waziristan, Southern Waziristan, and Kurram. To these, Pakistan later added a sixth, Mohmand.
6. In the NWFP the Congress Party of India, which was the ruling party in that province during those turbulent years, was referred to as the Frontier Congress.
7. Fletcher, *Afghanistan*, 251.
8. Sir George Cuningham, "The North West Frontier and the Tribes," *Sunday Statesman*, (Delhi), 29 May 1949.
9. *Official Records of the Plenary Meetings of the U.N. General Assembly*, Ninety-Second Plenary Meeting of the U.N. General Assembly, 30 September 1947.
10. Fletcher, *Afghanistan*, 254.
11. Ibid.
12. Dupree, *Afghanistan*, 492.
13. Quoted by Anthony Hyman in *Afghanistan Under Soviet Domination, 1964–81* (London: The Macmillan Press, 1982), 45.
14. Dupree, *Afghanistan*, 492–93.
15. Anthony Arnold, *The Russian Invasion in Perspective*, (Stanford, Calif.: Stanford University, Hoover Institute Press, 1981), 30.
16. Fletcher, *Afghanistan*, 244.
17. Ibid.
18. Quoted in Henry S. Bradsher, *Afghanistan and the Soviet Union* (Durham, N.C.: Duke University Press, 1983), 18.
19. Ibid., 17.
20. Quoted by Leon B. Poullada in "The Failure of American Diplomacy in Afghanistan," *World Affairs*, vol. 145 (3) (Winter 1982–83), 233.
21. Study prepared by the National Security Council, Index of Declassified Documents, No. 377A (Arlington, Va., 1978).
22. Fletcher, *Afghanistan*, 256.
23. Ibid.
24. Department of State, *Foreign Relations of the United States, 1950*, 5: 1, p. 448.
25. Conversations with the late Mohammad Naim, former Afghan ambassador to Washington and London, former deputy prime minister and foreign minister, and brother of Mohammad Daoud, in early 1974.
26. Conversations with Mohammad Naim.
27. Poullada, "Afghanistan and the United States," 186.
28. Bradsher, *Afghanistan and the Soviet Union*, 20.
29. Poullada, "Afghanistan and the United States," 186–87.

30. For a detailed account of the Iranian–Afghan dispute over the waters of the Hilmand River and the final 1972 agreement between the two countries, including comments on the provisions of the Hilmand agreement, see A. H. H. Abidi, "Irano–Afghan Dispute over the Hilmand River Waters," *International Studies* (July–September 1977).

31. Fletcher, *Afghanistan*, 267.

32. Conversations with a number of Afghan high officials including Abdul Samad (a former deputy foreign minister) and Abdur Rahman Popal (a former director general of political affairs) during the 1960s.

33. In connection with Vice President Nixon's stay in Kabul, this amusing episode was recounted to me by a former official of the Afghan Foreign Ministry. An ancient and elaborately decorated bed was brought for Nixon from the royal palace to the house where he was staying. In the middle of the night the boxspring fell noisily from its frame, shaking the sleeping vice president badly. The official firmly believed that Nixon's arrogant and offensive mood the following day was due to that unfortunate incident.

34. Poullada, "Afghanistan and the United States," 187.

35. Pakistan had entered SEATO in September 1954, and, in the following year, it joined CENTO.

36. Dupree, *Afghanistan*, 510–11. In case what has been reported to Dupree by American diplomats is accurate, the reader will note the interesting similarity between this Afghan demand and King Amanullah's demarche to the British in the 1920s informing them that he was willing to sever his ties with the Soviets provided the British gave assurances they would defend the northern borders of Afghanistan against Soviet aggression. The British government, as discussed in this book, decided against giving Amanullah those assurances.

37. Nikita S. Khrushchev, *Khrushchev Remembers* (Boston: Little, Brown, 1970), 560–62.

38. Fletcher, *Afghanistan*, 269.

39. According to Arnold, *Afghanistan: The Soviet Invasion in Perspective*, 34:

> The terms were generous: Afghan repayment was to be made in its natural exports, wool and cotton, and was to start only three years later, on January 1, 1957, it was to consist of five equal payments bearing an interest rate of 3 percent.

Subsequent Russian loans generally bore the same 2% to 3% interest rate.

40. Pakistan was constituted of two parts: West Pakistan and East Pakistan. The components of West Pakistan were the provinces of the NWFP, Punjab, Sind, and the Baluchistan States Union, plus a few princely states. East Pakistan was comprised of Bengal, which years later seceded and became the independent state of Bangladesh.

41. Poullada, "Afghanistan and the United States," 189.

42. Ibid.

43. Dupree, *Afghanistan*, 507.

44. Ibid., 507–8.

45. Bradsher, *Afghanistan and the Soviet Union*, 27.

46. Dupree, *Afghanistan*, 508.

47. Ibid., 508–9.

48. According to Bradsher, *Afghanistan and the Soviet Union*, 25, by 1979 Soviet military aid to Afghanistan was roughly $1.25 billion. About 3,725 Afghan military personnel had received military training in the Soviet Union.

49. N. A. Bulganin and N. S. Khrushchev, *Visit to Burma and Afghanistan* (New York: New Century Publishers, 1956), 34.

50. Ibid., 37.

51. Ibid., 23.

52. Conversations with Mohammad Daoud in late 1973.

53. Fletcher, *Afghanistan*, 285.

54. Bradsher, *Afghanistan and the Soviet Union*, 28.

55. Ibid.

56. Ibid., 29.

57. Kandahar International Airport was built with American financial aid and technical assistance. Once completed, this project became a "white elephant." For an interesting account of it, see ibid., 29–30.

58. Arnold, *The Soviet Invasion*, 38.

59. Ibid., 39. According to Arnold, during "the period 1950–1959, U.S. assistance totaled $148.3 million, while Soviet assistance came to $246.2 million. While most of the U.S. assistance was in the form of outright grants, the USSR concentrated on long-term loans." Arnold gave the following assessment of U.S. aid to Afghanistan: "Although the United States did not try to match the volume of Soviet assistance, the impact of the U.S. projects was considerable, and most Western analysts seem to feel that the Afghans benefited as much from the U.S. aid as from the Soviet." According to Bradsher, *Afghanistan and the Soviet Union*, 24–25, on the other hand, up to the time of the Communist coup in 1978, the USSR had extended $1.265 billion in economic aid to Afghanistan. The American aid had totaled $532.87 million, 71% of which was in outright gifts, whereas the Soviet assistance was almost entirely in the form of loans. However, interest and repayment terms on loans by Russia to Afghanistan were more generous than those accorded to other Third World countries. East European countries had also extended $110 million in aid to Afghanistan.

60. "The Eisenhower Doctrine loosely guaranteed all the States of the Middle East American protection against Communist invasion." Dupree, *Afghanistan*, 511.

61. Arnold, *The Russian Invasion*, 40.

62. *New York Times*, 24–28 June 1958.

63. *New York Times*, 25 June 1958.

64. *New York Times*, 10 December 1959.

65. Bradsher, *Afghanistan and the Soviet Union*, 26.

66. Louis Dupree, *The Mountains Go to Mohammad Zahir: Observations on Afghanistan's Reactions to Visits by Nixon, Bulganin–Khrushchev, Eisenhower and Khrushchev*, American Universities Field Staff Report (AUFS), South Asia Series, vol. 4, no. 6, May 1960, LD-6-60, 25.

67. Dupree, *Afghanistan*, 506.

68. Ibid.

69. Conversation with Abdur-Rahman Pazhwak, who was, at the time of the visit, the director general of political affairs in the Ministry of Foreign Affairs.

70. Dupree, *Afghanistan*, 539.

71. Ibid.

72. In 1961 the Afghans once again proposed to the Americans the building of a transit route from the port of Chahbahar in Iran to Zahidan on the Afghan–Iranian border and from there to Kandahar, which would have been shorter than the Tehran–Herat route. But the Iranians and the Americans did not agree with this proposal. Instead, the Americans expressed their readiness to improve the port of Khurmashahr and build an all-weather road from Herat to Islam–Qala to link with the Iranian road system.

73. John C. Griffith, *Afghanistan: The Key to a Continent* (Boulder, Colo., Westview Press, 1981), 149.

74. Dr. Mohammad Yusuf, Mohammad Hashim Maiwandwal, Noor Ahmad Etemadi (twice), Dr. Abdul Zahir, and Mohammad Mussa Shafiq.

75. A detailed account of the adventurous history of the PDPA can be found in Anthony Arnold, *Afghanistan's Two-Party Communism: Parcham and Khalq* (Stanford, Calif.: Stanford University, Hoover Institution, 1983). This book is a useful source of biographies of leading Afghan Communists.

76. In its first issues, *Khalq* stated, among other things, that "the main issue of contemporary times and the center of class struggle on a worldwide basis, which began with the great October Socialist revolution, is the struggle between international socialism and international imperialism." Quoted in Dupree, *Afghanistan*, 608.

77. Arnold, *The Russian Invasion*, 49.

78. Dupree, *Afghanistan*, 565.

79. Ibid.

80. Louis Dupree, *An Informal Talk with King Mohammad Zahir Shah of Afghanistan*, American Universities Field Staff, July 1963, LD9-63, 6.

81. *New York Times*, 6 September 1963.

82. *New York Times*, 8 September 1963.

83. Dupree, *Afghanistan*, 631.

84. Ibid.

85. Ibid., 631, 641.

6

The Advent of the Republic

On July 17, 1973, the people of Kabul slowly awoke to the realization that a military coup had taken place in the predawn hours. Many of those who had left home before sunrise in pursuit of their daily routine hastily returned to inform their families and neighbors that tanks and army vehicles had positioned themselves around the royal palace, at government buildings, and at important crossroads. Radio Afghanistan-Kabul, which usually started its daily summer program at six o'clock in the morning, was silent until 6:40 A.M., when it began broadcasting martial and *attan* (Pashtun tribal dance) music. As it became known later, speculations were running high as to who had launched the coup. Prime Minister Mussa Shafiq and General Abdul Wali, King Zahir Shah's son-in-law, were mentioned as possible leaders of the insurrection. The thought that some unknown colonel, profiting from the king's absence, might have ventured to assume power was not dismissed lightly.[1] At 7:15 the radio announcer informed his listeners of an imminent announcement. At 7:20 he announced that, in a few minutes, his Royal Highness Sardar Mohammad Daoud (the former prime minister and cousin and brother-in-law of the king) would address the nation.[2] It was suddenly realized by those listening to the announcement that it was Daoud who had launched the military takeover and that, in all likelihood, he was now in control.

A group of friends and I, who had hastily gathered around a radio, were startled. After all, there had been no indication in recent months, even in the circles close to Daoud, that he was seeking a political comeback or was willing to abandon his ten-year-old seclusion. But the mere mention of his name brought welcome relief from the feelings of uneasiness and tension usually associated with such sudden convulsions of the established political order. Daoud's name must have had the same soothing effect on the people at large, who, in those early hours of uncertainty, had understandably feared the consequences of a breakdown in law and order. They must have immediately reasoned that, if Mohammad Daoud were associated in any way with what had happened, then there was no cause for alarm. The country could not be in better hands than his. Quickly a flow of confidence replaced the spasms of apprehension.

It was almost 7:40 when Daoud started to speak to the people. He briefly described how his reform proposals for the progress of Afghanistan, as embodied in his last presentation to the king ten years ago, had been shattered by the coming into being of a pseudodemocracy. The prosperity and advancement of Afghanistan, he said, depended on the establishment of a true and reasonable democracy whose basic purpose would be to serve the Afghan people as a whole by securing the totality of their rights and by safeguarding Afghanistan's national sovereignty. He explained that the society he envisioned was to be built with the participation of all Afghans without discrimination. The past regime, he maintained, failed to achieve anything in this regard. That pseudodemocracy, he said, rested on personal and class interests and thrived on intrigues and falsehood. He further said that democracy, which should have benefited the people, was instead choked by anarchy, and the constitutional monarchy had fallen victim to the most abject form of authoritarian rule. All the distortions propagated during the last ten years by the government, he continued, had not succeeded in hiding from the Afghan people and the outside world the total collapse of economic, social, political, and administrative conditions, brought about by the incompetent regime. He mentioned that the deterioration of the situation at all levels had distressed Afghan patriots, especially the Afghan army. Daoud said that they had therefore decided to put an end to the corrupt regime and save the fatherland from its scourges. He then informed the nation that the old order had been replaced by a new one, a republican regime, which was in conformity with the true spirit of Islam. He conveyed his congratulations and those of his colleagues to the people of Afghanistan upon the advent of the Afghan republic and asked for their support and cooperation.

Thus by eight o'clock in the morning, the first Afghan Republic was officially born. Its coming into being had been remarkably painless. In the short span of a few hours, centuries of monarchy in the country of the Hindu Kush, which until then had not known any other form of government, were replaced by a republican order.

On the afternoon of July 17, 1973, the foreign ambassadors residing in Kabul were invited to the Ministry of Foreign Affairs. Director General of Political Affairs Abdul Wahed Karim officially informed them of the bloodless military takeover that had occurred the previous night and of the advent of the republic. He asked them to convey the goodwill of the new regime to their respective governments and expressed the wish that the republic be recognized by them as soon as possible.

During the course of the same day, it was announced that Mohammad Daoud had assumed the title of Head of State, that the Constitution of 1964 was suspended, and that a Central Committee had been formed to carry out the everyday tasks of the government. The president of the committee was

Mohammad Daoud, and its members were mostly leftists, military and civilian, who had assisted him in his coup d'état. Not much was subsequently heard of this committee, and it gradually fell into oblivion after the formation of the first republican cabinet in late August.

The leftist complexion of the Central Committee generated speculation that Mohammad Daoud was only a figurehead used by the Communists in their ascension to power. The reality, however, was quite different. He was, in fact, the one who had masterfully used them to gain control of the country. He could well have dispensed with their help, but ten years of separation from the army inclined Daoud to believe that his name and prestige were no longer sufficient to pull the traditional Afghan officer corps with him in the coup that he was preparing. He therefore opted to draw on the services of a small coterie of restless Russian-trained Communist officers, ready to oblige whenever a coup or a *putsch* was in the offing.[3] The cynical might suggest that the lack of support for the Communists within the country, which he believed would make it easy to eventually discard them once they had outlived their usefulness, also inclined Mohammad Daoud to retain their services.

Much has been said about the extent of the Soviet Union's involvement in Mohammad Daoud's coup d'état. I am, however, convinced, after years of association with Daoud and his colleagues, that the coup of July 17, 1973, was definitely not a Russian initiative. It was an Afghan venture in pursuit of purely Afghan aims.[4] But it can be reasonably assumed that Moscow was kept informed of its preparation and launching by at least some of the Communist participants, as part of their unquestionable allegiance to Russia. Daoud once told me that he was almost certain that the prospect of a larger Communist role in an Afghan government born of the coup was tantalizing enough for the Soviets not to create any obstructions to its successful conclusion. Daoud was undoubtedly confident that he would be able to keep the Communist influence checked once power was seized.

The resumption of power by Mohammad Daoud was welcomed by the majority of Afghans. Strong leadership was needed; they new that he could provide it. The accelerated pace of economic development during his ten years as the king's prime minister had left a positive and lasting imprint on the country. It was anticipated that his return would give new impetus to the sagging economy and that his dynamism and dedication would put the government back on to the right track. Anthony Hyman has given his view of Daoud's earlier decade of power in the following terms:

Daoud's decade of power from 1953 to 1963 had brought improved changes in Afghan society as well as in the economy. Although critics of Daoud often asserted that he was interested only in economic development to the exclusion of social reform, much in that area too had been accomplished by the end of the decade.[5]

Of these social reforms, the abolishing of the veil and the emancipation of women were not the least important.

To the Afghans, Mohammad Daoud was also the man who had brought Afghanistan out of the shadows in the fifties and, by his statesmanship, had succeeded in attracting the friendship and assistance of major world powers. It was during Daoud's prime ministership that Afghanistan had participated in the first Afro–Asian Conference in Bandung and its representatives had taken an active part in the formulation of its famous declaration. It was also in this era that the nonaligned movement had been founded, and Afghanistan had been one of its founding members. Thus, there was no doubt that, while Daoud's years of prime ministership had been a period of remarkable growth internally for Afghanistan, externally the country had also gained considerable prestige and recognition. It was, therefore, understandable that the people, judging Daoud's past record, received his political comeback with enthusiasm.

The republic came into being by the sole will of Mohammad Daoud. He perceived of it as a more appropriate means of promoting Afghanistan's progress and ensuring its survival at that time. However, in those respects he was unable to achieve much. In the span of a few short years, the first Afghan republic fell to Soviet ambitions, and its founder, together with his family and a number of his close associates, was massacred by the Communists in a Soviet-directed coup d'état on April 28, 1978. The collapse of the first Afghan republic also ended the existence of Afghanistan as an independent entity.

Notes

1. King Zahir Shah had gone to Italy for medical treatment.
2. It was the last time that Mohammad Daoud was referred to as His Royal Highness or *Sardar*. Subsequently, in the media and in all official correspondence and acts his name was preceded only by *Shaghalay*, which in Pushto means mister.
3. Conversations with Mohammad Daoud and Waheed Abdullah in October 1973.
4. As corroboration of this view, see, among other sources, the narrative by former KGB major Vladimir Kuzichkin, *Time Magazine*, 22 November 1982, 33; and the article by former Afghan diplomat Abdul Madjid Mangal, *Sunday Telegraph (London)*, 24 June 1984. Mangal's assertions are especially credible because of his close association with the Communist rulers of Afghanistan during their first years of rule. This association must have given Mangal ample opportunity to ascertain certain facts.
5. Anthony Hyman, *Afghanistan Under Soviet Occupation, 1964–81* (Hong Kong: The Macmillan Press, 1982), 51.

7

Foreign Relations of the Republic

In his address to the people of Afghanistan on July 17, 1973, Mohammad Daoud announced the underlying principles of his foreign policy.

The foreign policy of Afghanistan is based on neutrality, non-participation in military pacts, and independent judgment of the issues by the people themselves. Emanating from our national aspirations, this policy is designed to fulfill the material and spiritual needs of the people. More than anything else the fulfillment of these needs requires a world in peace. No country can attain its legitimate national aspirations except in conditions of tranquility. As we in Afghanistan endeavor to develop our country we aspire to the consolidation of world peace and security. The strongest pillars of Afghanistan's policy of non-alignment are its frankness and sincerity which stem from the national free will of the Afghan people. Thus, Afghanistan's friendly relations with other countries will retain their unshakable foundations, and through diplomacy, personal visits, and promotion of international cooperation, efforts will be exerted to consolidate these ties further. It is our hope that these efforts will bear positive and practical results. . . . This regime observes and respects the principles of the United Nations Charter, the main goals of which are the welfare of mankind and global peace.[1]

The policies outlined in this speech were viewed by Mohammad Daoud as essential elements of his plans for the survival and continued modernization of the Afghan state. In particular, the expansion and improvement of relations with Afghanistan's neighbors, major Arab countries, and the United States were considered important goals of the republic.

Pakistan

In the speech referred to, Mohammad Daoud said, "Pakistan is the only country with which we still have a political difference, the question of Pashtunistan. Our constant efforts to find a solution will continue."[2] A few days later, in his first press conference, which was attended mostly by foreign journalists, Daoud again spoke of the Afghan–Pakistani difference.

We hope that in grasping this reality [the existence of an Afghan–Pakistan dispute with regard to the legitimate rights of the Pashtuns and the Baluchi people] and with mutual good will, both sides [Afghanistan and Pakistan] will be able to find an amicable, peaceful and honourable solution to this problem in accordance with the hopes and aspirations of the Pashtun and Baluchi people and their leaders.[3]

Daoud's main reason for stressing the existence of the Afghan–Pakistani dispute at the very outset of the republic was to stimulate a solution to the problem, which, in his view, had to be settled as soon as possible in order for the new regime to devote all its energies to the overwhelming tasks of social and economic development. However, Daoud's initial references to Afghanistan's difference with Pakistan, conciliatory as they were, did not find a favorable echo in Islamabad. The Pakistani leadership, headed by prime minister Zulfikar Ali Bhutto, reacted with unrestrained anger to what had been said by the Afghan head of state. Instead of seizing the occasion to make a fresh start at solving the problem, the government of Pakistan was quick to denounce the new regime as anti-Pakistani and even anti-Islamic. A huge propaganda campaign was mounted by Islamabad, depicting Pakistan as the defenseless victim and Mohammad Daoud as the sinister predator bent on undoing Pakistan. Not long after, he was accused of being behind the new phase of the revolt in Baluchistan that had started in the early part of 1973 and acts of sabotage in the NWFP.

Although the new regime in Afghanistan was recognized by Pakistan on July 22, 1973, it was clear that Daoud's resumption of power had very much upset Pakistani leaders. In their deliberate negativism toward the issue of Pashtunistan, they had always perceived of Mohammad Daoud as the most serious hard-liner among the Afghan leaders. The impression was being created by Islamabad that the Afghans in the latter part of the monarchy had toned down their declarations on the subject of the "Pashtunistan stunt" (as it was still called by the Pakistanis) and had ultimately shelved it altogether and that it was now the dangerous and irresponsible Daoud who was unnecessarily reviving that so-called issue for his own ulterior motives.

Very few influential foreign friends of Pakistan bothered to check the record of past Afghan declarations on Pashtunistan and compare them with Daoud's statements. Had they done so, they would have learned that Mohammad Daoud's initial pronouncements concerning the republic's policy toward Pashtunistan were no more stringent than those that had been made regularly by the king and his ministers. They would have been convinced that, during the monarchy, Afghanistan did not abandon the Pashtunistan issue. Even the "internationalization" of the problem of Pashtunistan by Afghanistan, a development that had chagrined the Pakistanis considerably, occurred during the monarchy, while Daoud had no say in the affairs of state. It was in 1968, during the twenty-third regular session of the General Assembly of the United Nations, that Abdur-Rahman Pazhwak, the Permanent Representative of Afghanistan to the United Nations, put before the world body the issue of Pashtunistan and warned that it was one of those problems that, if left unresolved, would threaten peace and security in Asia.[4] The problem of Pashtunistan was subsequently raised often in the General Assembly by the Afghans, to the great disappointment of the Pakistani establishment, who considered this an immature and foolish act. Daoud did not "reopen an old wound" as was claimed by the London *Times*; rather, the wound had never healed.[5]

After Daoud's policy statement on Pashtunistan, Pakistan's media and diplomatic apparatus attempted to convince those not well acquainted with southwest Asian realities of Afghanistan's desire to dismember Pakistan (with the assistance of India and the Soviet Union). They asserted that the Afghan rulers had created the myth of Pashtunistan to divert their people's attention from their daily miseries. They stressed that, under the guise of self-determination for the Pashtuns in Pakistan, with which the Pakistani Baluchis were now banded together, the Afghan rulers were in fact aiming to end the existence of Pakistan as an independent entity.

Pakistani officials eagerly explained to anyone willing to listen that India had engineered the severance of Bangladesh from Pakistan in 1971. What Afghanistan intended now was to achieve the complete disintegration of Pakistan. Pakistani leaders also often stressed the vulnerability of their country, made up of a mosaic of different and often antagonistic peoples held together only by the cement of the Islamic faith. Those officials played on the fears of both their own people and Muslims at large by painting a gloomy picture of the future, in which, as a result of Afghan machinations, only the Punjab would remain in Pakistan, until it was in turn swallowed by Hindu expansionism. As at the time of the creation of Pakistan, the appeal of Islam was once again used by Pakistani leaders to inspire support for their position, especially among the oil-rich Islamic countries.

After the establishment of the republic in Afghanistan, Pakistani leaders frequently portrayed their country as a small, peace-loving nation surrounded by a hostile world bent on its total destruction. None of the Pakistani leaders, however, surpassed Prime Minister Zulfikar Ali Bhutto in these lamentations. He was a master at conveying to the outside world the image of a "beleaguered" and "victimized" Pakistan. Listening to Bhutto's diatribes against Afghanistan, one got the impression that the dismemberment of Pakistan through anti-Islamic machinations was imminent, and that, with the fall of Pakistan, the whole Islamic world would go under! Fantastic as they were, these accusations nevertheless convinced some Arab and Islamic countries. Diplomatic contacts with Iran and several Arab states who were viewed by the Afghans as potential donors to Afghanistan's developmental efforts left the Afghans with the impression that, while those countries were receptive to Afghan overtures for financial assistance, they wished that Afghanistan would make an effort to allay Pakistan's imagined or real fears. Although no conditions were attached to their financial help, it was clear that they felt deescalation in the intensity of the Afghan–Pakistani dispute would bring about a better climate for the availability of those funds. Beneath the subtle diplomatic language lay the unmistakably clear message: Take steps for the betterment of relations with Pakistan.

During this period, Pakistani authorities often spoke alarmingly of Afghan troop deployments in sensitive border areas, clearly implying that the Afghans were preparing for a war against Pakistan. However, not a single unit of the Afghan army moved to a position that threatened Pakistan. In the winters of 1974 and 1975, regularly scheduled Eastern Army maneuvers did take place in Nangarhar province, but they were simply war games and did not justify the Pakistani overreaction. It was clear that allegations concerning Afghan troop movements were part of Pakistan's overall effort to attract the sympathies of Islamic states to the "plight" of "vulnerable" Pakistan and alarm the Western countries as well. The Afghan media countered Pakistan's propaganda war against Afghanistan to the best of its abilities. This hostile exchange intensified as time passed and became extremely virulent.

By the beginning of 1974, Afghan relations with Pakistan had worsened considerably. This was largely due to intensification of the revolt in Baluchistan and the mounting unrest in the North-West Frontier Province, which had resulted in a ruthless war of subjugation in the former and increased Pakistani repressions in the latter. Alleged Pakistani involvement in Maiwandwal's antiregime plot (see Chapter 8) also contributed to the stiffening of the Afghan position. Gone were the conciliatory tones of the official Afghan statements of the first days of the republic and the deliberate omission of any reference to the specifics of the Afghan claim. The existing difference between Afghanistan and Pakistan was increasingly explained in greater detail and in harsher language by Afghan spokesmen such as the Deputy Foreign Minister Waheed Abdullah.

The Deputy Foreign Minister declared in an interview on November 5, 1973, that Afghanistan could not remain indifferent to Pakistan's "use of force and arms" against Pashtuns and Baluchis and that Afghanistan regarded this [the fate of the Pashtuns and the Baluchis] "as a national issue." He added that his country did not recognize the Durand Line, established during British rule of India, as a frontier with Pakistan. When asked about his Government's attitude to demands by Pashtun nationalists in Pakistan's North West Frontier Province for an independent state of Pashtunistan, he replied, "we demand the right of self-determination for the Pashtuns and Baluchi people." Asked whether this meant formation of a separate State or States or creation of a greater Afghanistan, he said, "it is for the people themselves to determine their future."[6]

Bhutto himself was adding fuel to the fire with his inflammatory statements. In a provocative speech in the tribal areas in mid-November 1973, after accusing the new Afghan regime of interference in the internal affairs of Pakistan, Bhutto told the tribesmen "that some people had advised him to invite the ousted Afghan ruler King Mohammad Zahir Shah to visit Pakistan's tribal areas. But how could this be done, as Pakistan did not want to interfere in the internal affairs of its neighbor?" Bhutto added, "If, however, King Zahir Shah wants to come to Pakistan as a guest we would welcome him. After all Mr. Abdul Ghafar Khan had lived in Afghanistan for eight years."[7] He then went on to say, in a paternalistic tone, that ties with Afghanistan "could be developed in trade and other sectors only if Afghanistan had the same desire and refused to be misled by others."[8]

Mohammad Daoud could not let such statements pass unanswered. In an interview with *Le Monde* in early February 1974 he gave the Pakistanis a foretaste of how unconciliatory the Afghans could become if the situation were left to deteriorate. He said that Pakistan's North-West Frontier Province had always been an integral part of Afghanistan and that the British, through imposing unequal treaties unacceptable to his government, had severed these regions from Afghan sovereignty.[9]

Daoud was under some pressure at the time from the Communist members of the Central Committee to change the traditional Afghan demand for self-determination for the Pashtuns to a clear-cut territorial claim. Although inconsistent with the Afghan position taken since the creation of Pakistan, a territorial claim with regard to the Pashtun lands may have been historically more justifiable. But Daoud, sensing at that time the inadvisability of such a shift, managed to maintain the official Afghan position emphasizing self-determination.

The simmering antagonism between the Baluchis and the Pakistani establishment, with its periodic violent eruptions, had come to a head after Bhutto's February 1973 dismissal of Baluchistan's provincial governor, his ouster of that province's government (constituted essentially of National Awami Party [NAP] members), and the subsequent imprisonment of NAP's Baluchi leadership.[10] Soon the outspoken NAP governor of the NWFP, Arbab Skandar Khan Khalil, was also fired by Bhutto and replaced by Alsam Khattak, onetime ambassador to Kabul. As a result of these events, the alliance ministry of NWFP, headed by the late Mowlana Mufti Mahmoud and made up of a coalition of NAP and *Jamiat-i-Ulama-i-Islam* (JUI) members, resigned in protest against Bhutto's actions in the two provinces.

Bhutto had agreed in 1972, as a consequence of the secession of Bangladesh and the uncertainties of that traumatic period, to the formation of provincial governments in Baluchistan and the NWFP on the basis of electoral mandates the parties had received in the two frontier provinces. Now he justified the measures taken against the NAP in Baluchistan by asserting that the Baluchistan government had dangerously exceeded the autonomy provisions of the federal constitution and that the NAP's Baluchi leaders were plotting the dismemberment of Pakistan and Iran with the help of Iraq and the Soviet Union. Strangely, whenever Bhutto spoke of the dismemberment of Pakistan and Iran together, he did not include Afghanistan among the culprits involved in the sinister task of undoing the two allies. Be that as it may, Bhutto, under pressure from the Punjab and the shah of Iran, probably had had second thoughts about putting into practice the autonomy provision of the federal constitution and was seeking a pretext to stem spreading Baluchi and Pashtun nationalism, which had found new impetus after the NAP's electoral victory in 1970. His interpretation of the developments in Baluchistan had provided him with such an opportunity. Undoubtedly, Bhutto knew that the ouster of the Baluchistan government would be followed by the resignation of the NWFP alliance government. He forced the issue and was thus able to kill two birds with one stone.

The savage war waged by the Pakistani army against the Baluchi people resulted in an increasing number of Baluchis' fleeing to Afghanistan. They found refuge in parts of Kandahar and Kalat provinces, as they had found it in the past during Baluchi upheavals against Ayub Khan's regime. While these Baluchis were considered freedom fighters by Afghanistan, the government of Pakistan referred to them as fugitives from justice. Bhutto relentlessly accused Afghanistan of aiding and abetting the Baluchistan insurgency, which he claimed could not have continued without Afghan help. These allegations held little credence with those well acquainted with the history of Baluchi relations with the Pakistani establishment. It was clear that, once again, Pakistan had to find a scapegoat for the blunders committed, and Afghanistan was the natural choice.

As in the past, the Afghans could not remain indifferent to the plight of the Pashtuns and the Baluchis, who were their kith and kin. The help extended to the Baluchi refugees was quite in line with established Afghan policies, of which the Pakistani government was well aware. On occasion, however, groups of fighting Baluchi tribesmen entered Afghanistan for rest and recuperation or to elude Pakistani patrols. These groups usually returned to Baluchistan and resumed their struggle against the Pakistani army. The government of Afghanistan neither wished to nor could hamper this transborder traffic.

Sardar Akbar Bugti, chief of the Baluch Bugti tribe, was appointed governor of Baluchistan, but in November 1973 he resigned in protest against Pakistan's atrocities in the province. Because none of the Baluchi appointees as governors of Baluchistan had entirely satisfied the expectations of Islamabad, the central government established direct rule over the province. Successive amnesties proclaimed by Bhutto for the tribes at war with the Pakistani army yielded no result; the Baluchis had no faith in the central government's promises. Besides, the immediate purpose of the struggle was release of the Baluchi leaders, reestablishment of home rule on the basis of the 1970 elections, and restoration of provincial prerogatives. None of these concerns seemed to be given serious consideration by the central government. The trial of the NAP's Baluchi leaders lingered on, while Bhutto and some of his aides had secret meetings with them in jail, trying to prod them to persuade the rebels to lay down their arms. But no agreement could be reached. The leaders remained in jail, appearing occasionally before the magistrate, and the war in Baluchistan continued.

Apart from providing $300 million annual assistance to Pakistan at this time, Iran in mid-1974 contributed to Pakistan's war effort in Baluchistan by sending thirty U.S.-supplied Huey Cobra military helicopters. Although Afghanistan's relations were developing satisfactorily with Iran, the government of Afghanistan recorded its disapproval of what had taken place in a diplomatic demarche to the government of Iran. The Iranian response was predictable. It asserted that the insurgency in Baluchistan was a Communist plot and that whatever support Iran was providing for Bhutto's war in

Baluchistan was aimed at stemming the spread of communism in that province and from there to southern Iran. According to Baluchi sources, the Huey Cobras affair was only one of many episodes of Iranian military assistance to Pakistan. Those sources strongly maintained that the Pakistanis had been receiving military hardware and ammunition from Iran regularly since the beginning of the insurgency. Although Kabul did not doubt the accuracy of those reports, no evidence surfaced to fully substantiate the allegations.

Several times prior to mid-1976, the shah of Iran reiterated the pledge of his government to the territorial integrity of Pakistan in strongly worded public statements and interviews. In private conversations with Afghan leaders, however, the shah never even insinuated that what Bhutto was saying about Afghanistan's purported efforts to undo Pakistan was true or that the Afghan claims with regard to Pashtunistan were threatening the existence of that country. Given the close relations between Iran and Pakistan, his under-standing of Afghanistan's posture and his apparent evenhandedness were indeed remarkable. One thing, though, on which the shah always insisted was the necessity for Afghanistan and Pakistan to compose their differences as quickly as possible, so that the Soviets could be denied the opportunity to exploit the situation for their own benefit.

It is important to record these Iranian attitudes not only because of Iran's friendship for both Afghanistan and Pakistan but also because Iran played and would continue to play a major role in attempting to find a solution to the Afghan–Pakistani dispute. Likewise, the reactions of two other Asian countries to the Afghan–Pakistani conflict are worth mentioning. The first of these countries is China, a close ally of Pakistan; the second is India, Pakistan's arch rival in the region.

It appeared to Afghan officials that China was unhappy with the establish-ment of the republic in 1973, let alone its championing of the right of self-determination for the Pashtun and Baluchi people living inside the borders of its close ally, Pakistan. But after the visit to China early in 1974 of President Daoud's brother and special emissary Mohammad Naim, on which he met his old ailing friend Chou En-lai, the Chinese attitude became more tolerant toward the republic. The new regime was no longer considered by China a product of Russian machinations, and the Chinese started to listen patiently to Afghan presentations about the issue of Pashtunistan.

Because the Indians had their own axe to grind with regard to Pakistan, their private expressions of support for the Pashtunistan issue and their opportunis-tic public silence did not impress the Afghans. The Indians were reluctant to even include any clear reference to the dispute between Afghanistan and Pakistan and the need for its resolution by peaceful means in Indo–Afghan joint communiqués. When pressed by the Afghans to be more specific in their public support of the Afghan stand, the Indians resorted to their oft-repeated argument that a more unambiguous public position would not be entirely in accordance with their endorsement of the Indian Independence Act of 1947 and their recognition of Pakistan as presently constituted. The Afghans felt that the question of Kashmir, which the Pakistanis insisted was a matter of self-determination and the Indians maintained was a matter of accession, also inclined India to shy away from publicly supporting the Afghan stand, which aimed at securing the right of self-determination for the Pashtuns and the Baluchis.

Although India was not forthcoming with support for Afghanistan's stand, both countries, given their strained relations with Pakistan, at times exaggerated the importance of their friendship for political reasons. Thus, no great significance was to be attached to passages like the following in an Indo–Afghan joint communiqué: "The two countries agreed to keep in close contact with each other on *political*, economic, and other developments in the region."[11] That kind of language was intended primarily to make Pakistan uncomfortable. The same was true of the so-called Mohammad Naim–Sarawan Singh (the minister of external affairs of India) understanding of 1974, which was rumored by some Indian Foreign Office officials to be a major step toward achieving the coordination of Indo–Afghan activities regarding Pakistan. In fact, that "understanding" was nothing more than an exchange of views between the two men during which they expressed the desire that Afghanistan and India inform each other of Pakistan's troop movements and other hostile activities on their respective frontiers with that country. To my knowledge, that exchange did not result in any significant action.

In his attempt to establish Pakistan as the champion of Islam and to endear himself to the Arabs, Bhutto organized an Islamic summit meeting to be held in Lahore on February 21, 1974. It was the second time that such a conference was to take place in Pakistan within a few years. Among the Islamic heads of state invited to Lahore was Mohammad Daoud. His invitation to attend the meeting was delivered in late January by Aziz Ahmad, the Pakistani minister for defense and external affairs. He was the first Pakistani high official to visit Afghanistan in an official capacity since the establishment of the republic. Daoud told Aziz Ahmad during a brief audience that he would try to go to Lahore but that, in all likelihood, affairs of state might prevent him from doing so.

Given the state of relations with Pakistan and the ongoing war in Baluchistan, Daoud deemed it inadvisable to attend the Lahore summit in person. The veteran Afghan diplomat Adbur-Rahman Pazhwak was chosen to represent the head of state as his special envoy. (I was also a member of the Afghan delegation.) Almost all of the heads of state of Islamic countries came to Lahore; however, the shah of Iran was conspicuous by his absence. The summit was chaired by Bhutto himself.

In his main policy statement at the summit, Pazhwak, after elaborating on the position of his government regarding the problems facing the Islamic world in general, drew the attention of the gathering to the upheaval in Baluchistan and also explained in some detail the existing political dispute between

Afghanistan and Pakistan. He expressed the wish that the assembly of Islamic nations understand the threat that those problems posed for peace and security in the region. He voiced his hope that the Islamic countries would help in the search for peaceful solutions to those issues. His statement was listened to in total silence. At its end, it was clear from the facial expressions of those present that the assembly would have been much happier if those matters had not been raised by the Afghans.

A few weeks before the Afghan delegation departed for Lahore, an exchange of views had taken place among the Afghan leadership about the advisability of addressing the war in Baluchistan and the dispute between Afghanistan and Pakistan at the Lahore meeting. During that exchange, some Afghan officials thought that, as a courtesy to the host country and to please the Arab and other Islamic friends of Pakistan, it would be better not to bring up those bilateral issues. Other influential members of the government argued that, if Islamic solidarity meant anything, the summit was the most appropriate forum in which to raise the issues of Baluchistan and Afghan–Pakistan relations. If the plight of Islamic Baluchistan and a dispute between two Islamic neighbors were of no concern to the Islamic summit, then whose concern were they? Besides, they maintained, to keep silent about the situation in Baluchistan in such an important Islamic gathering could be interpreted as a weakening of Afghanistan's support for the cause of the Baluchi freedom fighters, who were then enduring great hardship and sacrifices. Therefore, in spite of a certain skepticism about the usefulness of this act, it was decided that the Lahore gathering should be informed of these issues and of the danger they represented for peace in the region. This was not the first time that these issues had been raised in an international context since the establishment of the republic. The war in Baluchistan and the existing Afghan–Pakistani problem had already been put forth with much emphasis by the Afghans at the Fourth Conference of Heads of State and Governments of the Non-Aligned Countries in Algiers in September 1973 (Pakistan was not a member of the movement at that time) and at the UN General Assembly in October of that year.

The Afghan statement in Lahore did not prompt much public reaction, favorable or otherwise. It is likely that most delegates did not want to irritate the host country or take issue with a fellow Islamic state over something about which they knew little. The late President Boumedienne of Algeria, who was always ready to volunteer his advice, took the floor and requested the members not to raise bilateral issues during the summit, lest they lose sight of their main duty, which was to deal with the Arab–Israeli conflict and related issues. As the representative of Pakistan, Bhutto briefly exercised his right of reply to the Afghan statement, characterizing it as a perfect example of Afghan intervention in the internal affairs of Pakistan. He assured the assembly that no political differences existed between the two countries and that the situation in Baluchistan had never been better. In private, most Arab representatives expressed the wish that Afghanistan not bring up such controversial bilateral issues in Lahore. The Arabs were assured by the Afghans that they had no intention of pursuing the matter any further at that time.

This negative response to the Afghan presentation was not unexpected. However, if the whole affair is viewed as part of overall Afghan diplomatic endeavors to bring the war in Baluchistan and the state of relations between Afghanistan and Pakistan to the attention of the outside world, there was cause for some satisfaction on the part of the Afghans.

After the Afghan statement, the Afghan delegation was blackballed by the Pakistanis for the remainder of the summit. Suddenly the secretariat of the conference, controlled by the Pakistanis, grew reluctant to make adequate and speedy secretarial services available to the Afghan delegation. Documents were no longer regularly distributed to the Afghan delegation, and important draft documents submitted by the Afghans for reproduction and circulation during a particular meeting were instead handed out at the end of the meeting. The Afghans were no longer informed by the secretariat of the times of the informal regional group meetings so important in organizing the work of the conferernce, and the Afghans ceased to be invited to receptions hosted by Pakistan.

An unexpected side effect of the Afghan presentation to the Lahore summit was the sudden interest of Moamar Kaddafi in ending the Afghan–Pakistani conflict. The erratic Libyan leader called Mohammad Daoud from his residence in Lahore at two o'clock in the morning, a few hours after he had listened to the Afghan statement. Daoud narrated that rather amusing episode to me when I returned from Rawalpindi. He was fast asleep when the telephone woke him up. At first he thought that a member of the Afghan delegation was calling him from Lahore for instructions. It took him a good two minutes to realize that Kaddafi, of all people, was on the other end. In broken English that Daoud understood with difficulty, Kaddafi expressed the wish that the Afghan head of state came the following day to Lahore and said that he would send his personal plane to bring him to the summit. Kaddafi added that the preservation of Islamic solidarity was much more important than those petty conflicts to which the Afghan delegate had referred. Moreover, Pakistan was the bulwark of Islam and deserved much affection from all Islamic countries. Daoud understood Kaddafi to say that, if he came to Lahore, Kaddafi was sure that Afghanistan could be persuaded to abandon its dispute with Pakistan, because the matter was really not that important.

In a mixture of English and Arabic, Daoud explained to Kaddafi that, owing to previous engagements, it would be impossible for him to fly to Lahore. With respect to the dispute with Pakistan, Daoud told him that it would prove difficult to solve a problem that antedated the creation of Pakistan itself in just one short visit to Lahore. But he indicated his belief that, if a serious and unbiased interest were taken in the matter by Islamic leaders such as Kaddafi, a way out of the existing impasse could be found. Daoud assured Kaddafi that he had much affection for the people of Pakistan and that they need not have any fears about Afghanistan's designs. Daoud thanked Kaddafi for his telephone call and hoped that at a future date they would be able to meet either in Kabul or in Tripoli. It was never learned how much of Daoud's reply Kaddafi understood. Daoud jokingly added to his summary of that unusual diplomatic contact: "I only hope that he did not think I was talking in my sleep."

Kaddafi's interest in the matter did not wane with the end of the summit. In the following months he sent first his foreign affairs adviser Ali Tureiyki and then his top aide Abdul Salam Jaloud to Kabul to explore the possibility of using Libya's good offices to settle the dispute between Afghanistan and Pakistan. Kaddafi's flagrant bias in favor of Pakistan, however, prevented any serious talks from taking place between the Afghans and the Libyan envoys.

The then secretary general of the Permanent Secretariat of the Islamic Conference, Hassan El-Tohamy, was also unable to make any progress toward a solution of this problem in attempts made during June and September of 1974. These failures further emphasized that the core of the dispute between Afghanistan and Pakistan was of such a nature that its eventual settlement did not allow the interposition of a third party. Certainly a catalyst was needed just to bring about the essential direct contact between the two countries.

The major stumbling block preventing direct talks was Pakistan's refusal to recognize the existence of a political difference between the two countries, which, according to the Afghans, concerned the restoration and safeguarding of the rights of the Pashtuns and the Baluchi people. In Pakistan's view, that country's concurrence with the existence of a political difference with Afghanistan would mean that the fate of the Pashtuns and the Baluchis living inside Pakistan had not been definitely settled and was still open to negotiation with Afghanistan. Such a position would have been contrary to Pakistan's claim of sovereignty over the Pashtuns and the Baluchis. Pakistan contended that "differences" related to trade, transit, nomads, and even recognition of the Durand Line by Afghanistan existed between the two countries. It would not, however, accept any talks regarding the basic issue of the rights of the Pashtuns and the Baluchis, which it considered to be exclusively within its domestic jurisdiction. Afghan leaders maintained that they had no problems with Pakistan except one: the question of the restoration and safeguarding of the rights of the Pashtuns and the Baluchis. This could be resolved only if both parties would shed their sensitivities and approach the problem with a reasonable amount of patience, broad-mindedness, and vision. Afghanistan was of the view that, until the Pashtun–Baluchi problem was satisfactorily solved, relations between the two countries could not improve. Pakistan agreed that the reversal of the downward trend in relations between the two countries was a necessity but held that the deterioration of the situation had been brought about by Afghanistan's own volition and not by Pakistan's actions.

Since the establishment of the republic in Afghanistan, the government of Pakistan had maintained that Daoud's regime was supporting the Baluchi insurgency and was responsible for bomb explosions and acts of terrorism in the NWFP and other parts of Pakistan. During an official visit to Moscow from October 24 to 26, 1974, Bhutto shared his conviction with the Soviet leadership that Afghanistan was actively involved in the Baluchistan uprising and that, in connivance with the NAP, it was behind the wave of violence that had swept the NWFP. Assuming that the USSR wielded great influence in Kabul, he urged the Soviet leaders to ask Afghanistan not to interfere in Pakistan's domestic affairs. Although, at a banquet on October 24 Soviet Premier Kosygin stressed his government's wish that Pakistan normalize relations with "our friendly neighbor, Afghanistan,"[12] the joint communiqué published at the conclusion of the visit seemed to give due consideration to the Pakistani position by referring to "differences" between Afghanistan and Pakistan, instead of restricting them to "a political difference," which was the fundamental Afghan position. The communiqué also expressed the hope that the Afghan–Pakistani differences could be settled by peaceful means "on the basis of the principles of peaceful coexistence."[13] Needless to say, the Russians did not pressure Afghanistan to alter its stand vis-à-vis Pakistan, as Bhutto had hoped. It should also be noted that, in the joint Soviet–Afghan communiqués of this period, the Russians accepted the existence of "a political difference" between Afghanistan and Pakistan in accordance with the Afghan position.

As 1974 drew to an end, an atmosphere of violence had become commonplace in the NWFP. Pashtuns, discontented with the provincial government, which was now headed by Inayatullah Khan Gandapur, further fanned the strong movement of solidarity with Baluchistan that had already emerged in the NWFP. (The Gandapur government was a coalition of Abdul Kayum Khan's ex-Muslim Leaguers and Bhutto's People's Party of Pakistan [PPP].) Bombing incidents, acts of terrorism, and train derailments occurred frequently. This wave of unrest was spreading to Sind province, too, where an independence movement called *Sinduh-Desh* (independent Sind) was beginning to take shape. Even the Punjab was not immune; bombing also occurred there. The Pakistani government accused Afghanistan of creating these disturbances with the help of the NAP.

Bhutto, probably annoyed by the stability of the Daoud regime in the face of several coup attempts (see Chapter 8), resorted to arming fundamentalist Afghan dissidents, most of whom belonged to *Ikhwan-al-Muslimin* (the Muslim Brotherhood), and encouraging them to raid various localities in Afghanistan from bases inside Pakistan. These raids occurred during 1974 and reached their climax in the summer of 1975, when some Ikhwani elements (as the Ikhwan-al-Muslimin adherents were popularly called) succeeded in striking deep inside the Panjsher Valley, northeast of Kabul. Although the Panjsher incursion failed miserably and the people themselves succeeded in routing the raiders before the arrival of security forces, it nevertheless showed the seriousness of Pakistan's anti-Daoud intentions.

Apart from Ikhwani incursions into Afghanistan, Pakistani aircraft frequently violated Afghan air space. In this context, the following incident might amuse the reader: In August 1974 a Pakistani military helicopter that had run out of fuel and landed at Narray, a remote village in Nangarhar Province, was captured by Afghan police. Documents and maps seized in the craft proved that it was on an intelligence-gathering mission and was carrying out a survey of parts of Nangarhar and Laghman provinces. After two months of investigation, the helicopter and its crew, minus the documents and the maps, were returned to Pakistani authorities, who, until the end, maintained that their helicopter was assigned to a survey mission inside Pakistan, had run out of fuel, and had had to land on Afghan territory. It could never be ascertained from Pakistani authorities why the helicopter landed so deep inside Afghanistan on a clear summer day if it had in fact run out of fuel in Pakistani territory. As to the documents and maps, the Pakistanis insinuated that they were clever Afghan forgeries planted in the chopper immediately after its capture by the Afghans. As a result of these events, relations between Afghanistan and Pakistan grew even worse. The two countries seemed set on a collision course.

In August 1974, Abbas Ali Khalatbary, the foreign minister of Iran, visited Kabul. He suggested that, if some kind of lower-level, perhaps even unofficial, dialogue started between the two countries, it could help prevent further deterioration of the situation. He believed that some contact was better than no contact and that, with luck, periodic lower-level talks could smooth the way for a high-level meeting. This idea was also taken up by Ishan Sabri Chaylayangil, the foreign minister of Turkey. Bhutto's consent with regard to this suggestion was probably sought and obtained. As things were going badly for Pakistan in Baluchistan, Bhutto was willing to see Afghan–Pakistani tensions defused. Gradually the idea began to appeal to the Afghans. They hoped that, during these informal meetings, Pakistan could be persuaded at least to restrain its actions in Baluchistan. Moreover, it was felt in the Ministry of Foreign Affairs that, if handled properly, these informal meetings, during which, according to Afghan understanding, any matter could be raised, might lead in time to political reconciliation between the two countries.

Afghanistan made it known to the Iranians and Turks that it was willing to give lower-level, informal talks a try, provided no preconditions were attached to them. It was tentatively agreed that the first such contact would take place in March 1975 in Kabul between the deputy foreign minister of Afghanistan and the Pakistani foreign secretary. The Pakistani diplomat was to visit Kabul unofficially as the guest of the Pakistani ambassador, to avoid undue publicity.

Also in early 1975, U.S. Senator Charles Percy arranged a meeting between Mohammad Naim, Afghanistan's envoy, and Aziz Ahmad in Katmandu, where the three men were attending funeral ceremonies for the king of Nepal. Naim and Aziz Ahmad had a friendly exchange and agreed that, as a beginning to the betterment of relations, they would propose to their respective governments a scaling down of their hostile radio propaganda. Both governments agreed to accept these proposals made by their representatives.

On February 8, 1975, the NWFP home minister, Hayat Mohammad Khan Sherpao, a personal friend of Bhutto and a former member of the central government, was killed by a bomb while attending a ceremony at Peshawar University. Eighteen other people, most of them students, were injured, one of them fatally.[14] Measures taken by the government of Pakistan in the wake of Sherpao's death made the proposed unofficial meeting between Afghan and Pakistani officials in Kabul impossible and caused the Afghan government to cancel the agreed-upon gesture of curbing its anti-Pakistan propaganda campaign.

These measures included the arrest and imprisonment of hundreds of NAP members, including Khan Abdul Wali Khan, its president; dissolution of the NAP; banning of its publications; confiscation of its assets; placement of the NWFP under direct central government rule; institution of increased authority to detain people; and declaration of a state of emergency. Khan Abdul Ghafar Khan, the venerable Pashtun nationalist and Wali Khan's father, who was not an NAP member and who had gone back to Peshawar from his exile in Kabul, was also arrested. The government of Pakistan, accusing the NAP of being the culprit in Sherpao's murder, deemed these measures appropriate. It further justified them on the basis that a "neighboring foreign power" was disrupting law and order in the NWFP and creating a situation that was "beyond the Provincial Government to control." This announcement added that, by interfering in Pakistan's internal affairs, the foreign power in question was "totally betraying the principles of peaceful coexistence of sovereign States."[15]

Although Afghanistan was not specifically named in this first official statement, Pakistani Minister of the Interior Abdul Kayum Khan made it clear who the foreign power in question was when he accused Afghanistan at a press conference on February 17 "of being directly responsible for all the subversive activities in Pakistan" and alleged that, after failing to secure its objectives in Baluchistan, it had diverted all its energies to subversion in the NWFP. He added that, if Afghanistan did not cease its "constant intervention in Pakistan's internal affairs, Pakistan would be forced to take 'countermeasures.'"[16] Pakistani measures greatly reduced the NAP's effectiveness as a Pashtun–Baluchi political organization. A crackdown on the NAP was expected, because that party had emerged as the main opposition party and as a serious threat to Bhutto and the PPP in Pakistan-wide politics. Moreover, the NAP's enhanced stature had boosted Pashtun and Baluchi nationalism above a level the Pakistani establishment could possibly tolerate. Sherpao's murder gave Bhutto an excellent pretext to move against the NAP.

The government of Afghanistan reacted strongly to the imprisonment of NAP leaders and the dissolution of the party. A Foreign Ministry statement expressed Afghanistan's "deep anxiety and concern" about Pakistan's "arbitrary measures" against the NAP and stated that Pakistan resorted to these measures "without any proof against NAP and its leaders." The Foreign

Ministry's statement "charged that the Pakistani action was politically motivated. It also reiterated that the only solution to the problem lay in respecting the 'aspirations of the Baluchi and the Pashtun people.'"[17]

The crisis in the NWFP further worsened relations between Afghanistan and Pakistan. Anti-Afghan demonstrations outside the Afghan embassy in Islamabad became frequent. In one of these demonstrations, the ringleaders tried to deliver a letter to the embassy denouncing "the Afghan Government's alleged support of terrorists and the shelter given to Ajmal Khattak who was living in exile in Kabul at that time."[18] Members of the Afghan embassy identified some of the demonstrators as plainclothes policemen who had previously completed a routine tour of duty as guards at the embassy. The Afghan chargé d'affaires in Islamabad received anonymous death threats by mail and telephone demanding that Afghanistan officially renounce its Pashtunistan claim and that Ajmal Khattak be delivered to Pakistani authorities. The Afghan government did not accede to these demands.

Intensely aggravated by Islamabad's actions in Baluchistan and the NWFP, Pashtun nationalism could not be blamed for its violent reaction against the government of Pakistan. The imprisonment of NAP leadership and the dissolution of the party had particularly angered the people in the frontier province and in the tribal areas. Afghanistan could not remain indifferent to what was happening, especially since representatives and deputations from tribal areas were continuously coming to Kabul to seek help and guidance. They received ample moral and material help from the Afghans, as they had in the past. So far as guidance was concerned, the government made it clear that, whatever the Pashtuns and their leaders decided about their future, Afghanistan would accept and support their stand.

A number of Mohammad Daoud's associates, chief among them the remnants of the Parchami ministers in the cabinet and some influential Pashtun leaders, were demanding that Afghanistan demonstrate its extreme displeasure with Bhutto's actions in the NWFP by breaking diplomatic relations with Pakistan and changing its traditional Pashtunistan policy to an outright territorial claim. Those pressures were real and substantial. Daoud, however, managed to convince the hawks in his entourage of the inadvisability of such moves at that time. Credit is his alone for averting the total collapse of Afghan–Pakistan relations and for avoiding, as one of its eventual consequences, the reversal of the favorable trend in relations between Afghanistan and the Arab/Islamic states.

Even in that period of acute crisis, the mutual friends of Afghanistan and Pakistan, Iran and Turkey, did not give up their attempts to encourage a dialogue between the two neighbors. However, discussions between Afghanistan and Pakistan could not take place in the atmosphere of crisis brought about by suppression of the NAP. Afghanistan took the position that, unless the NAP leaders were freed and the ban on the party withdrawn, it would be impossible to begin bilateral contacts. Islamabad retorted that the dissolution of the NAP and the imprisonment of its members were internal affairs of Pakistan, and return to the status quo ante could in no way be invoked by Afghanistan as a precondition for talks. Abdul Wali Khan's and some of his codetainees' cases were before the courts, and, according to Pakistani authorities, it was up to the judiciary to decide their fate no matter how long it took. Thus Afghanistan and Pakistan were once again at square one.

Beginning in September 1974 and continuing into 1975, a number of letters describing Afghanistan's position toward Pakistan and deploring the latter's actions in Baluchistan, the NWFP, and within Afghanistan were sent by Mohammad Daoud to Kurt Waldheim, secretary general of the United Nations. These communications, and Bhutto's reply to them, were circulated at the request of the authors as UN documents. They reflect well the state of tension between the two countries during that critical period. On September 25, 1974, for example, Mohammad Daoud expressed in his letter to Waldheim, after deploring Pakistan's violations of human rights in Baluchistan, his support "for the demand by the Baluchi freedom fighters in Pakistan for an international fact-finding investigation of the situation in Baluchistan."[19] Bhutto's reply characterized this expression of support as "intervention in the domestic affairs of Pakistan," called Afghanistan a "medieval state" where no respect for human rights existed, and indicated that it should first put its own house in order before advocating human rights elsewhere.[20] Several more increasingly acerbic letters were sent to Waldheim by both countries in the months that followed.

One day late in 1975, Daoud asked me if I did not think that this letter-dispatching affair had lasted long enough. When I replied in the affirmative, he said, "We started it and it's up to us to end it." Thus, Bhutto's last letter was left unanswered, and the episode, after lasting for almost one and a half years, came abruptly to an end.

Afghanistan's support for the rights of the Pashtun and Baluchi people and the causes of the downturn in the relations between the two neighbors continued to be raised by Afghanistan, prior to the fall of 1976, at meetings of the UN General Assembly and at other forums, prompting heated verbal exchanges between the delegations of Afghanistan and Pakistan. Another matter that was usually put forward by Afganistan in appropriate international conferences, and that unnerved the Pakistanis tremendously, was the securing of the right of the landlocked countries to free and unhampered access to the sea. The Pakistanis saw this primarily as Afghan mischief intended indirectly to question their sovereignty over the NWFP and Baluchistan, through which the trade routes to and from Afghanistan passed, and to blame Pakistan's unwanted presence in those provinces for Afghanistan's difficulties in maintaining cheap and secure trade links with the outside world via the sea. The Pakistanis always fought tooth and nail not to allow Afghan proposals related to the rights of landlocked countries to be incorporated in formal documents.

The U.S. decision to resume arms sales to Pakistan provided another occasion for the Afghans to fire a volley at Islamabad. In addition to the statement of disapproval made by the Ministry of Foreign Affairs, Mohammad Daoud, at a state banquet in India on March 10, 1975, voiced his government's deep concern over the U.S. lifting of its arms embargo against Pakistan at a time "when Pakistan is engaged in shedding blood in Baluchistan."

He warned that it would lead to an imbalance in the region and promote an armaments race. . . . Afghanistan expects that the Government of the United States, as it has declared, will really support peaceful efforts aimed at creating stability in South Asia so that the people in this region, instead of spending their limited resources on arms, may devote attention to their development and economic programs. . . .[21]

As time passed, the government of Afghanistan, wary of Pakistan's hostile intentions, highlighted by the Panjsher incident of the summer of 1975 among others, and anxious to secure favorable conditions both internally and externally for speedy economic development (which was expected to be substantially financed by Arab and Islamic countries very friendly to Pakistan), became inclined to seek deescalation of the tensions between Afghanistan and Pakistan. Likewise, Bhutto, bogged down in a seemingly interminable war in Baluchistan and plagued by mounting unrest in the NWFP, was reportedly unwilling to see further deterioration in Afghan–Pakistani relations. Pakistan's traditional fear of India, despite the conclusion of the Simla Agreement between the two countries in July 1972, also encouraged it to avoid facing antagonism on both fronts. Furthermore, Bhutto was preparing for general elections in Pakistan, and, having eliminated the NAP, he was probably confident that, in more tranquil conditions, he would be able to further the prospects of the PPP candidates in all provinces, thus realizing his aim of transforming the PPP into a Pakistan-wide ruling party under his direct command.

During the latter part of 1975, Iran and Turkey once again began working behind the scenes to draw Afghanistan and Pakistan into a dialogue. A significant procedural difficulty arose over Afghanistan's preconditions for holding talks with Islamabad, particularly the release of NAP leaders. Bhutto was willing to release one or two of them as a gesture of goodwill but was unwilling to link his action with the beginning of the talks.

It was in the interest of both parties to move ahead expeditiously before an unexpected development once again poisoned the atmosphere. The Afghan Ministry of Foreign Affairs, therefore, got around this difficulty by adopting the view that the whole purpose of the talks was the restoration of the legitimate rights of the Pashtun and the Baluch people, which *ipso facto* included the release of their arbitrarily imprisoned leaders and the reentry of those leaders into the political mainstream of Pakistan. I remember the words of a colleague who jokingly said,

The whole of Pashtunistan is Pakistan's prisoner, it is not for nothing that we call it Pashtunistan-i-Mahkoom (the occupied or condemned Pashtunistan). Why not propose as a precondition for talks the liberation of Pashtunistan as a whole? In that case, if we insist and Pakistan accepts, the problem will be solved and there will be no need for holding the talks at all!

The views of the ministry in this regard were endorsed by Daoud. Word reached Kabul that some of the influential NAP leaders were also in favor of talks between Afghanistan and Pakistan, which could result in their release from jail before the elections. Although, on the basis of legislation passed after Sherpao's assassination, they could not stand for election for a specific period of time, they wanted to be in their constituencies during the elections. The Iranians and the Turks were informed that Afghanistan no longer insisted on its preconditions. It was, of course, made clear to them that Pakistan's precondition must also be dropped. Pakistan had always insisted that its internal affairs as defined by Islamabad, the fate of the Pashtun and Baluchi people being one of them, were not to be raised in any negotiations with the Afghans. Unexpectedly, Bhutto stated on October 31, 1975, in a radio broadcast "that he was prepared to visit Kabul for talks with President Daoud, on the condition that the dialogue was concerned solely with relations between the two countries and not with Pakistan's internal affairs."[22] The Afghan Ministry of Foreign Affairs' spokesman replied on November 3 that, "a visit by Mr. Bhutto would be a welcome gesture, provided it was not used as 'yet another means of confusing world public opinion about the real cause that has kept the two countries apart.'"[23] It seemed that the two countries still had a long way to go before sitting down for talks. To make things even more complicated, Bhutto alleged on November 29, 1975, without apparent reason, "that Afghanistan had ordered the mobilization of its troops" and declared "that Pakistan was prepared to face any eventuality."[24] Once again all movement toward talks stopped.

Winter had come and passed. The trial of Khan Abdul Wali Khan and other NAP leaders was lingering on. Mutual friends of Afghanistan and Pakistan renewed their oft-repeated proposal that the two countries try to scale down their hostile propaganda. They were of the view that this would encourage the holding of talks by bringing about a calmer atmosphere in relations between the two countries. Although Afghanistan was not unwilling to heed this request, such a decision at the time would have benefited only Pakistan, which was known to be having a hard time countering the effectiveness of Afghan radio and press propaganda in the Pashtun lands and Baluchistan. It was felt that giving up such an effective retaliatory instrument without a Pakistani quid pro quo was inadvisable. However, Pakistan passed word to the Afghans that it was ready to deescalate its hostile propaganda unilaterally, which it promptly did. Within a few weeks the Pakistani radio and press had lost much of their anti-Afghan venom. It was clear that the Pakistani decision was intended to force the Afghan hand and, because of inter-Islamic considerations, this gesture could not remain unreciprocated.

Through their embassies in Kabul and Islamabad, the Afghans and the Pakistanis quickly worked out a code of conduct for the media in both countries, aimed at reducing and eventually eliminating propaganda against each other. This "gentleman's agreement," announced simultaneously in

Kabul and Islamabad, was, to a great extent, observed satisfactorily by both sides. It was at about this time, in April 1976, that Bhutto offered Pakistani aid (grain, tents, and blankets) to the victims of floods and earthquakes in northern Afghanistan. Although there was some opposition to receiving Pakistani aid, Mohammad Daoud overruled the objections and ordered that it be accepted.

Early in May 1976 Mohammad Daoud told Waheed Abdullah and me that he had decided to extend an official invitation to Bhutto to visit Afghanistan, because he believed that conditions were ripe for responding favorably to Bhutto's gesture of goodwill. This quick decision might have stunned an outsider. But to us in the ministry, who since the latter part of 1975 had been probing the possibilities of a meeting between Daoud and Bhutto, it was cause for relief rather than surprise.

Daoud's invitation to Bhutto was promptly accepted by the Pakistani prime minister, and it was agreed that his visit would take place from June 7 to June 10, 1976. It was understood by both sides that they had dropped their preconditions for talks. On the eve of his journey to Kabul, Bhutto released the Pashtun leader Khan Abdul Ghafar Khan from jail as a token of goodwill and a gesture of reconciliation. Bhutto arrived at Kabul international airport on June 7, 1976.

Daoud and Bhutto held their talks tête-à-tête, with the exception of one meeting, which was also attended by some of their aides. I, serving at the time as the director general of political affairs in the Ministry of Foreign Affairs, was present during all these talks, interpreting for Mohammad Daoud.

In his talks with the Pakistani Prime Minister, the Afghan head of state explained the Afghan position regarding its difference with Pakistan, which was the same as had always been officially advanced by Afghan governments. Daoud told Bhutto that it was his sincere desire to see the dispute that had for so long marred relations between the two Islamic countries satisfactorily settled, lest the deterioration of the situation result in consequences detrimental to the security and well-being of both Afghanistan and Pakistan. There were countries, he said, without specifically naming them but clearly referring to the USSR, that did not want to see the amelioration of Afghan–Pakistani relations. It was imperative that those quarters be denied the satisfaction of witnessing the worsening of relations between Afghanistan and Pakistan. Daoud stressed geographical, historical, and other unshakable ties, as well as the indissoluble link of Islam, which enhanced the innumerable affinities between the two neighbors. He said that Afghanistan and Pakistan both needed peace and tranquility for their economic advancement, indicating that, so far as Afghanistan was concerned, the betterment of economic conditions had become the primary concern of the government. Without speedy and substantial progress in this field, he continued, the very survival of Afghanistan as an independent entity would be in jeopardy.

Daoud mentioned that contemporary preoccupations compelled Afghans and Pakistanis, as neighbors and Muslims, to work together for their mutual interest. Opportunities for economic cooperation between Afghanistan and Pakistan were so vast and exciting that both governments should make a very sincere effort to take advantage of them by creating a better climate of mutual understanding. There was no reason, he said, why Afghanistan and Pakistan could not become the closest of friends, once the existing difference between them was realistically and honorably solved. Close friendship between Afghanistan and Pakistan, he added, would not only be beneficial to both countries but also contribute to stability in the region.

Daoud stated that, contrary to the opinion of some circles in Pakistan, Afghanistan had no intention of seeing Pakistan destroyed or weakened. The existence of a strong Pakistan was in Afghanistan's interest, but because of past Pakistani rulers' extreme suspicion of Afghanistan's motives, they never bothered to ponder and understand this self-evident Afghan geopolitical concern. Twice in the recent past, during Indo-Pakistani wars, Afghanistan could have taken advantage of the situation and "stabbed Pakistan in the back." However tempting the situation may have seemed to many, and in spite of encouragement from some quarters, the government refrained from taking any anti-Pakistani action. Could such an attitude be construed as hostile and destructive? Daoud told Bhutto that "when you assumed the presidency of Pakistan and visited Kabul in January 1972, you yourself conveyed to the King Pakistan's appreciation for Afghanistan's restraint in 1965 and 1970 and informed him of your commitment to the establishment of cordial relations between our countries." Daoud told Bhutto that no serious effort had ever been made by the Pakistanis to understand the Afghan claim, which had always been dismissed out of hand as detrimental to Pakistan's integrity. Had such an effort been made, he was certain that areas of agreement between the two governments could have been found. Daoud mentioned to Bhutto that a bold and novel approach required the abandonment of the chauvinistic near-sightedness that a man of vision like Bhutto had at last succeeded in overcoming.

Daoud stated that Afghanistan's interest in the welfare of the Pashtuns and the preservation of their rights and identity could never be abandoned. To foreswear such an interest would go against the grain of the Afghan nation. What was happening to the Baluchis, for whom the Afghans nourished profound neighborly feelings, he said, also pained the Afghans. They wanted Pakistan to stop the war in Baluchistan and seek the means of restoring the rights of the Baluchi people.

At this point, Bhutto interrupted Daoud and solemnly said, "the government of Pakistan recognizes as legitimate the interest of Afghanistan in the welfare and the preservation of the rights of the Pashtuns living in Pakistan." He then smilingly added, "We want you to be interested in the welfare of all the peoples of Pakistan, not only in that of the Pashtuns." To this Daoud replied, without pause, "Please let me first be concerned about the welfare of our kith and kin. The turn of other Pakistani nationalities will come later."

Daoud suggested that Pakistan should not fear Afghanistan's expansionist designs because it did not entertain such ambitions. What Pakistan should be concerned about was the alienation of the Pashtuns and the Baluchis, which could very well harm the territorial integrity of Pakistan. It seemed to Afghanistan, Daoud said, that the aim of Pakistani authorities in suppressing the rights of the Pastuns and the Baluchis was to prevent the disintegration of Pakistan. This policy, he added, could very well be counterproductive and bring about precisely what the Pakistanis wanted to prevent.

Daoud mentioned that NAP leaders had been accused of secessionist designs. "While nobody can know what is in a man's heart," he said, "to us none of the ones with whom we have spoken, including Wali Khan, said that they wished to separate from Pakistan." By accepting the constitution of Pakistan and participating in Pakistani national elections, Daoud told Bhutto, the Pashtuns and Baluchis had demonstrated their desire to achieve their rights within the framework of Pakistan. He went on to say that the triumph of Pashtun and Baluchi leaders in the provincial elections showed that they enjoyed the support and the trust of their people. Afghanistan, Daoud said, faithful to its declared policy, would accept whatever NAP decisions were acceptable to the Pashtuns and the Baluchis. It was a pity, he went on to say, that a promising beginning to the betterment of relations between the Pashtun and Baluchis on the one hand, and the government of Pakistan on the other, had been reversed when the entire NAP leadership was arrested and measures that further suppressed the rights and freedoms of the Pashtun and Baluchi peoples were adopted. Daoud told Bhutto that a reconciliation between Pashtuns, Baluchis, and the government of Pakistan was necessary and that such a development would be in the interest of all parties concerned. If the parties so wished, Daoud said, Afghanistan could offer its help in this process of reconciliation. He added, "In any case we don't want to pressure you. You can choose your own time and your own ways of negotiation. What counts for us are results acceptable to our brethren." Daoud added that he was certain the prime minister of Pakistan attached sufficient importance to better relations between Afghanistan and his country to do his utmost in finding ways and means of accommodating Pashtun and Baluchi demands and settling their grievances.

Prime Minister Bhutto expressed his joy at being in Afghanistan and said that, on his way to Kabul, he had stopped in Peshawar, where he had addressed a huge gathering of Pashtuns and had assured them that the purpose of his journey to Kabul was to improve relations with Afghanistan. Bhutto stated that he was profoundly committed to the betterment of relations between Pakistan and Afghanistan and expressed his regret that, since he had last visited Kabul to convey to King Zahir Shah his gratitude for Afghanistan's admirable neutrality in Indo–Pakistani wars, relations between the two countries had worsened. It was particularly vexing to see two countries bound by so many ties and having so much in common drifting so dangerously apart. Bhutto stated that he recognized that misunderstandings had frequently clouded Pakistani perceptions, but he was certain that talks and contacts such as these would create a favorable climate conducive to allaying fears and misgivings. He agreed with the Afghan head of state that friendship between Afghanistan and Pakistan would not only benefit the two countries but also strengthen stability and peace in the region. He said that, "In the dangerous world in which we are living, cordial relations between our countries are worth striving for."

In explaining the events in Baluchistan and the NWFP, Bhutto said that the Baluchi leaders had far exceeded the autonomy provisions of the constitution and refused to change course when they were pressed to do so. In this they were encouraged by the Pashtun leaders and the NAP–JUI coalition in the Frontier. Bhutto said that he was sincere in his desire to let the autonomy provisions of the constitution become a working reality, but unfortunately NAP leadership proved extremely uncooperative and, thus, a positive step had to be reversed.

Bhutto said that the situation in Baluchistan had become so complicated that even "the shah of Iran asked us to resort to stronger means to achieve a speedy normalization, and we had to give him satisfaction." When the insurrection grew, the army had to go in, but in several instances it went beyond the restraint that it had been instructed to observe and dealt with Baluchi populations with extreme heavy-handedness. Although the insurgency was drawing to an end, the generals were still adamant about withdrawing the army from Baluchistan and opposed the release of the Pashtun and the Baluchi NAP leaders. "We in Pakistan," Bhutto said with a smile, "have to be careful about the mood of our generals. But I am sure that in due time I will be able to get around this difficulty." Bhutto contended that the idea of provincial autonomy was strongly opposed by some influential circles in Pakistan and that it had received a further setback with the secession of Bangladesh. He said that he himself was in favor of provincial autonomy, which he viewed as a suitable arrangement to hold Pakistan together, provided a balance between the rights and obligations of the central and provincial governments could be found and the provincial leaders agreed to cooperate sincerely and responsibly in the system.

Bhutto added that he recognized that the continuation of the crisis brought about by the arrest of NAP leaders was harmful to Pakistan and that it had to be brought to an end. He had taken the initiative, he said, of discussing with the NAP leaders, some of them presently in jail, how their grievances could be accommodated and the present crisis resolved. But he stressed that it was very difficult to bargain with them: "one day they will agree on one point, and the next day they will go back on their agreement." He said that Wali Khan, even before going to jail, when he served in the Assembly as leader of the opposition, never showed a semblance of willingness to compromise. Bhutto blamed the Pashtun leaders' negative and obstructive attitudes for what he termed the "abnormal and unwanted situation" in Pashtun areas. While refraining from any comment on Daoud's offer of help in the process of reconciliation between the government of Pakistan and the Pashtun–Baluchi leadership, Bhutto added that he would continue in earnest his efforts to reach an accommodation with the Pashtun and Baluchi leaders "especially now that I know the extent to which Your Excellency's Government attaches importance to the matter of their release, and accommodation of their views." Bhutto said the government of Pakistan could ask the courts to accelerate the judicial proceedings concerning Wali Khan and other political prisoners.

The prime minister of Pakistan said that, although he was certain that Afghanistan did not entertain any territorial claims concerning Pakistani territory, he had noted with satisfaction the reaffirmation of this position by the Afghan head of state. He was pleased, he stated, that Afghanistan would sanction whatever agreement the Pashtuns and Baluchis reached with his government. Mohammad Daoud immediately added to Bhutto's comment, "Agreement reached freely and their consent expressed openly." Bhutto replied, "Of course." He then reiterated his earlier assertion, saying, "apart from the fact that it is my duty to seek an accommodation with the Pashtuns and the Baluchis, the friendship of Afghanistan in itself is of such importance to us that I have decided to permanently remove this irritant from the path leading to better harmony between our two countries." At his point as if thinking aloud, Bhutto said that when the time came why should the Pashtuns not be allowed to call their land Pashtunistan as the Punjabis, the Sindis, and the Baluchis called their provinces respectively Punjab, Sind, and Baluchistan. Daoud unhesitantly replied that it would be up to the Pashtuns themselves to choose whatever name they wished for their land.

It was toward the end of the first meeting that Bhutto produced a sheet of paper from his pocket and presented it to Daoud. After reading it attentively, Daoud gave the paper to me. I looked at it and discovered that it contained the text of a draft joint communiqué. I was a little surprised because we had not expected any joint communiqué to be issued at the end of this series of talks in Kabul; the Afghan–Pakistani dispute had scarcely been discussed. Daoud good-humoredly told Bhutto that, in his recollection, all day long they had only been discussing *one* difference that prevented the development of close ties between Afghanistan and Pakistan, and that was the problem of the Pashtuns and the Baluchis. Daoud added, "You refer in the your text to the discussions between the two sides for the purpose of solving 'their differences.' Would it not be more accurate therefore, to say 'their political difference' or 'their only difference'?" Bhutto smiled and said, "What about combining the two by saying 'their political difference and other differences'? You see we have become quite used in Pakistan to the 'differences' with an *s* in relation to the Afghan–Pakistan situation and it would be a disappointment to our bureaucrats not to see it in the text." Daoud expressed his agreement with Bhutto's formulation regarding this point and laughingly added, "It seems that now we have a variety of differences when until now we had only one." He then told Bhutto that the Ministry of Foreign Affairs needed to have a look at the text before he gave his final approval. Bhutto readily concurred with Daoud's suggestion.

After Bhutto left for his residence, I told Mohammad Daoud that it seemed that he (Daoud) had accepted in principle the issuance of a joint communiqué. He replied that "if a joint communiqué pleases the Pakistanis, let us have a joint communiqué. We are sincere in our efforts to move ahead. Let there be no ambiguity in our attitude now that we have chosen to settle the problem." The long-standing problem of the "naughty *s*," as it was known in the Afghan Ministry of Foreign Affairs because the Afghans would not accept it at the end of *difference* and the Pakistanis would not drop it from that word, having been settled so rapidly and satisfactorily by Daoud and Bhutto, the members of the Afghan and Pakistani delegations addressed themselves to the rest of the draft text.

The Afghans expressed reluctance to accept language in the text that implied that Afghanistan and Pakistan aimed to solve their political difference at that stage on the basis of the five principles of peaceful coexistence. They took the position that it was premature to refer to the five principles in any search for a solution when the Pakistanis had not yet taken a single step to redress Pashtun–Baluchi grievances, when not a single NAP leader had been freed, and while the Pakistani army continued to wage war in Baluchistan. The Afghans contended that a general commitment by both sides to solve their problem peacefully through negotiations was sufficient. But the Pakistanis insisted on retaining a reference to the five principles. The Pakistanis were always anxious that the observance of the principles of peaceful coexistence be mentioned whenever a text referred to the solutions of their problems with Afghanistan. They probably thought that the inclusion of those principles in a text was sufficient to bar Afghanistan's interference in their internal affairs, as they defined them, and would nullify any territorial claims the Afghans might have. It was decided to put aside the reference to the five principles of coexistence in the text and leave it to be tackled by the heads of the delegations.

The penultimate paragraph of the Pakistani draft stated, "With a view to preserving and promoting the present favorable and friendly atmosphere, and for the purpose of arriving at a final solution of these differences, the two sides agreed to refrain from hostile propaganda against each other in the press, media and broadcasts." The Afghans proposed that, if the solution were going to be final, it should also be honorable. Furthermore, knowing the impact of Afghan radio broadcasts and the media in Pashtunistan and Baluchistan, the Afghans stated that they could not commit themselves to an indefinite postponement of "hostile propaganda" if a satisfactory solution did not emerge within a reasonable period of time. It was therefore necessary that the words "for the time being" be inserted between the words "refrain" and "from." While the Pakistanis accepted the first Afghan suggestion, they hesitated to accept the second set of amendments. After a while, they informed the Afghans that they accepted those changes as well.

Deputy Foreign Minister Waheed Abdullah had gone to inform Daoud about the discussions between the two delegations concerning the draft text. It was after two o'clock in the morning when he returned to the Ministry of Foreign Affairs. He told me that Daoud had agreed with the draft text as amended by the Afghan proposals and that even the original Pakistani reference to the five principles was acceptable to him. Daoud had told him that the observance of the five principles of peaceful coexistence was binding on both sides and that nobody in the government "wants the Pakistanis to repeat their incursions of last year into our territory." "Besides," he had said to Waheed Abdullah,

to those who do not recognize Pashtunistan as part of Pakistan, interference from our side in support of the Pashtun cause would not be deemed infringing on Pakistani sovereignty, in spite of our acceptance of the five principles. In reality, the five principles will have no relevance for us unless we recognize the Durand Line as the frontier between Afghanistan and Pakistan. However, we who are committed to a peaceful solution of our problem with Pakistan have to be realistic in our perspective and pragmatic in our approach. For us, what other alternative is there but to refrain from any act that the Pakistanis, who consider Pashtunistan an integral part of their territory, may construe as interference in their internal affairs? To proceed otherwise, whether we accept Pashtunistan as part of Pakistan or not, will simply block the settlement, and we might as well not have embarked on the present negotiations.

What is relevant under the circumstances is the securing of the rights of the Pashtuns, to the maximum extent possible. After all, let us not forget that Wali Khan has said that he is a Pakistani and that even his father Ghafar Khan considers himself a national of that country. As things stand presently, it is therefore not harmful for our cause to mention the five principles in the text and, by doing so, assure the Pakistanis of our sincerity. It would be up to them to prove their goodwill by delivering on their promises.

We have to develop a final solution to our dispute gradually. That solution has to be endorsed by the people of Afghanistan. We have to acquaint our people with the other dimensions of Afghan–Pakistani relations and the new compelling realities that have emerged. We will encounter many difficulties, both internally and externally, in this task of bridge-building with Pakistan, but we have to move ahead and succeed eventually. The situation in the region and in the world is such that we cannot afford another stalemate in our relations. The vital interests of Afghanistan militate for an accommodation with Pakistan.[26]

Early the next morning the Afghan Ministry of Foreign Affairs informed the Pakistani delegation that the Afghans had no objection to a reference in the text to the five principles of coexistence. Later, at a meeting between Daoud and Bhutto, the two leaders formally expressed their approval of the joint communiqué, which was published simultaneously in Kabul and Islamabad upon Bhutto's return to Pakistan.[27]

Daoud's and Bhutto's formal statements at the state banquets reflected the optimistic mood of the two leaders and their pleasure that the talks had taken place in a friendly atmosphere. In their statements, both leaders expressed their determination to pursue the dialogue until a satisfactory solution to the problem had been found.

At the conclusion of this first round of talks in Kabul, relations between the two countries improved dramatically. There was suddenly an abundance of Pakistani railway wagons for Afghan transit trade. Fundamentalist skirmishes stopped altogether. There were no more violations of Afghan air space by Pakistani aircraft. Thus, the ice was broken, and what came to be called the "Spirit of Kabul" was born. It was now up to the two parties not only to preserve that spirit but also to let it inspire and guide them in their search for a settlement.

Apart from the compelling necessity felt by Afghanistan and Pakistan to settle their long-standing dispute, a number of shifts in the positions of the parties had facilitated first the holding and then the continuation of Afghan–Pakistani talks. Two important initial decisions by Pakistan, both procedural and substantive, had unlocked the door to the kinds of negotiations that Kabul had wanted. These decisions were (1) the admission by Pakistan that *a* dispute existed between the two countries, and (2) its recognition that Afghanistan had the right to be concerned about the fate of the Pashtuns living east and south of the Durand Line and, consequently, that it could discuss the fulfillment of their aspirations with the government of Pakistan.

The decision of the Pashtun leaders to opt for autonomy within Pakistan by accepting the Pakistani constitutions of 1970 and 1973 and participating in Pakistan-wide elections as Pakistani politicians also rendered more flexible the Afghan stand on the Pashtunistan issue. The Afghan aim became, therefore, the consolidation of this autonomy through talks with Pakistan, rendering it functional and lasting so that the Pashtun culture and identity could be preserved and their social, economic, and political rights safeguarded. It was hoped that Pakistan could make genuine concessions to Pashtun autonomy because it had decided to seek Afghanistan's friendship and knew that that friendship was not possible without giving satisfaction to the Pashtun people. Once the Pashtuns "openly and freely" expressed their satisfaction with the autonomy arrangements, Afghanistan's endeavors with regard to the restoration of their political rights would be deemed to have come to an end. It was envisaged that at that stage the matter would be placed by the Afghan government before a Loya Jirga that would take cognizance of the Pashtun decision and would ultimately determine the Afghan stand with respect to the Pashtunistan claim and the status of the Durand Line. Meanwhile, Afghanistan would also continue to press for justice for the Baluchi people. It was assumed that relaxation of Pakistan's control in Baluchistan would further clear the atmosphere and contribute to a more speedy solution of the Afghan–Pakistani difference.

The second round of talks between Daoud and Bhutto took place in Pakistan (Islamabad, Lahore, and Murree) from August 20 to August 24, 1976, following the Afghan head of state's participation in the nonaligned summit conference in Sri Lanka.[28] Although Daoud thought the invitation to visit Pakistan followed too closely on the heels of the talks in Kabul, and Pakistan had not yet taken any significant steps toward a solution, he nevertheless decided to go because he wanted to maintain the momentum started in Kabul.

While the ceremonial side of Bhutto's visit to Afghanistan two months earlier had been subdued and low key, Daoud's reception at the Rawalpindi airport, where he was welcomed by Pakistani President Fazel Elahi Choudhry and Prime Minister Bhutto, was an extravagant display of pomp and fanfare.

All the functions he attended during his stay in Pakistan were no less grandiose and elaborate than the pageantry at his arrival. Daoud was a simple frugal man who disliked such displays of wealth and magnificence, but he went along patiently. Only his lopsided smile betrayed his state of mind to those who knew him well.

The civic reception organized by the Pakistanis in the magnificent Shalimar gardens outside Lahore, where thousands of Lahore citizens had gathered to honor Daoud, was undoubtedly the climax of their efforts to please, or perhaps dazzle, their guest. Daoud addressed the Shalimar gathering, and his speech, emotional at times, was received enthusiastically by the people of Lahore. He told them how happy he was to be able to convey directly the best wishes of the people of Afghanistan to the people of Pakistan.

> . . . all of whom they [the Afghans] consider brothers. . . . This brotherhood is not a mere worldly brotherhood emanating from proximity or generated by requirements of the time, but it is based in spirituality . . . which is inspired by the tenets of Islamic brotherhood and the holy teachings of Islam. . . . The wish of the government of Afghanistan and my person is that our political difference be resolved, and our relations be brotherly and friendly, and permanently based on good will. . . . The government of Afghanistan and the government of Pakistan have the means of resolving this difference at their disposal. . . . For the realization of this we have no way but understanding and serious and direct negotiations through peaceful means. . . . I am certain that on this path the grace of God will be with us. . . . One cannot solve all difficulties in one or several talks, but every negotiation with good will and seriousness can be expected to take us one step closer to our objective.[29]

If nothing else, this speech was an excellent exercise in public relations for Daoud, delivered in the heart of Punjab, where, for more than three decades, he had been portrayed and denigrated as Pakistan's nemesis.

Most of the talks between Daoud and Bhutto again took place in private. Only I, interpreting for the Afghan head of state, was present at the private talks. On Pakistan's request, a couple of meetings were held between delegations in Lahore and Murree. At the outset, Bhutto informed Daoud that, since their meeting in Kabul, he had made efforts to reach an understanding with the Pashtun and Baluchi leaders but had not yet succeeded. Bhutto contended that the situation had improved substantially in Baluchistan, and law-and-order conditions were much better in the NWFP. But, Bhutto said, the generals believed that the pacification of Baluchistan had not yet reached the point where the army could be withdrawn, and they still opposed the release of political prisoners. "However," Bhutto stated, "if the courts decide their release, it is difficult to see how the generals could oppose it." Bhutto added that the leaders were elusive in their demands and that it was not at all easy to hammer out an agreement with them. Daoud commented,

> I am not going to ask what your proposals were to the Pashtuns and the Baluchis, and why these could not satisfy them. This is your own business. But what I am going to stress is the necessity for a satisfactory agreement and the termination of the present state of affairs, which is to nobody's advantage. Pashtun and Baluch lack of trust in the government of Pakistan is not something imaginary. Perhaps confidence-building measures have to be instituted by your government. I am sure that you appreciate the usefulness of such a move. The leaders are in prison. They can always

say, and legitimately so, that whatever agreement is reached with them behind bars was extracted under duress. I suggest that your government, in order to show its goodwill, should enable the Pashtun and Baluchi leaders to negotiate with it in freedom and equality.

Bhutto replied that he concurred with what had been said but he wanted Daoud to appreciate the difficulties that slowed progress toward an understanding. "However," Bhutto said, "these difficulties are temporary and to a large extent will disappear with the restoration of peace in Baluchistan."

Bhutto reiterated what he had said in Kabul about the significance he attached to the betterment of relations with Afghanistan. He mentioned that, in this regard, he fully realized how important it was to reach an agreement with the Pashtuns and the Baluchis. He added that it would be a happy day for him when he could inform Afghanistan of a clear and unambiguous agreement with them. Bhutto then said that, although Daoud had left it entirely up to Pakistan and the Pashtun and Baluchi leaders to reach an agreement, his government would be happy to seek the consent of Afghanistan regarding that agreement. Daoud replied that Afghanistan was the well-wisher of all the parties involved. After approval of the agreement was announced by the Pashtuns and the Baluchis, he said, Afghanistan could publicly declare its endorsement of the accord, or, if the parties wished, it could join in a tripartite declaration of approval.

As anticipated, during meetings at the delegation level, the Pakistanis brought up the question of the Durand Line in an oblique fashion. Since the creation of Pakistan, the Pakistanis had publicly adopted the position that, so long as they and the rest of the countries that mattered recognized the Durand Line as Pakistan's international frontier with Afghanistan, the negative attitude of the latter did not bother them. But, in reality, behind that self-righteous and disinterested facade, they craved Afghanistan's acquiescence. In real terms this meant more to them than the recognition of the Durand Line by all other countries combined. Afghanistan's recognition of the line would have completed Pakistan's sovereignty and would have given full meaning to its territorial integrity. Without that recognition there was something missing, and the Pakistanis felt uneasy so long as that loose end had not been tied up. That suppressed frustration has often sprung into the open when Pakistani officials held talks with Afghans, even on nonpolitical matters.

At the first meeting of the two delegations, Aziz Ahmad, the Pakistani minister of state for defense and external affairs, proposed that, at this stage, both countries agree on a package deal, which according to him, meant that Afghanistan and Pakistan agree to simultaneously take certain reciprocal steps to normalize their relations. Afghan Deputy Foreign Minister Waheed Abdullah looked at me and smiled. We both knew what was coming next. Ahmad said that such a package deal would include, for example, freeing of political prisoners by Pakistan and recognition of the Durand Line as the international frontier by Afghanistan. He also alluded to certain other obligations that should be fulfilled by the countries if the package were accepted. Chief among them was the necessity of a formal declaration by Afghanistan that it had abandoned the issue of Pashtunistan. That declaration was to match the agreement that would be reached between the government of Pakistan and the Pashtun–Baluchi leaders concerning the safeguarding of Pashtun and Baluchi political rights. That agreement would necessarily be well within the framework of the constitution of Pakistan, Ahmad said, since the leaders had accepted that constitution.

Waheed Abdullah replied to Ahmad that, so far as the Afghan delegation was aware, the leaders of the two delegations had not discussed a package of matching obligations to be performed simultaneously by the parties. What had emerged from the discussions so far was Bhutto's determination to move toward better relations with Afghanistan and, to that end, his desire to find ways of accommodating the Pashtun and Baluchi demands. Given the importance that the release of political prisoners had acquired, Bhutto had expressed his willingness to try to solve this problem as the essential first step. Aziz Ahmad was clearly not happy with this reply but remained silent. Both sides, sensing that the meeting might turn sour, agreed that it should be adjourned.

By the second meeting between the delegations, the Pakistanis had spelled out their proposal on paper. Copies of that working paper, as they called it, containing the elements of a package deal, were distributed to us. Ahmad said in his presentation that the prime minister of Pakistan was sincere in his decision to move quickly toward freeing the Pashtun and Baluchi leaders. He added that, although Bhutto was prepared to take appropriate measures, their release from jail presented complications. For the prime minister to be successful in his plea to the courts and the legislature, he had to have popular support, and such support for leniency could only materialize if the Afghan government were to take a substantial conciliatory step by recognizing the Durand Line. Explaining the contents of the Pakistani paper, Ahmad said that Bhutto's task in redressing Pashtun–Baluchi grievances would be greatly facilitated if Afghanistan formally abandoned the issue of Pashtunistan. Such steps, he said, would clear the atmosphere.

Although in the working paper the release of the prisoners was to be matched by Afghan recognition of the Durand Line, and the agreement between the Pashtun and Baluchi leaders and the government of Pakistan by Afghan abandonment of the Pashtunistan claim, Ahmad had implied in his presentation that Afghanistan should take such initial steps to "clear the atmosphere," in other words, prior to any corresponding Pakistani move.

The direction the discussions had taken was certainly not in conformity with the course adopted by Daoud and Bhutto. After listening to Ahmad, I stated that what Afghanistan considered to be of the utmost importance at that time was the freedom of Pashtun and Baluchi leaders, followed by their reentry into the political mainstream of Pakistan. Realizing the importance Afghanistan attached to this matter, Bhutto had graciously agreed to release them. Clearing the atmosphere in the suggested one-sided manner was unrealistic. Even if the two countries adhered to the simultaneous implementation of a list of matching obligations as contained in the working paper, the outcome could be quite problematic. For example, what would happen to the list of obligations in the package deal if, after their release, for whatever politically motivated pretext, the leaders were jailed again? Should Afghanistan in that case denounce its recognition of the Durand Line, if it had already recognized it in order to fulfill its part of the bargain? I reminded the Pakistanis of the difficulty that might stem from confining the two governments at this stage to a strict package of mutual obligations.

I added that what had kept the two countries apart was the suppression of Pashtun and Baluchi rights by the government of Pakistan. To move ahead and break the present deadlock, I said, something positive had to be done, and that obviously could be done only by the government of Pakistan. Such a step would not only remove Afghanistan's distrust but, more importantly, that of the Pashtuns and the Baluchis. When Pashtun and Baluchi rights were restored, and if the parties were still willing and sincere, all the pieces of a final settlement would gradually fall into their proper places. What Afghanistan wanted was more than a *modus vivendi* between the two countries. It was determined to settle the difference once and for all and to develop the closest possible ties with Pakistan. Was not the prospect of close Afghan–Pakistani relations, which according to Bhutto himself would open many vistas of cooperation between them, attractive enough for the government of Pakistan to make a substantial gesture of goodwill and understanding toward the Pashtuns and the Baluchis?

Ahmad replied that agreement on a list of matching obligations to be performed by the parties was advisable, otherwise Pakistan would feel itself surrendering to external pressure. He then added that, if the freed leaders flouted the law, they would of course go back to jail like any other Pakistani. At this point Abdullah retorted, "You will have us committed to a fundamental decision [recognition of the Durand Line], while in effect nothing would have been achieved for safeguarding the rights of the Pashtuns and the Baluchis. You may appreciate that the question of simultaneous action with regard to a list of matching obligations is irrelevant in the present situation." Aziz Ahmad was obviously not happy with the tone of these exchanges.

Wishing to pursue further the question of the release of the Pashtun and Baluchi leaders, I said that once the leaders were freed, guarantees were needed to ensure their unhampered political and civic activities. I added:

All that brings to the forefront the unavoidable question of the rights of the Pashtuns and the Baluchis, which has to be attended to before anything else can be undertaken by Afghanistan. It is the core of the matter, as the question of Palestine is the core of the Middle East problem. If I understood the prime minister of Pakistan correctly, he had admitted the significance of this reality and had decided to try his utmost to satisfy Pashtun and Baluch aspirations. Mr. Bhutto has also concurred with the Afghan head of state that the freeing of the imprisoned leaders would be the first step in that direction. But Afghanistan suggests that their freedom, important as it is, will be of little significance if they are prevented at any time from freely serving their people.

Ahmad replied that reference to guarantees implied that Pakistan was to change some of its laws. He added that it was an internal matter and concerned Pakistan alone. If anything could be undertaken in this field, he said, it would be based only on goodwill and, in the absence of an Afghan quid pro quo, would be quite difficult to achieve.

At that point, Waheed Abdullah told the Pakistanis that the prime minister of Pakistan had expressed his determination to bring Afghanistan and Pakistan closer to each other, and, in order to do so, he wanted to remove the obstacles that blocked the friendship between the two countries. Waheed Abdullah added that, should Bhutto, in his search to do away with the impediments to Afghan–Pakistani friendship, determine that some Pakistani laws had to be changed or even some new constitutional arrangements had to be made, he would probably decide whether or not the betterment of relations between the two countries was worth those steps. The timing of such steps, should he decide to take them, had been left entirely to Bhutto's discretion.

Since it was felt that nothing constructive was resulting from the meetings at the delegation level, we told the Pakistanis that it was too early to get involved in discussing details and that it was necessary at that point to seek the advice of our leaders as to the direction the talks should take. Aziz Ahmad concurred with that suggestion.

When we briefed Daoud about the proceedings, he commented that the Pakistanis were rushing forward toward a settlement without bothering to create the necessary environment, a course he considered unwise and harmful. Daoud shared these views with Bhutto when they resumed their talks. Bhutto immediately agreed and said that haste was not advisable. He added that animosity between the two countries had been going on for so long that they both needed time to prepare their people for a settlement. Bhutto stated that he was certain the process for the betterment of relations was irreversible and that what really counted was the preservation of this atmosphere of confidence and goodwill. He said that the present talks "formed part of the continuing dialogue envisaged by the two leaders," which, in due time he was sure, would lead to a final settlement satisfactory to all concerned. Daoud agreed that, in an atmosphere of true friendship, differences lose their relevance and gradually disappear.

A joint communiqué was issued at the conclusion of Daoud's official visit to Pakistan, in which both sides reaffirmed the principles in the earlier Kabul communiqué and pledged to continue their discussions in "the spirit of Kabul," with a view to achieving a settlement. At the state banquet the previous evening in honor of Mohammad Daoud, Bhutto had said,

Please believe in our sincerity and please believe the efforts we are making along with you to reach a solution, because once our differences, or difference as you like to put it, are resolved we know that many vistas will open up for the betterment of our peoples and the peoples of Afghanistan and Pakistan will mutually benefit.[30]

On the way back to Kabul, I could not help asking Daoud what he thought of Bhutto. He unhesitatingly replied, "Bhutto is certainly a statesman and an extremely intelligent person, but I don't know to what extent he can be trusted."

After Daoud's visit to Pakistan, relations between the two countries improved even further. Transit trade was flowing smoothly. Even wheat from India's surplus crop was allowed to be transported overland from India to Afghanistan. On March 2, 1977, Afghanistan and Pakistan agreed to restore air service between them, which had been suspended since early 1974.

The next time we saw Bhutto was on June 9, 1977. (By then I had been promoted to the rank of deputy foreign minister.) He was returning from Tehran and stopped overnight to see Daoud. Bhutto had rigged the 1977 Pakistan-wide elections and was in deep trouble politically. In his informal conversation with Daoud before and during dinner, he tried to minimize the impact of the demonstrations and unrest that had surfaced in Pakistan as a reaction to his manipulation of the elections. He also said that those so-called irregularities were highly exaggerated by the opposition, which, profiting from the hysteria, was out to get him.[31] He regretted that, because of the emergence of that somewhat abnormal situation in Pakistan, he had not yet succeeded in freeing the political prisoners. Daoud listened to him quietly and at the end urged him not to stall on the freeing of the Pashtun and Baluchi leaders. Bhutto replied that he had not forgotten this most important issue and that he would deal with it on a priority basis as soon as the confused situation returned to normal.

Unfortunately, the situation never did return to normal for Bhutto. He was toppled by the military on the night of July 5, 1977. The chief of staff of Pakistan's army, General Zia-ul-Haq, took over as chief martial law adminis-trator. Martial law was proclaimed in Pakistan, and political activities were banned.

Remembering the difficult times that previous Afghan governments had had with past Pakistani military regimes, our initial reaction to this military takeover was one of displeasure. But, as time went by and contacts were established between President Daoud and General Zia-ul Haq, we discovered in the latter, to our delight, the most affable, well-disposed, and farsighted Pakistani leader we had ever met.

Soon after the advent of the military regime in Pakistan, General Zia informed President Daoud that his government accepted the two joint com-muniqués issued by Afghanistan and Pakistan and wished not only to preserve the "spirit of Kabul" but also to promote and strengthen it. He expressed a desire to meet with Daoud, who invited him to come to Kabul at his earliest convenience. By that time Daoud had appointed Noor Ahmad Etemadi, a former prime minister and one of the most able and respected Afghan statesmen, as ambassador to Pakistan.[32] This appointment indicated the importance attached by Afghanistan to the process of steady normalization of relations with Pakistan and was perceived as such by the Pakistanis.

General Zia visited Afghanistan in October 1977. Because of protocol considerations, Zia was received at the Kabul Airport not by President Daoud but by a senior cabinet minister, and his reception was by mutual agreement extremely low key.[33] The two meetings in Kabul between Daoud and Zia took place in private; I was the only other person present.

The general told Daoud of developments in Pakistan and what prompted the military to do away with Bhutto's government. He also explained in general terms his program for the future of Pakistan. Daoud summarized his discussions with Bhutto regarding Afghan–Pakistani relations and expressed the hope that efforts to reach an honorable solution to the existing difference would be continued by both sides. Showing a remarkable understanding of the Afghan position, the general offered his commitment to removing the obstacles from the path of a speedy Afghan–Pakistani reconciliation. He said that he realized that there were many compelling factors that prompted the two Muslim neighbors to live like brothers. The general added that continuing enmity between Pakistan and Afghanistan spawned great dangers for both countries.

Although this informal round of talks in Kabul was not expected to result in any significant breakthrough, it was useful in the sense that it allowed the two leaders to get acquainted and to learn about each other's policies and aspirations. It was quite clear that an excellent rapport had been established between the two men. President Daoud and General Zia agreed to continue their talks in Pakistan early the following year. No joint communiqué was issued.

In the meantime, the war in Baluchistan drew to an end in 1977, and, by the beginning of 1978, the situation there had become almost normal. In the months following General Zia's visit to Kabul, Ambassador Etemadi had developed good relations with him and his government and had been urging the general to make a substantial gesture regarding the Pashtuns and Baluchis before the next round of talks. By the time Daoud decided to make his second official visit, General Zia had made that substantial gesture by freeing all the imprisoned Pashtun and Baluchi leaders. Thus, the first concrete step toward normalization of relations between the two countries had been taken. The freed leaders had not reentered the political mainstream of Pakistan, because all political activities were banned under martial law, but they had regained their status as leaders and spokesmen of their people.

President Daoud arrived in Rawalpindi from Delhi on March 5, 1978, at the end of official visits to several countries.[34] He was welcomed by General Zia and other Pakistani dignitaries. The reception at the airport was dignified but simple. This visibly pleased and relaxed the Afghan president.

The talks between the two leaders were again held in private; only I was present. General Zia spoke at length of events in Pakistan, of his plans for the future of his country, of his efforts at reconciliation, and of the necessity to weed out those elements that, in his view, had corrupted Pakistani society. He expressed his happiness that the Pashtun and Baluchi leaders were free once again and that the politically motivated judicial proceedings against Wali Khan and others had been suspended.

Daoud thanked General Zia for his comprehensive description of developments in Pakistan and conveyed to him his pleasure about the release of the Pashtun and Baluchi leaders. He said that it was a gesture of Islamic brotherhood that was greatly appreciated by Afghanistan and by the Pashtuns and the Baluchis. He expressed the hope that, in due time, the leaders could resume their political activities for the benefit of their people. He said that the future of the Pashtun and Baluchi people was entirely their own; Afghanistan in that respect abided by their decision. Daoud mentioned that there were countries who viewed with displeasure the thaw that had begun in Afghan–Pakistani relations and that there existed dangerous undercurrents in this strategically important region that could harm the stability of both countries. Again, Daoud was referring to the Soviet Union without specifically mentioning it. He added that, in unity and brotherhood, the two countries could, perhaps, better counter these threats and preserve their independence. Daoud stated that establishment and preservation of cordial relations between Afghanistan and Pakistan was of primary importance.

Daoud emphasized that, when Pakistan had been established, the Afghans had become very hopeful about the settlement of the long-standing dispute regarding the Pashtuns. They thought that it would be much easier to reach an agreement with Islamic Pakistan than with Britain. But, unfortunately, as time passed, these hopes had been shattered. Relations had been allowed to disintegrate. Layers of suspicion, misrepresentation, and misunderstanding had gradually covered the relatively simple issue at stake. Meanwhile, Pakistan and Afghanistan chose different paths. Undoubtedly owing to imperatives perceived by its leaders, Pakistan threw in its lot with the West. Afghanistan, in view of its isolation in the region, embarked on another course, which in itself contributed to Pakistani uneasiness. But, Daoud said, had it not been for the existence of the difference with Pakistan that had became an emotion-packed national issue, Afghanistan might not have taken the path that it took (Daoud was referring to Afghanistan's closeness with the Soviet Union). Referring also to Afghanistan's nonalignment, Daoud added that their political stance was in conformity with Afghanistan's aspirations; however, strong ties of friendship between Afghanistan and its Islamic neighbors, although allied with the West, were politically important for Afghanistan's survival, and the lack of these ties had always been felt by the Afghan government. "But," Daoud said, "We are not here to ascribe blame to anybody for past mistakes, misrepresentations, and suspicions. If we succeed in cementing our unity, the benefits deriving from it will make up handsomely for the years lost and the opportunities missed." He went on to say that "now that Afghanistan and Pakistan have left aside their sensitivities and sincerely desire to resolve their dispute, it is essential that they should not allow another wedge to be driven between them." Daoud said that the way to a final settlement was not without difficulty, but he was certain that Afghanistan and Pakistan, by working sincerely together, would be able to remove all the obstacles. He said it was essential that each step toward the final settlement be taken cautiously and cooperatively, to ensure success and popular acceptance.

For the present atmosphere of goodwill to evolve into friendship and better understanding, President Daoud said that it was necessary to adopt concrete and meaningful measures such as institutionalized economic and cultural cooperation. He proposed that a high-level joint economic commission be created to promote economic cooperation between the two countries, including the establishment of joint economic ventures. Further, he said, competent authorities in both countries should jointly study the possibilities of broader cultural exchanges and launch programs to that effect.

General Zia told President Daoud that their views were identical regarding the necessity of close ties between the two Islamic neighbors. Zia mentioned that the benefits of cooperation between the two countries were well understood by the government of Pakistan. Cooperation would bring prosperity to both nations, he said, and solidarity would enhance their mutural strength. The general expressed his satisfaction that the Pashtun and Baluchi leaders were released. He added that, once conditions in Pakistan allowed, he saw no reason why Pashtun and Baluchi representatives could not participate on an equal footing with others in the political life of Pakistan. Zia said that he had held talks with Pashtun–Baluchi leaders to that effect and intended to continue his contacts with them.

General Zia expressed his agreement with the suggestion made by the president that both governments watch for pitfalls on the road to a final settlement and proceed step by step with caution and vigilance. The Pakistani leader said that what was important was total understanding between the two countries. This, he believed, had been achieved, and the process of reconciliation, in his view, had now become irreversible. The final settlement would emerge, he said, in due time, when conditions were ripe. He also welcomed Daoud's proposals concerning steps to be taken in the field of economic and cultural cooperation and said that he considered such a move extremely useful in strengthening understanding and friendship between the peoples of Afghanistan and Pakistan.

President Daoud thanked General Zia for his explanations and told him that it was his cherished hope that one day the Pashtuns, instead of being a source of contention, would become a unifying link between Pakistan and Afghanistan. President Daoud and General Zia agreed that the next round in the continuation of the bilateral talks would take place in Kabul some time during the ensuing summer.

One of the highlights of President Daoud's second official visit to Pakistan was his meeting with the Pashtun and Baluchi leaders, including Abdul Wali Khan, Ghaus Baksh Bizenjo, Attaullah Mengel, and Khair Bakhsh Marri. To make the congregation appear less parochial and at the same time infer that the

Pashtun and Baluchi leaders were mainstream Pakistani politicians, the host government had added prominent political figures belonging to other ethnic groups and Pakistani political parties to the list of attendees. The president greeted and talked with each one of the political leaders and wished them success in the service of their people. Some of the recently freed Pashtun leaders were old acquaintances of his; he expressed joy at seeing them again free and in good health and recalled old memories. This meeting, during which General Zia was present, took almost an entire day. The president seemed to enjoy the lengthy meeting and told us later that he had profited from the views expressed and was happy to have seen his old friends.

Interested in meeting the people of Pakistan, Daoud accepted with pleasure an invitation by General Zia to address once again a civic reception at the Shalimar Gardens in Lahore. Amid enthusiastic applause, he told the people of Pakistan,

Your strength is our strength, your welfare is our welfare and your stability is our stability. . . . Let's walk hand in hand in the warm glow of brotherhood and sincerity to cover the distance lying ahead of us. I pray that the day may come soon when brotherly ties already existing among us will transform themselves into a permanent . . . reality. I hope the friendship between Pakistan and Afghanistan will be permanent and everlasting.[35]

After a pause, he cited a Dari poem written by Pakistan's poet laureate Allama Iqbal a few years previously:

The continent of Asia made of water and clay is but one body
In that body the heart is the Afghan nation
The destruction of that nation will result in the destruction of Asia
The prosperity of that nation will bring about the prosperity of Asia
As long as the heart remains free, the body will be free,
Otherwise, it will become like a straw on the path of the wind.[36]

I was surprised by that extemporaneous recitation of poetry, which was not quite in line with Daoud's habitual reserve. At the time, I thought he must have been carried away by the enthusiastic mood of the audience and the warmth of the welcome. However, in retrospect, one cannot dismiss the thought that Daoud, finding himself suddenly in rapport with the people at Shalimar and suspecting the dire events that were in the offing, had wished to sound an alarm about the impending danger to Afghanistan and, perhaps also, to its eastern neighbor. After all, it was only a few weeks after that memorable afternoon that the Russian empire resumed its southward advance.

Speaking at the state banquet that evening, Mohammad Daoud pointed out that talks on bilateral relations, particularly about the political difference between the two countries that "had clouded the relations with suspicion and doubt for 30 years, had proved extremely useful and productive."[37] He said he was happy that, with the renewal of the talks, a new chapter of goodwill and understanding had been opened. Zia, in his speech earlier, had expressed his optimism about the future prospects of the two nations' working together for their common prosperity.

It was late on the eve of Daoud's departure for Kabul when the Pakistani foreign ministry invited the members of the Afghan delegation to a hastily arranged meeting. As soon as we arrived, Agha Shahi, the Pakistani Foreign Secretary, gave us the text of a draft joint communiqué that Pakistan had prepared. A quick look at the text confirmed that it was in fact not a joint communiqué but a veritable draft treaty that the Pakistanis wanted us to approve and sign. According to the text, Afghanistan would recognize the Durand Line as the international frontier between the two countries and abandon the issue of Pashtunistan, both sides would pledge noninterference in each other's internal affairs, both sides would commit themselves not to resume hostile propaganda against each other, and both parties would agree to an expanded program of economic and cultural cooperation.

Waheed Abdullah told the Pakistanis that Afghanistan supported a pledge of mutual noninterference in each other's affairs and welcomed economic and cultural cooperation between the two countries not only as a necessity but also as a means of preparing the Afghans and the Pakistanis for reconciliation. He said that the Afghans were also willing to accept nonresumption of hostile propaganda. But, Waheed Abdullah said, Afghanistan could not at this stage accept the first two elements of the Pakistani text, namely recognition of the Durand Line and abandonment of the Pashtunistan issue. It was undeniable, he told the Pakistanis, that those matters should eventually find a satisfactory solution, but the dialogue so far had been aimed essentially at softening the ground, and the two leaders in their wisdom had not felt it opportune to tackle those questions of substance. He added that, although the release of the Pashtun–Baluchi leadership was a substantial gesture of goodwill, it should be borne in mind that Afghanistan had always stressed their release *and* their return to the political mainstream of Pakistan. Waheed Abdullah pointed out that this aspect of the matter had not yet been resolved. Waheed Abdullah went on to say that the Pakistanis were always eager to raise the question of recognition of the Durand Line, but did they realize that the line had been abrogated by a decision of the Afghan Loya Jirga and that only that supreme representative body could revoke its previous decision? Neither the president of Afghanistan nor anybody else present was empowered to make a decision concerning the Durand Line or Pashtunistan. Such decisions belonged to the people of Afghanistan and could only be made by them.

Waheed Abdullah told the Pakistani Foreign Office officials that, to his knowledge, no understanding had been reached between the government of Pakistan and the Pashtun and Baluchi leaders with respect to the future of their people, although Afghanistan agreed that such an understanding could fall within the framework of Pakistan's constitution. According to General Zia, he had only begun talks with the leaders and intended to continue his contacts with them. Perhaps a restructuring of Pakistan's constitution would be necessary to prevent the recurrence of events that took place in Pashtunistan and Baluchistan during Bhutto's tenure. Perhaps both sides (Pashtuns and

Baluchis and Pakistanis) would agree on some novel approach. It was hard to tell what would be the nature of their arrangements. Afghanistan had to be reasonably sure about what had been accepted, particularly by the Pashtuns, before taking such substantial steps as those proposed by the Pakistani Foreign Ministry. Waheed Abdullah advised caution and a great deal of patience. The senior Pakistani officials present, raised in an atmosphere of suspicion and distrust of Afghanistan, were visibly annoyed. They obviously doubted Afghanistan's professions of sincerity about its desire to reach a satisfactory and honorable solution to the problem. We had heard rumors that they referred to Afghanistan's expressed determination to keep on talking until the problem between the countries was settled, as "the Afghan charade." Their facial expressions at this meeting left no doubt that these were not merely rumors.

We told the Pakistanis that we would accept the issuance of a joint communiqué, but it had to be simpler and more generally worded to reflect the reality of what had been discussed and what had been agreed upon. But the Pakistanis were reluctant to accept our suggestion. We, therefore, told them that we had to refer the matter to the president and seek his instructions.

When briefed about this latest development, the president expressed his utter opposition to such a course and instructed us not to accept the Pakistani text. He told us that he would take it up with General Zia in the morning. An unscheduled meeting between the president and General Zia was arranged for early the next day. When the two leaders met a few hours later, Daoud, obviously totally relaxed, told Zia that the Pakistani Foreign Office had been giving the members of the Afghan delegation a tough time. Zia laughed and said that he knew that his bureaucrats were being unnecessarily zealous. He told the president that they were both aware of the ground covered and the progress made, and, when the time came, other appropriate steps would be taken by both sides. Zia added that there was no need for texts or documents between two brothers. We never heard anything more about the joint communiqué.

At the conclusion of his stay in Pakistan, President Daoud told a press conference on March 8 that his visit had been "an important step towards the betterment of relations between the two countries."[38] He was asked "if the political difference between the two countries figured in his talks with General Zia-ul-Haq. Mr. Daoud Khan said, 'Everything was discussed and with the passage of time everything would fall in its proper place and time would take care of everything.'"[39] In response to another question, Daoud said, "We [Afghanistan and Pakistan] understand fully each other's position and . . . to what extent our future is common."[40] He informed the press conference that both sides had agreed to set up a joint economic commission and to enlarge the scope of their cultural cooperation. He also informed those present that the next round of talks would be held between Zia and him in Kabul the following summer.

Before boarding the plane bound for Kabul, President Daoud was in a visibly good mood. I asked him about his impression of the trip to Pakistan and what he thought of General Zia. "On the whole," he said, "I am satisfied with the visit. The general is an honest man; I think that with him we can move forward." That was my impression, too. Unfortunately, the two men were not to meet again. A few weeks after his return from Islamabad, Mohammad Daoud and his regime were wiped out by the Communist onslaught.

Having been intimately associated with the Afghan–Pakistani talks during the republican period, there is no doubt in my mind that the leaders of the two countries, by the unique method they had devised, would ultimately have succeeded in achieving an honorable solution to the difference between Afghanistan and Pakistan. The timing of a solution would naturally have depended on a variety of factors, but I believe it is safe to say that in three to four years the Afghan–Pakistani dispute would have ceased to exist. The remarkable aspect of the Afghan–Pakistani talks had been the unorthodox manner in which they had been carried out. This approach necessarily required a great deal of patience and understanding, which perhaps only men of vision and farsightedness could muster. The Afghan–Pakistani dispute was so subtle in nature and kindled such profound emotions that a frontal attack favored by those technocrats enamored of quick results would have reversed the process of normalization and further hardened the position of the parties. The most important factor in bringing about a settlement between the two countries was the determination of the parties to forge ahead for a durable friendship. That determination stemmed from the realization that they needed each other in the turbulent world that they lived in and that their enmity was harmful to both sides. The Afghan and Pakistani leaders had tacitly agreed that the establishment of a durable friendship based on mutual trust and community of interest would bring about an environment in which an honorable solution of the difference between the two countries would peacefully emerge by itself.

The talks between President Mohammad Daoud and Zulfikar Ali Bhutto and between the former and General Zia-ul-Haq never lost their sophistication, indeed their elegance. They assiduously avoided reaching agreements to the detriment of third parties. In his book, *In Afghanistan's Shadow*, Selig Harrison stated with surprising certainty, "Shortly before his assassination in 1978, he [Daoud] was on the verge of concluding a deal with Islamabad providing for *forcible* return of all Baluchi 'refugees' to Pakistan."[41] I can assure him that nothing of the kind ever occurred, and his assertion is totally false. Likewise, it has been suggested that Afghanistan's position in the bilateral talks mellowed because of the offer by Paskistan of free and uninterrupted access to the sea, including port facilities in Karachi or some other Pakistani port. Undoubtedly the question of the right of Afghanistan to free access to the sea and its related problems would have come up for discussion at an appropriate time, probably in the joint economic commission, but it was never raised at the high-level meetings between the Afghan and Pakistani leaders.

From the fall of 1976, Afghan representatives' speeches in the General Assembly of the United Nations and other international gatherings reflected the positive trend in relations between Afghanistan and Pakistan.[42] The bellicose tone of the past had been replaced by an optimistic mood. Out of deference to Pakistani sensitivity, the annual Pashtunistan Day celebrations on August 31 became more subdued, and the statements made were devoid of confrontational character. On that occasion, Afghan, Pashtun, and Baluchi speakers expressed their satisfaction at the improvement of relations between Afghanistan and Pakistan and hoped that the betterment of these relations could help the Pashtuns and Baluchis attain their inalienable rights.

Unfortunately the Communist coup in April 1978 put an abrupt end to the considerable efforts toward reconciliation embarked on in the latter years of the republic by Mohammad Daoud and his counterparts in Pakistan that came so close to resolving the long-standing dispute between the two neighbors. The strong possibility that this dispute was finally going to be settled was perhaps one of the underlying causes that hastened the Communist takeover of Afghanistan.

Iran and Major Arab Countries

Throughout the republican period, Mohammad Daoud sought to diversify and expand Afghanistan's sources of economic assistance and to reassert its independent, nonaligned, Islamic stance. To achieve these goals, he made extensive efforts to expand and further develop relations with Iran and major Arab countries.

In July 1974 Mohammad Naim and Waheed Abdullah toured Iran, Iraq, Libya, Algeria, Egypt, Saudi Arabia and Kuwait. All those who were approached for financial assistance responded sympathetically, and in some cases warmly, to Afghan overtures, although most of them made it known that the improvement of Afghan–Pakistani relations would facilitate the furnishing of that assistance. The countries visited showed great interest in the preservation and consolidation of Afghanistan's independence and appreciated the importance of its nonaligned and Islamic stance. As time passed, countries like Iran, Saudi Arabia, Kuwait, and Iraq committed themselves firmly to extending financial help to Afghanistan.

Iranian–Afghan relations became very close during the republican regime. In the first months of the republic, a clash occurred between Afghan and Iranian frontier guards concerning the ownership of a stretch of land created some time back by a shift in the Hilmand River's course in the lower Hilmand frontier region. Two Afghans and one Iranian were killed. However, the two governments, desirous of cultivating friendly relations, rapidly contained the problem and cooperated in solving it amicably. Later, as a result of the disappearance of a frontier demarcation pillar in the Islam–Qala frontier region, a controversy arose between Afghan and Iranian technical experts as to the lost pillar's exact location. This had some significance, because the new pillar's emplacement determined whether a small triangle of land belonged to Afghanistan or Iran. There was a suggestion that the matter be submitted to third-party Turkish arbitration. But the Afghan and Iranian governments decided to solve it between themselves, and to make every effort until a solution satisfactory to both sides emerged. To that end, work was still going on by Afghans and Iranians when the Communist coup put an end to those endeavors. Although these two occurrences were not of major importance, the way they were handled by the two governments was a reflection of their intentions to have cordial relations.

In April 1975 Daoud visited Tehran. During this visit Iran agreed to extend to Afghanistan a credit of $2 billion, $1.7 billion for the construction of a railroad from Herat to Kandahar and Kabul (linked to the Iranian railway system) and $300 million for other projects in the Afghan Seven Year Plan. The importance of the railroad, giving landlocked Afghanistan access to Iranian seaports, and the significance of Iranian economic assistance to Afghanistan, which was bound to bring about new economic and political alignments in central Asia, were lost to no one. In March, Daoud had also visited President Ahmad Assan al-Bakar in Baghdad. The Afghan head of state had offered his good offices to Iraq, as he did later to Iran, to enable them to solve their dispute over Shatt-el-Arab. Both countries initially accepted his offer, but, after some time, Iran lost interest in the matter.

In late 1977 the shah of Iran accepted an invitation to pay a state visit to Afghanistan in July 1978. It was also in 1977 that the instruments of ratification of the Hilmand Treaty was exchanged between the two countries, bringing it legally into force and finally ending the dispute over the sharing of Hilmand waters.

Apart from the expanded economic and financial assistance from Iran, that country's contributions to the betterment of relations between Afghanistan and Pakistan had a positive impact on the development of Iranian–Afghan friendship. Since the establishment of the republic, Afghan leaders had felt that Iran could play an important role in bringing Afghanistan and Pakistan closer together, so they kept the shah and his government fully informed regarding the Afghan–Pakistani situation. In order not to hamper Iran's freedom of movement in its search for a rapprochement between the two nations, the Afghans never asked the Iranians to make any official pronouncement in favor of Afghanistan's position with respect to the dispute. It was in this spirit, for example, that the Afghans did not insist on a reference to the difference between Afghanistan and Pakistan and the need for its speedy solution in the Iranian–Afghan communiqué issued at the conclusion of Mohammad Daoud's visit to Tehran.

During 1977, events in Iran increasingly attracted the attention of the Afghan government. It seemed that the oil boom had come and gone, and now Iran, faced with its own colossal economic problems, was finding it difficult to fulfill its pledges of assistance to other countries. Although the shah of Iran had stated in early 1977 to Mohammad Naim, Waheed Abdullah, and me that Afghanistan remained at the top of the list of recipients of Iranian aid, it was decided in Kabul that certain readjustments had to be made in the Seven Year Development Plan in case Iranian pledges did not materialize. It was in this context that the initial phases of the construction of the railroad from Islam–Qala to Kabul were postponed, although the railroad's survey had been completed by a French company on a grant of $10 million from Iran. Other aspects of the plan would not be affected by Iran's eventual default because of the firm financial commitment of donors like Saudi Arabia and Kuwait and the still substantial input by the Soviet Union. While the slowdown in Iranian assistance, which gradually became a reality, did not create undue concern, the rising tension between the shah and his people was genuinely disturbing.

Both Mohammad Daoud and Mohammad Naim were of the opinion that the emergence of the Shiite clergy at the forefront of the antimonarchist struggle did not augur well for the shah of Iran. They held the view that Mohammad Reza Shah's moderation and reforms were coming too late and were not sufficient to turn the tide in his favor. The two brothers, however, believed that, if the shah's position became critical, the United States would intervene in Iran in order to keep the Pahlevi dynasty in power. Further, they felt that this might be accomplished not just through a CIA-sponsored operation but also, if necessary, by resorting to military force.

Daoud did not wish to see Iran plunged into turmoil. More importantly, he thought that even the Kremlin's perception of such an American action could result in a forceful Russian reaction in the region. He told me that the Russians would never allow an American military deployment so close to their borders, not only because of security considerations but also because of the politics of superpower competition. Daoud was quick to add that, in his view, the moment the Russians determined that the time had come for them to act, they would position themselves more advantageously in the region in order to preempt or more effectively counter the American move. The Russians might even take action, Daoud said, if they thought that the scope and intensity of the Iranian disturbances were becoming a threat to the tranquility of their southern flank. He shared the view held by some high officials of the Ministry of Foreign Affairs that, under the circumstances, a move by the Russians to assume more direct control of Afghanistan would be their most logical option. That would be, in all likelihood, a low-risk operation that would substantially increase Soviet clout and bring its power closer to the Persian Gulf and the Iranian hinterland. In fact, such a move would place Iran well within the Russian pincer. This being the perception of the Afghan leadership, it was, therefore, understandable that it watched so carefully the unfurling of the Iranian political crisis and, in that context, worried about the future of Afghanistan.

In the beginning of 1978, there were extensive anti-regime demonstrations in

Qum and Tabriz, where hundreds of Iranians were killed and injured by the security forces. Alexander Puzanov, the Russian ambassador, in a meeting at the Foreign Ministry, expressed to me the serious concern of the Soviet government with regard to these developments in Iran. On another occasion he told me that it would be very difficult for the Soviet Union to remain indifferent should the conflict in Iran acquire an international dimension. He did not elaborate, but we both knew what he meant.

Although by that time the shah of Iran had become entangled in Iran's internal crisis, he nevertheless on several occasions conveyed to Mohammad Daoud his pleasure with the positive turn that relations between Afghanistan and Pakistan had taken and expressed his belief that this improved situation would unquestionably evolve into close and beneficial cooperation in all fields among the three Islamic neighbors, Iran, Afghanistan, and Pakistan.

The first months of 1978 were a period of intense diplomatic activity for Mohammad Daoud. His trips to Libya, Yugoslavia, India, Pakistan, Kuwait, Saudi Arabia, and Egypt were politically successful, and whenever the question of financial assistance to Afghanistan's Seven Year Development Plan was raised during these visits, it received a most favorable response. Whereas Saudi Arabia and Kuwait were already heavily committed to the plan, Libya was not and at this time announced its intended participation. It was decided that an economic mission from Libya would visit Kabul shortly in order to determine, in cooperation with the Afghans, the size of Libyan assistance.

The new era of goodwill and understanding between Afghanistan and Pakistan was hailed by the Arab leaders, who praised the president's wisdom and statesmanlike approach to the bilateral problem confronting the two Muslim neighbors. It seemed that one of Afghanistan's considerations in seeking better relations with Pakistan had been realized: The Arab and Islamic countries friendly to Pakistan were genuinely satisfied with what had been achieved, and they had become generally convinced that Afghanistan did not nurture any ill will toward Pakistan.

In Yugoslavia, India, Egypt, and Saudi Arabia, Daoud's view with regard to keeping nonalignment as geniune as possible was warmly welcomed. President Tito of Yugoslavia and Prime Minister Moraji Desai of India adhered more clearly than the other leaders of the nonaligned movement that we met during this period, to the position that the original concept of nonalignment, including the criteria for membership in the movement, should not be diluted if the movement were to function as a healthy force for peace.

Daoud, in his talks with President Anwar Sadat of Egypt, praised his courage and initiative in going to Jerusalem and opening a new era in the search for peace in the Middle East. But he cautioned him against any move that could jeopardize Arab solidarity. He told Sadat that Arab solidarity was the key to the just solution of the Palestinian problem that was at the core of the Middle East crisis and that, therefore, it should be preserved at all costs. It was rumored later that Daoud had asked Sadat how to get rid of the Russians and of their influence in his country, presumably to learn from Sadat's experiences. Nothing of the sort was mentioned by Daoud, although Sadat did catalog his grievances against the Russians and said that in the early 1970s they had become the virtual rulers of Egypt, dictating their will to the military and civilians alike.

After these hectic trips we devoted our attention in the Foreign Ministry to completing preparations for the Nonaligned Ministerial Meeting, which was scheduled to be held in Kabul in May 1978. The meeting, however, did not take place, for, by that time, the Afghan republic had ceased to exist.

The United States

Since the end of World War II the United States occupied a place of importance in Afghanistan's economic and social development and, to all intents and purposes, it seemed that America was genuinely interested in Afghanistan's independence and territorial integrity. So far as the Afghans were concerned, they believed that good and active relations with the United States were important not only for reasons of economic and social development but also for the maintenance of their policy of balance. The majority of the ruling elite was of the opinion that strong Afghan–U.S. ties would likewise serve Afghanistan's nonalignment policy and provide flexibility in its foreign affairs. Since Afghanistan did not have much to offer in return for U.S. friendship and support, it was hoped that the country's geopolitical situation and its continued nonalignment would work as plausible incentives for maintaining U.S. interest in Afghanistan and its future.

At the advent of the republic, Afghanistan–U.S. relations became uneasy for a brief period. This temporary uneasiness had two main causes. First, the United States, like many other Western countries and like China, adopted a wait-and-see attitude with regard to the political and economic orientation of the new Afghan regime before deciding on its attitude toward Afghanistan. Second, Mohammad Daoud was annoyed with the Americans, suspecting that the United States (in conjunction with Pakistan) had been involved in the Maiwandwal plot (see Chapter 8). His suspicions were stirred by the Communist functionaries of the Ministry of the Interior attached to the team of investigators of the plot, who were determined to show American complicity in the matter.

However, the slump in Afghan–U.S. relations was of short duration. Mohammad Daoud and Mohammad Naim, both firm believers in a meaningful American presence in Afghanistan to counterbalance that of the Soviet Union, were quick to overcome their misgivings regarding the perceived or real attitude of the United States toward the Afghan republic. Mohammad Naim assured the new American ambassador, Theodore L. Eliot, Jr., of Afghanistan's desire to have the friendliest of relations with the United States and stressed the need for a strong American economic presence in Afghanistan, not only to help the country's economic advancement but also to assist Afghanistan politically. He further told the ambassador that the Afghan government wanted to stem attempts by "young people imbued with leftist ideas" in the government apparatus and outside it who were bent on stirring up Afghan–U.S. tensions.[43]

In early 1974, Ambassador Eliot told me that his government attached great importance to Afghanistan's independence and nonalignment and was of the view that U.S. policy interests in the region were well served to the extent that those conditions were preserved in a stable Afghanistan. He had made it known to Washington, he said, that substantial development assistance by the United States could play a significant role in helping the Afghan government maintain its independence, nonalignment, and economic autonomy in the face of unavoidable pressures from the Soviet Union. He had recommended to his government that the Afghans be able to count on continued U.S. economic and political presence.

It was to the credit of Ambassador Eliot that he detected the true nature of the Afghan state and drew the attention of Washington to Afghanistan's continued nationalist and nonaligned posture despite the leftist complexion of the new regime in the early days of the republic. Soon Afghan–U.S. relations grew warmer, and cooperation between the two countries was reactivated.

Little more than one year after the inception of the Afghan republic, on November 1, 1974, U.S. Secretary of State Henry A. Kissinger paid an official visit to Afghanistan. He met in Kabul with high-ranking Afghan officials and Mohammad Daoud, with whom he had a cordial exchange of views on matters of mutual interest. Daoud thanked Kissinger for the valuable U.S. assistance extended to Afghanistan over the years and expressed the wish that this assistance in the economic, technical, and education fields not only continue but also be expanded. Daoud drew the secretary's attention particularly to the need to complete the Hilmand project and the necessity of increased U.S. financial and technical assistance for that purpose. Daoud praised Kissinger's efforts to bring peace to the Middle East and his role in consolidating detente.

Kissinger told Daoud that the United States valued Afghanistan's friendship and attached great importance to its stability, independence, and staunch nonalignment. However, he said, these could not be safeguarded unless Afghanistan was politically and economically strong. He added that the United States had decided to assist Afghanistan to the extent possible in its social and economic development. To that end, he announced that he was going to send a senior official of the U.S. Agency for International Development (AID) to Kabul in the near future to cooperate with Afghan authorities in considering new programs and seeking ways of accelerating the completion of existing ones, like the Hilmand Valley project.

Daoud explained to Kissinger the fundamental importance to Afghanistan of good Russo–Afghan relations and the extensive cooperation that existed between the two countries. He briefed the secretary of state about the Afghan moves to expand relations with Iran and the Arab states and to involve them in Afghanistan's economic development. Daoud also referred to Afghan–Pakistani relations, which he described as "regrettably quite bad." Kissinger expressed his satisfaction with regard to the widening of ties between Afghanistan and Iran and some of the Arab states. He said that the United States was aware of the constraints on Afghan foreign policy and realized that Afghanistan's policy of cooperation and neighborly relations with the USSR was based on unavoidable realities. He added that, in extending its cooperation to Afghanistan, the United States wanted to be careful not to create difficulties for the Afghan Republic; it was up to the Afghans themselves to determine the scoop of this cooperation in accordance with their own foreign policy imperatives.

The secretary of state seemed adequately informed of the basics of the Pashtunistan dispute and regretted that Afghan–Pakistani relations had not improved. He said that Prime Minister Bhutto was also very much disappointed with this state of affairs, adding that Bhutto had complained to him that Afghanistan was harboring Pakistani dissidents and training anti-Pakistani guerrillas. Bhutto alleged, he said, that these guerrillas were entering Pakistan to commit acts of sabotage in the NWFP and Punjab and were combating Pakistani troops in Baluchistan. Daoud replied that the Afghan government indeed harbored Pashtun and Baluchi dissidents who had found in Afghanistan a safe refuge from Pakistani persecution and that they were welcome to stay as long as they wished because Afghanistan was their own country. But, he added, Afghanistan was not training anti-Pakistani guerrillas. Because of the ongoing war in Baluchistan, he said, hundreds of Baluchi refugees had crossed into his country and were presently living in camps in parts of south and southeastern Afghanistan. Daoud added that, after rest and recuperation, young warriors from among these refugees regularly returned to Baluchistan to defend their land against the Pakistani onslaught. He made it clear to Kissinger that the Afghan authorities neither wanted to nor could prevent these Baluchis from reentering their country. Daoud told Kissinger that the unrest in the NWFP and other parts of Pakistan was the consequence of ill-advised Pakistani policies. People in those areas, he said, were angered by the government's oppressive actions and were reacting violently to Islamabad's denial of their rights.

Daoud stated that what was going on in Baluchistan was very serious. Apart from the suffering that it inflicted on the people of Baluchistan, he said, it was one of those episodes that invited manipulation from many quarters, with dire consequences for peace and stability in the region. It was, therefore, necessary for Pakistan, he continued, to cease its war of destruction in Baluchistan and seek a dialogue with Baluchi leaders. He said that Afghanistan viewed with concern the eventual resumption of U.S. military aid to Pakistan, which would not only encourage the latter to continue the war in Baluchistan but also upset the balance of arms in the region.

Daoud said that Afghanistan was not sending saboteurs and agent provocateurs into Pakistan but rather it was that country that engaged in such
practices. Daoud referred to the continuous violations of Afghan territory and
air space by Pakistani agents and military aircraft. He mentioned the capture
of a Pakistani military helicopter inside Afghan territory a couple of months
earlier as a case in point. Daoud assured Kissinger that Afghanistan had no
wish to undermine the Pakistani government. He told him that the Afghan
government was committed to a peaceful solution of the present dispute. But,
he said, Pakistan did not show any inclination to negotiate with Afghanistan for
the purpose of finding such a solution. It seemed, Daoud continued, that the
Pakistani authorities were waiting for the Afghans to abandon their support for
the rights of the Pashtuns and the Baluchis. However, he said, the Afghans
would never withhold their support for the fulfillment of the legitimate
aspirations of those people who were their kith and kin. Under the circumstances, the good offices of mutual friends of the two countries, Daoud
added, would perhaps be useful in bringing Pakistan to the negotiating table.

Kissinger expressed his satisfaction that Afghanistan was committed to a
peaceful solution of its dispute with Pakistan and hoped that soon the two
countries would be able to settle their long-standing difference. He said that
friendship between Afghanistan and Pakistan would contribute to the consolidation of peace and stability in this important region of the world and that such
a development would be highly welcomed by the U.S. government.

At the conclusion of Kissinger's visit, a joint U.S.–Afghan statement was
issued. This document reflected the warmth of U.S.–Afghan relations and
reiterated the U.S. commitment to cooperate with the Afghans in achieving
their economic-development goals.[44]

In the beginning of January 1975, a high official of AID, Assistant Adminis-
trator Robert Nooter, visited Afghanistan and held talks with the Afghan
minister of planning and other Afghan officials. It was decided to establish a
joint committee to develop a program for the Hilmand Valley. A great deal of
importance was attached by Afghan experts to the completion of an adequate
drainage system in the valley. This concern, of which the Americans were
fully aware, was once again explained to Nooter. He informed the Afghans that
the AID would provide technical assistance for maintenance of the existing
parts of the drainage system in the valley and finance completion of the
drainage system in the present project area, subject to Washington's approval
and provided some improvements were made by the Afghan government in the
administration of the valley. In a related action, Nooter signed with the
Afghans an additional $2 million loan agreement for the building of electrical
transmission lines between Kajakai (a dam on the Hilmand River) and
Kandahar.

On January 23 and 24, 1975, the head of AID, Daniel Parker, visited
Afghanistan and met with high Afghan officials. Parker's talks with the
Afghans further brightened the prospects of increased U.S. participation in

Afghanistan's development and confirmed, in particular, U.S. interest in completing the Hilmand Valley project.

As time went by, a number of agreements concerning U.S. assistance in the provision of school textbooks, the development of Kabul University, rural development, rural schools, rural health care centers, and construction of drains in the Hilmand Valley were signed between the Republic of Afghanistan and the United States. Although American assistance was still modest, its reactivation nevertheless pleased the Afghan leadership. By 1978, the United States had invested $532.87 million in economic aid to Afghanistan, of which 71% was in the form of grants.[45]

At the invitation of Secretary of State Kissinger, Mohammad Naim, in the capacity of special envoy of the Afghan head of state, paid an official visit to Washington from June 29 to July 1, 1976. I accompanied Naim on this visit. He held talks with Kissinger and President Gerald Ford and had meetings with several members of the cabinet. In addition to talks with these high administration officials, Naim met with members of the Senate Foreign Relations Committee and the House International Relations Committee. These meetings enabled Naim to give an appraisal of Afghanistan's foreign and domestic policies and further acquaint Americans with the republic's goals and aspirations. Although Mohammad Naim's official visit to Washington was mostly a goodwill trip, it nevertheless significantly contributed to strengthening conditions for further expansion of Afghan–U.S. cooperation.

One of the issues raised during Naim's visit by U.S. officials and members of the Senate and the House of Representatives was the problem of illicit traffic in narcotics in Afghanistan. This was not a new issue. In 1947, Afghanistan had banned the cultivation of opium poppies and the production and trade of opium, in response to an appeal from the U.S. Congress. But this law, enacted for the sake of international cooperation, could not be implemented satisfactorily, due to various difficulties. One such difficulty stemmed from the fact that opium was the only cash crop in many of the areas where opium poppies were grown, such as Badakhshan in northeastern Afghanistan. To eliminate this sole means of livelihood without substituting other cash crops or economic activities (e.g., cottage industries or animal husbandry) would have meant great hardship for the farmers concerned. The Afghan government believed that, in areas like Badakhshan, income substitution for the farmers, as part of a program of overall development, would be the only way to gradually eliminate the narcotics problem. The other main difficulty was the weakness of the law enforcement agencies dealing with illicit production of and traffic in opium. To become effective in controlling narcotic drugs, the police needed to be expanded, reorganized, and provided with modern equipment. All this required, obviously, substantial monetary expenditure far beyond what Afghanistan could afford.

Since Mohammad Daoud's reassumption of power, the Afghan government had increased its efforts to slow the opium traffic. A previously established

United Nations fund for drug abuse control received the strong backing of the new government. This fund, to which the United States, the Federal Republic of Germany, Afghanistan, and a few other countries were contributing, was helping to improve the law enforcement authorities' struggle against the illicit traffic. It was also mandated, in cooperation with competent Afghan departments, to study and recommend means of accomplishing income substitution in Badakhshan and other opium-growing regions.

Mohammad Naim explained all this to his American hosts. He added that the Afghan Republic, though faced with enormous developmental problems, was ready to discharge its moral obligations to the international community, but the paucity of Afghan resources and the magnitude of the problem warranted a truly international effort to deal with the problem of illicit drug traffic. It was apparent that U.S. lawmakers were not well informed about the Afghan predicament and the positive steps that had already been taken to curtail the illicit traffic in opium. They listened with great interest to what was said in this regard by Naim, and most of them promised to help the Afghan efforts.

The Ministry of Foreign Affairs was very keen to see the government achieve tangible and positive results in the eradication of opium poppy cultivation and the illicit traffic of opium and its derivatives. To that effect a coordinator of anti-narcotics activities was appointed within the Ministry of Foreign Affairs with the responsibility to coordinate activities on the national and international levels of various Afghan departments concerned with the narcotics problem. The coordinator, a senior Foreign Ministry official, made a remarkably good start in this difficult work, but soon the Communist coup put an end to this promising program to combat the cultivation of opium poppies and the production of opium and its illicit traffic.

By the invitation of the government of Afghanistan, Secretary of State Kissinger made a second official visit to Afghanistan on August 8, 1976. At that time a major step had already been taken by Afghanistan and Pakistan to improve their relations. Mohammad Daoud explained this development to the secretary of state at some length and expressed his optimism about future prospects. Kissinger conveyed his pleasure about the Afghan–Pakistani rapprochement and reaffirmed his government's deep interest in the normalization of relations between Afghanistan and Pakistan. Daoud welcomed the accelerated pace of U.S. involvement in Afghanistan's social and economic development. He particularly praised American efforts to speed up the progress of the Hilmand project. Kissinger reconfirmed his government's continued desire to participate closely in Afghanistan's development. Both sides noted with satisfaction the warmth of Afghan–U.S. relations and expressed their determination to further strengthen these relations. It was at this meeting that the secretary of state broached the idea of an official visit of the Afghan head of state to the United States. He added that, should such a visit be agreeable, President Ford would extend an official invitation to him. Daoud asked Kissinger to convey his thanks to President Ford and told the secretary that the matter of his visit would be discussed and finalized through diplomatic channels. A joint U.S.–Afghan statement was issued upon the secretary's departure that confirmed the "United States' strong support for the recent initiatives which have improved relations among the states of the region," expressed U.S. understanding of Afghan nonalignment and its support for Afghanistan's independence, and reaffirmed the "United States' interest in participating closely in Afghanistan's economic and social development."[46]

Neither during Kissinger's visit to Kabul nor in other contacts with the Americans was any indication given that Washington had exerted pressure on Bhutto to adopt a more conciliatory attitude toward Afghanistan. There was no doubt, however, that the United States was genuinely interested in an Afghan–Pakistan reconciliation for the sake of regional harmony. Therefore, the feeling among Afghans was that the United States could not have refrained from occasionally impressing upon Pakistan the necessity of making efforts to reverse the negative trend in Afghan–Pakistani relations. To what extent the Americans had been persuasive in this regard is not known, but any presentations of this kind that they may have made to the Pakistanis would have added significantly to the influence of mutual friends of Afghanistan and Pakistan, such as Iran and Turkey, concerned with deescalating tensions between the two Islamic neighbors.

Apart from exerting efforts to expand their own economic and technical assistance to Afghanistan, the Americans made clear to the Afghans their unabated encouragement of the friendly oil-rich Arab countries to help Afghanistan financially in its economic development. Ambassador Eliot told me that this kind of friendly persuasion was going on at various levels and that he himself had made it a habit of bringing it constantly to the attention of friendly Arab ambassadors in Kabul, particularly the ambassador of Saudi Arabia.

In the summer of 1977, President Jimmy Carter invited Mohammad Daoud to the United States for an official visit. In his letter to Daoud, Carter praised Afghanistan's nonalignment, welcomed the positive efforts of the Afghan president in improving Afghan–Pakistani relations, and expressed the hope that he could meet with Daoud in the near future to discuss matters of common interest. Daoud accepted Carter's invitation but, due to a heavy schedule that included a number of other state visits planned for 1977, it proved difficult for Daoud to undertake the U.S. trip that year. This was contrary to the wishes of the Ministry of Foreign Affairs, which wanted the trip to take place as soon as possible because of its perceived political impact, notably with regard to the ongoing Afghan–Pakistani negotiations, and the consolidation of Communist forces inside Afghanistan (see Chapter 8). The Americans apparently also had scheduling difficulties that precluded the possibility of a visit by Daoud in 1977. Early in 1978, after a trip to Washington, Ambassador Eliot informed the Ministry of Foreign Affairs that the State Department had tentatively planned Daoud's visit for September, the exact date of which was to be fixed later in consultation between the two parties. Daoud agreed with that schedule, and the Ministry of Foreign Affairs was of the opinion that the trip in September should coincide with the opening days of the United Nations General Assembly so that Daoud could address that world organization. I conveyed to the American ambassador this preoccupation of the ministry. He assured me that the matter would be taken into account by Washington planners.

But Daoud's trip, viewed by many as one of the highlights of Afghanistan's reconfirmation of its policy of balance, never took place, due to the Communist takeover. It has been said that Daoud's scheduled visit to Washington and the shah of Iran's forthcoming trip to Kabul in July 1978 were among the factors that contributed to Daoud's rapid undoing. While this could probably never be verified, it is certain that neither of those events was to Russia's liking.

The Soviet Union

The advent of the republic of Afghanistan was hailed by the Soviet Union, the first country to recognize the new regime, on July 20, 1973. The Russians considered Mohammad Daoud the architect of Afghan–Soviet friendship, and the fact that he had seized power with the help of leftist officers, most of them trained in the Soviet Union, was undoubtedly an added cause for delight in Moscow. On July 26th the Soviet leadership stated in a message to Mohammad Daoud its confidence that "the genuinely good-neighborly relations of friendship and all-around cooperation existing between the Soviet Union and Afghanistan will further successfully develop."[47] Alexander Puzanov, the Russian ambassador in Kabul, told Waheed Abdullah, then deputy foreign minister, at one of their first meetings (during which I was present) that the Kremlin leadership was quite happy about the change of regime in Kabul.

In the months following the establishment of the republic, the Russians, perceiving that the general orientation of the new regime was markedly leftist and that the disposition of the Afghan leadership was extremely favorable toward them, substantially increased their offers of assistance to Afghanistan. They had probably concluded that the return of Mohammad Daoud, surrounded by a solid corps of pro-Russian leftists, was a significant step in the furtherance of their interests in southwest Asia. It was therefore necessary not only to actively support the new "leftist" regime in Kabul but also to strive to increase Afghanistan's dependence on the Soviet Union, to extract maximum benefit from the unexpectedly fortuitous new conditions.

As the probing for economic and financial help from other quarters was only in its initial stages, the republican government was in no position to decline this

Russian largesse, which would also have unnecessarily provoked Russia's well-known sensitivities. It was decided to accept the Soviet offer of increased assistance but also to continue the search for other options, so that Afghanistan could diversify its sources of economic assistance. The decision to seek aid from other sources too, made by Daoud and his small circle of non-Communist collaborators, was reluctantly accepted by the members of the Central Committee, who maintained that reliance on the Soviet Union alone was sufficient for modernizing and developing a progressive Afghanistan.

If Daoud had been of the opinion in the 1950s that strong disincentives existed for the Soviet Union to take over Afghanistan in the foreseeable future and that Afghanistan's rapid advancement could be accomplished with massive Russian assistance without risking harm to Afghanistan's independence, he had unquestionably reassessed that opinion when I met with him a few days after he had begun his second tenure. He seemed to share the Afghans' innate suspicion of the Russians, and he adhered closely to the simple and unsophisticated belief that expansion toward the Indian Ocean was the ultimate regional goal of the Soviet Union. I was astonished when Daoud, speaking of Soviet intentions, suddenly recalled the reflection of a Russian regarding the purpose of their economic and technical assistance to Afghanistan, which he had read many years ago in an article in *Life*. What Daoud had smilingly paraphrased proved to be an accurate rendition of the Russian's disquieting remarks. The Russian (probably an expert working in Afghanistan in the 1950s) confided to an American in Kabul that the growing supply and communications facilities financed by the Soviets "will be useful to our armies when they will march."[48] I gathered from that conversation that the consequences of a Russian southward move for Afghanistan, whenever conditions allowed its realization, were not lost to Daoud. If he had ever been lax in his assessment of Soviet ambitions, he was certainly alert now to the Russian danger.

During subsequent exchanges with Daoud, I learned that he did not believe that Soviet use of economic assistance as a means of penetrating Afghan society was cause for great alarm. He once said that Russian economic assistance enriched the masses; therefore, by extending aid, the Soviets were in fact strengthening the forces that would oppose the propagation of their ideology. In Daoud's view, a well-to-do Islamic society was a powerful deterrent to the propagation of communism. He thought that, as peddlers of communist ideology, Russian economic and technical experts who came into daily contact with the staunchly Islamic masses of Afghanistan were not very effective, and their influence was easily outweighed by the benefits accruing from the material impact of Russian assistance. What worried Daoud most was the Soviet Union's systematic penetration of the army, disturbingly confirmed to him while he was preparing his coup, and that country's continuous involvement, although often lukewarm, with the PDPA. These Soviet actions, according to Daoud, not only demonstrated the disquieting intentions of the Soviet Union toward Afghanistan's non-Communist regime, but also constituted a serious breach of faith by the Kremlin leadership, which at periodic intervals had renewed its solemn pledge to him and to the king that Russia had no wish to interfere in the internal affairs of Afghanistan.

The essence of Mohammad Daoud's observations regarding Afghanistan's involvement with the USSR, noted over a period of several months, ran as follows: The need for a modern army arose when the question of Pashtunistan became heated in the second half of the 1940s. The national issue of Pashtunistan could not be abandoned, and the Pakistanis were seriously bent on destabilizing the Afghan regime. The appearance in Waziristan in 1949 of Amin Jan, one of ex-King Amanullah's half brothers, and the revolt of the Safi tribe west of the Durand Line were not the least of their continuous attempts in this regard. The Afghans decided that a modern defense, especially its air force component, would function primarily as a deterrent to Pakistani actions against Afghanistan.

The risks involved in opening the army to Russian influence by accepting Soviet military assistance were understood by the Afghans, but there were no alternatives because the United States had already turned down their request for arms. In addition, there were two other factors that operated as incentives for the Afghans to turn to their northern neighbors for the procurement of military assistance. First, it was clearly perceived that the Russians would not accept Afghanistan's military involvement with any other power while they themselves were providing massive economic assistance. In other words, if the Soviets were to extend meaningful economic assistance and Afghanistan still felt strongly about building a modern army, Russia would have to be its sole provider. Secondly, the close proximity of the Soviet Union to landlocked Afghanistan militated in favor of obtaining arms from Russia, especially if the intention was to build a modern army rapidly. Political and logistic difficulties involved in the transit of Western military equipment, especially heavy material, through Pakistan could easily be imagined.

King Zahir Shah and Mohammad Daoud both shared in all frankness, first with Khrushchev and Bulganin in 1955 and later with other Soviet leaders, their legitimate apprehensions about the dangers for Afghanistan inherent in the inevitable exposure of young Afghan army officers to the Russian way of life and Communist ideology. Russian leaders repeatedly assured the king, Daoud, and other Afghan leaders that the Soviet Union would refrain from any act that could be interpreted by the Afghan state as hostile and that they would see to it that Afghan officers and personnel trained either in Russia or Afghanistan would not be exposed to ideological indoctrination. They assured the Afghans that this discipline would be strictly observed. Russian leaders from Khrushchev to Brezhnev maintained that they were only interested in the nonalignment and the stability of Afghanistan and not in subverting its officer corps and preparing the ground for the advent of communism in that country. Unfortunately the Russians did not honor their word. They gradually but doggedly tried to transform the officer corps into an instrument of Russian policy. It was surprising, given the degree of Soviet involvement in the army and systematic efforts to subvert its loyalty, that the number of Communist recruits there remained proportionally so low.

The Afghan government in all sincerity offered Russia its friendship. By doing so it was theorized that it would gain Russia's confidence and ultimately eliminate the Russian need to Sovietize the army with a view to one day toppling the Afghan government. In a sense, it was hoped that Afghanistan's friendship with Russia would serve as a counterbalance to the potential dangers stemming from the latter's military assistance. But, over the course of the years, that hope proved to be no more than an illusion. The Russians continued their activity of recruitment among the young officers of the army. Even some noncommissioned officers were approached by Russian advisers and were known to have been won over to their side. It became increasingly clear that the Russians aimed beyond the narrow limits of the status quo in the region; otherwise they would not have busied themselves so assiduously in penetrating Afghan army cadres and establishing their network of subversion in a friendly country from which they had nothing to fear.

In spite of these Afghan concerns, it was hoped that Russian interest would not militate in favor of resumption of the Soviet southward move for a long time to come. It was also hoped that in the future Afghanistan could disengage from military cooperation with Russia without causing significant damage to Afghan–Soviet relations, while meaningful Western vigilance would increase, forcing the Soviets to restrain their aggressive impulses. For the time being, however, the Afghans thought it would be even more dangerous to attempt to disengage from Soviet military cooperation than to continue that relationship. Care had to be taken not to alarm the Russians and extra care taken not to provoke them.

It should always be kept in mind that Afghanistan has a long common frontier with the Soviet Union and that it therefore did not have the option of acting as Egypt had acted when Anwar Sadat ousted all Russian military and technical advisers from Egypt and abrogated the Russo–Egyptian friendship treaty in 1971. Besides, Afghanistan needed Soviet friendship and appreciated its economic assistance, its flaws and shortcomings notwithstanding. One way of eradicating, or at least limiting, Soviet influence in the army would be to scale down its size, but that would only be possible once the problem of Pashtunistan was solved and Afghanistan and Pakistan had achieved cordial relations. Only this development would obviate the need for a strong military deterrent and the Russian assistance that made it possible. It was difficult, however, to predict what Russia's position toward continued economic and technical assistance would be once the elimination or reduction of their military assistance was decided upon. Further, the effect of a negative Russian reaction on economic and technical assistance from other Soviet-bloc countries, already quite substantial, could not be easily ascertained.

In addition to consideration of Russia's sensitivities, the answers to these questions had to be found and weighed. No one was unaware of the imperial thrust of Soviet policies, but for Afghanistan it had always been a question of taking risks or remaining stagnant. Ultimately, the decision was made to move ahead fast, otherwise stagnation in itself would jeopardize the nation's survival. In the process, the Afghan leaders had no other option but to turn to Russia, no matter what the consequences.

The Russians would never have assisted Afghanistan had their interests dictated otherwise. Later, perhaps, Russia's favorable disposition might have changed. Afghanistan profited from Russian self-interest and attracted a sizable amount of economic aid that was put to good use. The army was also modernized and strengthened. What the future held was anybody's guess. For the Afghans, it was essential to concentrate on building the country. When the time came for the Soviet Union to move, nobody would be able to do much anyway unless the Americans found themselves at that juncture in a different frame of mind. This summary of Mohammad Daoud's observations well demonstrates the Afghan leaders' preoccupations with regard to Soviet economic and military assistance to Afghanistan.

Soon after the inception of the republic, Mohammad Daoud became upset with the ostentatious pro-Soviet bias, the excesses, the inefficiency, and the frequent insubordination of the leftists in various branches of the government, including the Central Committee and the cabinet. One anecdote from this period tells of Daoud's furiously adjourning a meeting of the Central Committee because most of its members, while discussing two offers of aid for the same project, one presented by the UN and the other by the Soviet Union, stubbornly insisted that the Russian offer should be chosen despite its higher cost and evident flaws.

Partly for these reasons, Daoud decided to bring to an end the growth of Communist influence in the state apparatus, something on which the Communists seemed inexorably bent now that they thought they had a solid foothold in the government and the administration. The military was to be spared a swift purge, although discrete measures aimed at controlling its suspect elements and hampering its infiltration by Russian agents were ordered.

When, in June 1974, Daoud embarked on his first official trip to Moscow since his return to power, the contours of his move to disassociate himself internally from the Communists had begun to come into focus. The shake-up in the Ministry of the Interior was well under way, one Communist cabinet minister had already been fired, and another had been sent to Bulgaria as ambassador. As for the leftist-dominated Central Committee, it had been pushed into the background, where it slowly perished from idleness and lack of attention.

The Afghans were watchful for any sign of Soviet annoyance with the change of outlook in Kabul but did not detect any, either before Daoud's visit to Moscow or during his stay there. One passage of President Podgorny's speech at the state luncheon in the Kremlin was construed in retrospect by some analysts as prodding Daoud to continue to work closely with the PDPA.[49]

Great and complex tasks (of renovating political, economic and cultural life) will have to be tackled. . . . But as experience shows, they can be solved successfully when the course chartered is pursued firmly, when broad popular masses are drawn into the work of building a new life, and when forces which are sincerely interested in strengthening the new system act vigorously and in close unity.[50]

This did not, however, impress the Afghans as an expression of Russian disappointment about the shift of attitude concerning the leftists. Indeed, the huge amount of public and private praise the founder of the republic and the new regime received and the largesse shown by the Russians regarding their economic and financial aid to Afghanistan did not leave any room for entertaining speculations of that nature. Another passage of Podgorny's same speech, however, did appear bizarre to the Afghans.

It should be hoped that [in] developing its international contacts . . . and making its constructive contribution . . . to the solution of international problems, including those of the Middle East and South Asia, the Republic of Afghanistan will become a really peaceful crossroad in Asia.[51]

Russian officials declined to furnish a clarification of this statement.

As was customary in these high-level Afghan–Soviet meetings, Brezhnev, Podgorny, and Kosygin profusely praised Afghanistan's nonalignment and its importance for the Soviet Union and characterized Russo–Afghan friendship as the most noteworthy example of peaceful coexistence and cooperation between states with differing social and economic systems. Here again, there was no hint of disappointment by the Soviet leadership about Afghanistan's attempt to diversify its sources of economic and financial assistance and forge new friendships.

The visit to Moscow went well. The leaders of the Soviet Union welcomed the establishment of the republic, both in their private talks with Mohammad Daoud and in their public statements, and expressed Russia's readiness to participate substantially in Afghanistan's forthcoming Seven Year Development Plan. Podgorny said in his speech to which reference has already been made that

With the establishment of the Republican system in July 1973 our friendly relations are rising to a still higher level. The Soviet Union was the first to recognize the new Republic and immediately after it was proclaimed it declared its readiness to develop relations of friendship and fruitful cooperation with it.[52]

In view of the Soviet commitment to increase its economic and technical assistance to Afghanistan and to contribute to the financing of its Seven Year Development Plan, both sides agreed to set up a joint commission for economic and technical cooperation. The commission's task was to identify those projects that could be implemented with the cooperation of the USSR, preferably within the framework of the plan; to deal with the question of trade and payments on the basis of existing agreements or new ones; and to settle differences that might arise between the two sides in the field of economic and technical cooperation. The Russians agreed to open a $600 million line of credit for financing various Afghan projects within the proposed Seven Year Plan. They also agreed to a moratorium on the repayment of loans from the Soviet Union.

On one economic matter, however, the Afghans did not receive a favorable response: the question of an increase in the price of natural gas exported to the USSR. The Russians were buying Afghan natural gas at well below the world price and were ignoring Afghan requests to negotiate a new price more in line with what prevailed internationally.[53] Daoud himself raised the matter with Kosygin, who told him that the redetermination of the gas price was a complicated matter that needed more study and probing by the experts. Daoud had to drop the matter after expressing the hope that the competent Russian authorities would accelerate their efforts in this regard.[54] It has to be noted that the exploitation of gas had started in the early 1960s with Russian help. Afghan gas was exclusively exported to the USSR by pipeline, and the meters registering the amount of gas exported were situated on Russian soil.

In the political field, Mohammad Daoud extensively briefed the Soviet leadership about the causes of Afghanistan's poor state of relations with Pakistan. The Russians listened carefully to his explanations and praised Afghanistan's restraint in its attitude toward Islamabad. However, the passage of Daoud's statement at the Kremlin luncheon that pertained to Afghan–Pakistani relations and Islamabad's treatment of the Pashtuns and the Baluchis was omitted from the *Tass* dispatch. This omission was probably a crude way of indicating the Soviet Union's increasingly ambivalent and even neutral stance in the dispute between Afghanistan and Pakistan. But in the joint Russo–Afghan statement at the conclusion of Daoud's visit, the Russians recognized the existence of "a political difference" between Afghanistan and Pakistan and the need for its peaceful resolution through negotiations in conformity with the basic Afghan position.

After his return to power, Daoud commented on Brezhnev's Asian collective security proposal to the effect that, "We like certain things in the doctrine but we do not like its emphasis on the inviolability of frontiers . . . that will mean accepting Pakistan's present frontiers which are the doing of the British."[55] Nonetheless, it was obviously difficult for the Afghans to change a position substantially, taken under the monarchy, during Podgorny's official visit to Kabul in May 1973.

Considering that observance of the principles of peaceful coexistence of states with differing social and political systems is an effective way toward establishing peace both in Asia and in other parts of the world, the USSR and Afghanistan again declare that in order to guarantee security in Asia it is essential for all the countries of the area to make joint efforts in that direction.[56]

At the delegation level, the Russians requested that, in the 1974 joint Russo–Afghan statement, the formulation relative to Brezhnev's proposal be rendered more streamlined and concise. The Afghans explained that the creation of a security system in Asia would necessitate the fulfillment of certain conditions. They proposed that their objections to the colonial frontiers and their adherence to peaceful settlement of disputes be reflected in an appropriate fashion in the relevant part of the communiqué related to Asian security if the Kabul formulation were to be altered. After some hard bargaining, the following text emerged from the deliberations, which adequately covered Afghanistan's preoccupations:

> The Republic of Afghanistan and the Soviet Union are deeply interested in securing peace and cooperation in Asia and consider that the creation of a security system by joint efforts of all the states of Asia would meet the interests of the Asian peoples. This would require the settlement of disputable issues through peaceful means and elimination of the remnants of colonialism.[57]

Interestingly, while President Podgorny stated in his speech that the idea of collective security in Asia was increasingly supported in Asian countries and that conditions were "gradually being created for the translation of the idea into life,"[58] Mohammad Daoud had this to say about it:

> Your Excellency referred to collective security in Asia. This is a commendable idea. But, Afghanistan is of the opinion that real peace is achieved only when the lawful rights of human masses are respected by all states, and colonialistic attitudes are condemned on the basis of the principles of the United Nations Charter.[59]

Further, the Afghans knew at this point that Brezhnev's proposal had little or no chance of being realized, since one of the most important contributors to any Asian collective security system, China (who believed that the Russian scheme was primarily aimed at isolating it), ridiculed the proposal and maintained that it would never get off the ground. Subsequently the Chinese were proved right.

Soon after Daoud's return to Kabul, the process of determining the scope of Russian participation in the Seven Year Development Plan, already begun, was further accelerated. In a few months, both sides had agreed on a number of projects that were to be implemented with Russian economic and technical assistance. These included irrigation and other agricultural projects, a second urea fertilizer plant, a second thermal plant, expansion of the Jarquaduq natural gas project, and an ambitious joint venture aimed at locating Afghanistan's natural resources and the extent of their reserves.

The Russians, however, did not commit themselves to three important infrastructural projects, although they had a long history of association with them. These were the construction of an oil refinery at Angot in the Saripul-Shiberghan area (northern Afghanistan); the exploitation of Ainak's copper deposits in Logar province, coupled with the construction there of a smelting and refining complex; and the development of the Haji Gak iron ore reserve in the central Hindu Kush.

The Russians had assisted over the years in oil exploration in the Saripul-Shiberghan area, apparently with no great success except for the Angot reserves, which in fact had been initially discovered by the Swedes after World

War II. The Russians maintained that the exploitable reserves at Angot did not justify the building of a refinery. When larger reserves of oil were found by the Afghan experts themselves in the same general area, it rendered the Russian argument untenable, but the Soviets still stalled, claiming that further in-depth studies were necessary to determine the feasibility of the project. It seemed that the Russians preferred for some reason that the Afghan oil remained underground for the time being.

The Russians had provided financial and technical assistance for geological surveys to determine the extent of Ainak's copper reserves. Their surveys had shown that Ainak's deposits were rich and of good quality. But when it was decided to include in the Seven Year Plan the exploitation of Ainak's copper and the construction there of a smelting and refining complex to produce copper for both domestic use and export, the Russians became less enthusiastic about the project. Although negotiations with the Russians for funding the project continued, it became apparent that what they wanted was for the mining of the ore and its concentration to be performed in Afghanistan and the concentrate to be shipped to the Soviet Union for smelting and refining.[60] Several times the Russians came close to accepting the Afghan point of view, but they refrained from making any firm commitment.

The Haji Gak iron ore development project was a colossal undertaking, the initial stages of which were to be dealt with in the first Seven Year Plan. Although a Franco–German company had prepared development and exploitation feasibility studies, important preliminary surveys to determine the extent of Haji Gak reserves had been done by Soviet geologists. According to plans established for the development and exploitation of Haji Gak, roads, railroads, mining facilities, a blast furnace, processing facilities, and manufacturing plants had to be built. The Afghan planners' intention was that, at the intial stages of production, Haji Gak would produce iron billets for export to Iran, Pakistan, and the Soviet Union. As Haji Gak was a huge project, necessitating the construction of a multitude of other supplementary facilities, it was hoped that the bulk of funding would come from a consortium of French, German, American, and Japanese sources. The Russians showed an interest in continuing to be financially and technically associated with certain aspects of the development of Haji Gak. However, as negotiations for their financial commitment went on, it was realized that they had the same plan for Haji Gak iron as they had for Ainak's copper: After the exploitation of the ore, it was to be transported to the USSR, where the production of iron and steel would take place.[61] It was clear that the Russians wanted Afghanistan to remain for them the provider of raw materials and the receiver of their manufactured goods, a classic example of colonial exploitation.[62]

From September 10 to September 14, 1974, Mohammad Naim and Waheed Abdullah visited the USSR, meeting with Brezhnev and Kosygin. Although talks between the two Afghans and the Russian leaders were primarily devoted to discussing the deteriorating relations between Afghanistan and Pakistan and the dangers that the situation presented for the region, economic matters did come up for discussion. Mohammad Naim in particular alluded to the need for Russian financial help to develop the Ainak and Haji Gak projects, but the Russians were vague and noncommital in this respect.

During these talks, Kosygin assured Naim and Waheed Abdullah that the Soviet government would strongly disapprove of any aggressive action by Pakistan against the Afghan republic. He further assured the Afghan envoys that the level of procurement of certain military hardware like tanks, antitank weapons, and aircraft could be raised if the Afghan side felt the need for such an increase at this time. He nevertheless expressed the hope that Pakistan's provocations would be countered by the Afghans with the same restraint as hitherto demonstrated. Naim told Kosygin that the Afghan government abhorred the idea of an armed conflict with Pakistan but, in the case of aggression, the Afghans would have no alternative but to defend themselves. So far as the proposed increase in Russian military support was concerned, Naim said that he would convey to Mohammed Daoud what Kosygin had told him.

In October of 1974, Soviet Deputy Defense Minister Marshal Moskolenko made an official visit to Kabul. His visit was part of a routine established at the beginning of the military cooperation between Afghanistan and the Soviet Union. The routine consisted of periodic exchanges of military delegations between the two countries for the purpose of reviewing and evaluating Afghan requirements for armaments and training. Occurring in the middle of an Afghan–Pakistani crisis, the marshal's visit sparked speculation that Afghanistan was being made ready for war with Pakistan. This speculation, however, was totally unfounded.

By the time Podgorny returned Daoud's visit on December 9, 1975, there had been a number of developments of concern to the Russians in Afghanistan. Daoud had begun to speak out against and to actively eradicate Communist influence in the government and the army. Further, Afghanistan's attempts to diversify and expand its sources of economic assistance by making overtures to Islamic, Arab, and other countries were well under way.

Apart from these developments, some of Daoud's uninhibited reactions to matters directly or indirectly involving the Russians could not have pleased the Soviet leadership. For example, Daoud did not conceal his profound disappointment with the nonaligned movement, which he thought had lost its sense of moderation and would further lose its effectiveness and even its raison d'être as a catalyst for peace if countries like pro-Soviet Cuba continued to be members of the movement. Daoud had said to several foreign visitors that, although he had nothing against Cuba, that country did not qualify for membership in the nonaligned movement, as it was subservient to Soviet policies and was geared to furthering the latter's interests, especially in Africa and Latin America. He likewise opposed the participation of Rumania in the movement. Responding politely to the Rumanian ambassador's request for

Afghanistan's support of his country's efforts to become an observer at the forthcoming Colombo summit meeting, Daoud said that, as things stood at the time, by no stretch of the imagination could he see Rumania associated with the nonaligned movement. He insisted, along with a few other nonaligned leaders, that strict observance of the criteria for membership was necessary; otherwise the movement would rapidly become a policy instrument of one or the other superpower.

It was also known that Daoud had criticized Russia's African adventure in discussions with his cabinet and had frequently expressed his disapproval of the role played in this respect by Cuba.[63] With regard to the conflict over the Ogaden Desert between Somalia and Ethiopia, which had provided the opportunity for Russo–Cuban intrusion into the Horn of Africa, Daoud had come out squarely in support of Somalia. The government of Afghanistan took the position that the Somali–Ethiopian dispute should be solved peacefully on the basis of self-determination by the people of Ogaden. This position was contrary to that of the Ethiopians, who were militarily and politically supported by the Soviet Union and Cuba. The Ethiopians considered Ogaden an integral part of their country and opposed any recourse to the process of self-determination.

In spite of these developments, once again no strains were detected in Russo–Afghan relations during Podgorny's two-day visit to Kabul (December 9–10, 1975). Talks between Daoud and Podgorny, during which I was present, were routine and uneventful. They centered mostly, as was customary in those meetings, on taking stock of the excellence of Soviet–Afghan relations. At no time did Podgorny ask about the availability of new sources of economic assistance to Afghanistan or the results achieved in securing these sources. While Daoud, as part of his exposition relating to Afghan foreign policy, was describing the deteriorating state of Afghan–Pakistani relations, Podgorny inquired whether the shah of Iran was still trying to help Afghanistan and Pakistan overcome their differences. When Daoud replied in the affirmative, Podgorny asked if the shah had been successful in his efforts. After listening to Daoud explain that the shah had not yet been able to bring the two sides closer together, he did not pursue the matter further. It seemed that he was only interested in knowing of the shah's involvement. He asked a few routine questions about the difficulties of Afghan in-transit trade through Pakistan and then alluded to a conversation with the Pakistani ambassador in Moscow he had had before departing for Kabul. Podgorny said that the Pakistani ambassador had asked him, as a gesture of goodwill toward Pakistan, to suggest to the Afghans that they refrain from fomenting trouble in Baluchistan and the NWFP, because the continuation of their interference would not only harm Pakistan but might also jeopardize the security of the region as a whole. After saying this, Podgorny added that he was only conveying to the Afghans what the ambassador told him without adding to or deleting from his words. After a pause, Podgorny, looking straight at Daoud, said that Afghanistan was a sovereign country with its own particular national interests that the Soviets respected. Afghanistan, he added, would decide whatever best suited those interests, and it was, of course, also aware of its extremely sensitive position in the region. To us, Podgorny's words could not have better emphasized Soviet ambivalence vis à vis the Afghan–Pakistani dispute.

When Daoud mentioned the dangers that threatened world peace and security, Podgorny put the responsibility for increasing international tension squarely at the doorstep of "American imperialism" and "Chinese hegemonism." Daoud, without directly commenting on Podgorny's statement, said that *all* big powers, without distinction, had great responsibility for the maintenance of world peace and security and that other countries, gathered within an ineffective UN system, watched silently and helplessly the performance of the big powers, which very often promoted their own selfish interests. Podgorny listened to Daoud without batting an eye.

Although Army General Ivan G. Pavlovsky, a Soviet deputy defense minister, was present at the talks, the only military matter mentioned was brought up by Podgorny himself when he said to Daoud that the military authorities in Moscow had informed him that all the tanks requested by Afghanistan would be delivered on schedule.

During the talks, Podgorny, on the basis of earlier Afghan requests, offered additional Russian credits for the Seven Year Plan, which was being finalized in part with the help of Russian experts. He promised that Soviet assistance for the Ainak project would continue but was noncommittal about the exploitation of Haji Gak iron ore. As a new series of feasibility studies was being carried out with regard to the Angot oil refinery, he refrained from offering any comments on that project.

Podgorny referred extensively to the Asian collective security scheme in his banquet speech, but Daoud glossed over it in his statement. With respect to Afghan–Pakistani relations, Daoud's speech was less stringent than his previous one in Moscow. However, in his statement, Podgorny did not refer to this issue at all.

The Kabul communiqué was agreed to a few hours before Podgorny departed for Moscow. Both sides expressed their firm "determination to do everything possible to develop still further Soviet–Afghan friendly relations and fruitful cooperation between the two countries in political, trade, economic, cultural, and other spheres." They regarded these relations as "the valuable property of the peoples of the two countries."[64] As far as the Asian collective security scheme and Afghan–Pakistani difference were concerned, the joint communiqué simply reconfirmed the formulations adopted in June 1974.

There were some differences in language between the Moscow communiqué of 1974 and the one issued at the conclusion of Podgorny's visit. Instead of the word *cordiality*, the communiqué spoke of "mutual trust, mutual understanding, *frankness*, and good will." Some analysts have stated that use of the word *frankness* by the Russians, according to Soviet diplomatic jargon, indicated trouble in Russo–Afghan relations.[65] However, the word *frankness* was used in conjunction with expressions that in no way could indicate the worsening of relations between the two countries. Besides, it is only fair to point out that the word *frankness* figured in the original draft communiqué prepared by the host country and was not included in the text by the Soviets. In retrospect, one can reasonably assume that the Russians had probably begun to reappraise their attitude toward Daoud, but at that stage there were no indications they had done so.

A protocol extending the 1931 Soviet–Afghan friendship and nonaggression treaty for a further period of ten years was signed by Daoud and Podgorny on December 10. The Russians, always fond of pompous ceremonies, seemed very happy about this rather hollow event.

By mid-1976, Moscow had become actively involved in bringing together the two rival factions of the PDPA, Parcham and Khalq, into one unified party (see Chapter 5). Undoubtedly this had been undertaken as a means of salvaging the Afghan Communist party and preparing it for more important tasks, after the Russians realized that the divorce between Daoud and the left was final. The Russians, who conceived of the PDPA as an instrument of their policy and were naturally concerned about its future prospects, could not tolerate its likely annihilation. So long as Russian interests warranted it, the PDPA could be kept on the back burner, but the moment it was sensed that a more firm Soviet presence in Afghanistan was necessary, the PDPA had to be called upon to discharge its responsibilities, as determined by Moscow.

Some Afghans close to the circle of power believed that, when the time came for the Russians to take over Afghanistan, they would want to avoid intervening militarily and occupying it by force of arms. They were of the opinion that the Russians viewed these as anachronistic options that could result in too many unwanted complications. These Afghans held the view that the Soviets would move into Afghanistan under the guise of a Communist takeover perpetrated by the local Communists. But such an undertaking would necessitate the existence of a strong and united PDPA that could shoulder the responsibilities of a Russian proxy and bring to fruition the Soviet Union's immediate and long-range aims in Afghanistan.

Viewed against the background of such perceptions, the intensification of Russian efforts to unite Parcham and Khalq were disturbing to many Afghans. Although Mohammad Douad was also concerned about the eventual union between Parcham and Khalq and viewed its purpose as hostile to the Afghan republic, he thought that the animosity between the leaders of the two factions of the PDPA was so deeply rooted that the fusion would be temporary and of no real use to the USSR. Mohammad Daoud held the view that, whenever the Russians decided to occupy Afghanistan, they would go about it through staging a coup by local Communists and would draw for that purpose exclusively from those in the military establishment. He believed, however, that, for administering the country and tightening their hold on it, the Russians would need to buttress rather quickly the military conspirators who had seized power by bringing into the governing apparatus a group of knowledgeable and well-disciplined civilian Communists. Daoud was of the opinion that the current leaders of neither Parcham nor Khalq, nor the combination of the two, could usefully serve Soviet interests, because of their extreme incompetence, their intrinsic weaknesses, and their lack of popular support. He did not think the Russians were foolish enough to rely on the present Parchami and Khalqi leadership for furtherance of their interests in Afghanistan. He inclined toward believing that, while the Russians exerted efforts to merge the Parchami and Khalqi cadres into one strong Communist party as an instrument of their policy, they would try at the same time to recruit and train an entirely new leadership for the PDPA. This thinking implied that the reconstruction of the PDPA into one effective Communist unit would take time.

Daoud differed in this opinion from many of his close associates, who believed that Russia, in propping up the Communist organization in Afghanistan, would put its weight behind a united PDPA under its present leaders because of their proven loyalty to Russia, a characteristic to which Moscow attached the greatest importance. They suggested that an added reason for the Soviets to cling to the Parchami–Khalqi leadership was that Russian conservatism abhorred experimenting with new ideas and new people, especially in a foreign country, where unknown pitfalls could slow down efforts at recruitment and organization and result in embarrassments.

While these differences of opinion regarding when the PDPA would be deemed ready to move into action were being aired, Mohammad Daoud was miffed by flagrant Soviet interference in Afghan internal affairs, as exemplified by their increasingly active and visible involvement with local Communists. Although not unaware of Soviet long-term designs, he somehow could not reconcile himself to the idea that Afghanistan's staunch friendship for the Soviet Union and its unswerving nonalignment were no longer appreciated, or at least understood, by that country. He once said that Afghanistan's sincere friendship, its proven reliability as a neighbor, and its firm nonalignment should be all that mattered to the Soviet Union, adding that what Afghanistan did internally and externally was none of Russia's business. This somewhat simplistic conception of Afghan–Soviet relations made sense if one viewed Russian policies in south and southwest Asia as static. But if a contrary view, based on Russia's historical reflexes, known ambitions, and geopolitical imperatives, were accepted, such a conception became irrelevant.

During the second half of 1976, intelligence reports were continuously coming in depicting Russian subversive activities aimed at organizing and revitalizing the Afghan Communist elements. Daoud adopted a wait-and-see attitude and continued to refrain from mentioning the matter of Soviet interference in Afghan affairs to the Russian ambassador; likewise, he did not authorize any of the officials in the Ministry of Foreign Affairs to do so. The intention was to not embarrass the Soviets prematurely, and to take action against local Communists whenever enough hard evidence of their anti-regime activities became available. This evidence had to be of such an incriminating nature that even the Russian mentors could not deny its credibility or take issue with the ensuing punishment.

Undoubtedly, the Russians had become increasingly disturbed by the emergence of new and expanded ties between Afghanistan and its Islamic neighbors, a situation they may have feared could result in the lessening of Afghanistan's dependence on the Soviet Union and consequently of the latter's influence in Kabul. However, the Russians were finding it difficult to move overtly to reverse this unwelcome trend. Russia's relations with both Iran and Pakistan were good and improving. In all likelihood, the Soviet Union did not want to jeopardize these relations by approaching the Islamic neighbors of Afghanistan and asking them to desist from strengthening their ties with it. On the other hand, the Russians could not directly request the Afghan government to refrain from seeking closer relations with Iran, Pakistan, and the Arab states. Such a request would have drawn a negative response from the Afghans and, besides, would have not been in line with Russia's avowedly profound interest in the improvement of relations among the Asian states, an important prerequisite for the implementation of their Asian collective security scheme.

In spite of the fact that the Soviet Union must have been concerned about what was happening to the Afghan Communists and about Afghanistan's relations with other Islamic countries (especially Kabul's rapprochement with Pakistan and its expanding economic ties with Iran), Russian officials carefully avoided any inquiries or comments about these matters in their contacts with the Afghan leadership and members of the Foreign Ministry. Obviously that disinterested attitude was adopted on Moscow's instructions. We knew how feverishly they were probing other diplomats in Kabul for information about these developments and that they had even expressed serious apprehensions to a few about the new orientation of Afghan political and economic policies. I recall only one instance when a departure from that self-imposed restriction took place. In November 1976, at the end of a meeting concerned with other issues, Ambassador Puzanov asked me, almost in a whisper, whether the Afghan government was sure that Iran would deliver on its pledges of assistance to Afghanistan. And could Afghanistan trust the shah and his promises? I replied that there was no reason to doubt the sincerity of Iran's pledges of assistance. This uncharacteristic Russian aloofness implied that Moscow was going through a period of introspection and in-depth assessment of this new, multifaceted, Afghan situation, and it did not want its thinking to be known until the ongoing reappraisal was completed.

Meanwhile, economic cooperation between the USSR and Afghanistan appeared to be progressing normally. The Soviets "gave the Afghans $437 million in economic credit during 1975. In 1976 the two nations signed a trade agreement calling for a 65 percent increase in commerce by 1980. By September of 1977, the Soviet presence in Afghanistan was greater than that of any foreign power."[66]

While Soviet clandestine activities with a view to reuniting Parcham and Khalq were going on, Russian officials still kept silent about the new trends in Afghan foreign and domestic policies. They were regularly professing their faith in Soviet–Afghan friendship and describing the relationship as a "perfect model of peaceful co-existence between countries with different social and economic systems." This Russian deception lasted until the day the Daoud regime fell victim to Communist subversion.

As time went by, Mohammad Daoud became increasingly annoyed with the covert Soviet operations in Afghanistan. A couple of days after his election as president of the republic by the Loya Jirga, in February 1977, Daoud mentioned to Waheed Abdullah and me that the time had come for him to inquire from the highest authority in the Soviet state, Leonid Brezhnev, whether Soviet subversive actions in Afghanistan had received his sanction or were carried out without his knowledge. He would tell him that what was being done could in no way be construed as conforming with the expressions of cordiality and friendship for the Afghan regime constantly uttered by the Soviet leadership. He said that Brezhnev would have to tell him frankly what the Soviets intended to achieve by pursuing this course.

Thus, when in March the Russians invited Daoud to make his second official trip to Moscow since his return to power, he gladly accepted their invitation. In consultation with the Russians, it was agreed that the visit would take place from April 12 to April 15, 1977. On the plane to Moscow, President Daoud instructed Waheed Abdullah to arrange a private meeting for him with Brezhnev some time during his stay in the Soviet Union. He said that he intended to use that meeting exclusively for discussing the issue to which he had previously drawn our attention in Kabul. He asked that the Russians be given no hint about what was going to be raised at that meeting. Immediately after the arrival of Daoud and his party in Moscow, Waheed Abdullah informed the Russian protocol officer that President Daoud wished to have one private meeting with Secretary General Brezhnev at his convenience, perhaps some time at the end of the official talks.

The first round of official talks was held at the Kremlin late in the afternoon of April 12 between Leonid Brezhnev, Nikolai Podgorny, Alexei Kosygin and the Soviet delegation on the Russian side and Mohammad Daoud and his delegation on the Afghan side.[67] Gavrilov, a Russian Foreign Office official who had spent long years in the Soviet embassy in Kabul and who knew excellent Dari, was interpreting for both sides.

The first thing that struck me as we sat across the conference table from the Russians was Brezhnev's unhealthy appearance. The man was visibly very ill, much more so than we had heard from various sources in Kabul. His face was ashen and blotted. He spoke with much difficulty and often abruptly stopped in the middle of a sentence as if he had forgotten what he had started to say. His eyes were glazed; there was no doubt that he functioned, if function he did, with the help of some potent drugs. A colleague sitting next to me said in a whisper that he wondered if Brezhnev would make it to the next meeting. Ironically, Brezhnev not only made it to the next meeting but lived long enough to preside a year later over the process of the absorption of Afghanistan by the Soviet Union.

After a few words of welcome by Brezhnev to the Afghans, Daoud took the floor and conveyed his gratitude for the Soviet Union's aid to Afghanistan, especially its assistance in setting up and partly financing Afghanistan's first Seven Year Development Plan. With regard to economic matters between the two countries, he said that he agreed with the draft of the treaty on the development of economic cooperation between Afghanistan and the USSR and had given instructions to Ali Ahmad Khurram, the minister of planning, to sign it. Daoud told the Soviet leadership that, although the issues related to Russian economic and technical assistance to Afghanistan and the problems of trade between the two countries would be discussed by the Afghan ministers with their Soviet counterparts, he wanted personally to mention once again the necessity of reaching agreement on a new higher price for the Afghan natural gas exported to the USSR.

Daoud briefed the Soviet leadership on the improvement of Afghan–Pakistani relations and the development of closer economic ties with Iran and the Arab states. He said that Afghanistan had embarked on the construction of a new and, it was to be hoped, prosperous society that demanded considerable efforts by the people and the government of Afghanistan. In this undertaking, he added, Afghanistan needed the disinterested help of all friendly countries and was actively seeking that help. Daoud said that the assistance extended by the Soviet Union was greatly appreciated by the people and the government of Afghanistan and to a great extent had helped the country on the road to progress. He expressed the hope that the friendly relations between Afghanistan and the Soviet Union, which were based on good neighborliness, mutual respect, and noninterference in each other's domestic affairs, would further expand and develop.

Daoud further stressed the irreversibility of Afghan nonalignment and its significance for Afghanistan. He added that strict adherence by nonaligned countries to the principles and criteria of nonalignment would strengthen the movement as a genuine force for peace and stability. He said that, although on the whole the proceedings of the nonaligned summit in Colombo were satisfactory, they showed that some aspects of nonalignment needed to conform more closely to the basic precepts of the movement, otherwise it would lose sight of its mission and degenerate into another debating forum. Undoubtedly, the Russians understood that Daoud was alluding to the attitude of countries like Cuba who were trying to push the nonaligned movement toward supporting Soviet policies.

Podgorny commented that the Soviet Union welcomed the improvement that had occurred in relations between Afghanistan and Pakistan, which he said contributed to normalization of relations between countries in southwest Asia. In his observations he completely ignored that part of Daoud's presentation relating to the expansion of Afghanistan's economic cooperation with Iran and the Arab states. I honestly expected from him some kind of subtle criticism of the new trends in Afghan economic relations, or at least some general remarks about the drawbacks of economic cooperation with capitalist countries as contrasted with the benefits to be derived from exclusive economic cooperation with the USSR and other socialist states. Any such allusion by Podgorny would have given Daoud a useful opportunity to elaborate further on the matter, and perhaps by doing so he would have succeeded in allaying to some extent the misconceptions that undoubtedly permeated the Russian mind with regard to the evolution of Afghan policies. Kosygin, who always seemed to listen attentively to what was being said around the table, told Daoud that the Soviet Union was aware of the importance that Afghanistan attached to the reassessment of the natural gas price and he hoped the Soviet side would be in a position in the near future to make a positive proposal to the Afghans, perhaps through the Soviet–Afghan economic commission.

Brezhnev, as if suddenly coming out of a trance, addressed the president and asked him if he could know his views about why the shah of Iran was stockpiling such massive quantities of armaments. He commented that the shah should not be afraid of the Soviet Union, since they had repeatedly assured him of their friendly and peaceful intentions. Did Iran, he asked, as a surrogate of the United States, intend to protect U.S. interests in the gulf area? If this were the case, he suggested it was an unwise policy. He pointed out that the United States was very far from the region, while the Soviet Union had a common border with Iran, and that, in case of a conflict, no arms buildup would counter this geographic proximity. Brezhnev inquired whether the smaller neighbors of Iran did not feel threatened by Iran's enormous arsenal of weaponry. Daoud replied that, in his view, Iran was not pursuing a militarily aggressive policy in the region, and Afghanistan certainly did not feel threatened by the Iranian arms buildup. He added that, although he did not approve of such disproportionate expenditure on armaments because it deprived Iran of funds needed for its social and economic development, he had not discussed the matter with the shah in the spring of 1975 or subsequently with any other Iranian official. Daoud said that, in his opinion, Iran's arms buildup could be explained by the shah's desire for Iran to be perceived as a strong military power, because that kind of perception would act as a deterrent to aggression, would give Iran a stronger voice in regional and Asian affairs, and would enhance its prestige, a matter to which the shah seemed excessively attached. Otherwise this arms buildup, he said, did not make sense, especially if viewed in the context of a Russo–Iranian conflict.

Daoud suggested that there was really no reason to be apprehensive about

Iran's alleged role as a "regional gendarme" or as an extension of American military power in west Asia. He observed that third world countries, including Iran, still suffered from so many structural flaws and organizational deficiencies that they could not possibly fulfill such expectations in an effective manner, even with massive infusions of military hardware. Daōud referred to the poor performance of Iran's military in suppressing the Dhofari uprising in Oman as a case in point. Although it was obvious from Brezhnev's facial expression that he did not agree with all that was said by the Afghan president, he did not pursue the matter further. At this point the talks were adjourned until the next morning.

The Kremlin banquet that evening was a cordial and sumptuous gathering. Brezhnev was present but did not speak much. Podgorny referred to the Asian collective security proposal in his speech, saying that "we want peace and cooperation to be established between the Asian countries so that their joint efforts should guarantee security on the Asian continent."[68] He added,

but one cannot fail to see that the supporters of the Cold War [probably the Chinese] do everything to counteract the policy of detente in Asia also. They try to maintain tensions between Asian countries, they sow mistrust between peoples in a bid to incite countries against each other and provoke conflicts between them. The militaristic forces [probably the United States and its European and Asian associates, such as Iran] clutch at blocs and war bases that they established in Asia. The activity of the imperialist reaction [probably U.S., Israeli, and Egyptian] continues in the Middle East also. The will power and efforts of the peaceful countries should counteract these intrigues.[69]

Then, in a rather singular way, he stressed that

The role of the Republic of Afghanistan, which is situated in the heart of Asia, and its favorable contribution are very important. The Soviet Union and Afghanistan have a common approach to many urgent problems related to the contemporary situation in Asia and the rest of the world.[70]

Some of the Afghans present at the state dinner thought that Podgorny's remarks about the importance of Afghanistan's contribution to the solution of Asian problems was in fact a reminder to the Afghans that their country's geographical closeness to Russia did not allow it diversions from a common approach by both countries to "many urgent problems" and that Afghanistan's active participation in Asian affairs should, therefore, remain more congenial to Russian interests.

Daoud did not refer to Asian collective security in his speech at the dinner. He stressed Afghanistan's nonalignment, which he said was based on "the strong foundations of peaceful coexistence, mutual respect, non-interference in each others' domestic affairs, [and] non-participation in political groupings and war blocs."[71] Daoud stressed that friendly and good neighborly relations between Afghanistan and the USSR stood on the firm foundations of good neighborliness, frankness, sincerity, and disinterested and worthwhile cooperation.[72] He welcomed the consolidation of détente and wished that it would spread to all countries and continents, taking into account their national interests and legitimate aspirations and hopes.[73] He hoped that détente could contribute to removing the problems that "our planet faces today, especially problems stemming from the existing unjust economic order."[74] Although Daoud mentioned that "a political difference" still existed with Pakistan and, as a result of that situation, Afghan–Pakistan relations were not yet "normal good-neighbor relations," he spoke of improvement in this regard and added that "if we succeeded in preserving the atmosphere established as a result of contacts between the leaders of the two countries we can hope that an honorable solution to the political disagreement will be found in the future . . ."[75]

Daoud further indicated that "the people of Afghanistan strive to liquidate all the remnants of backwardness in various aspects of their national life, backwardness created by the domestic or foreign reaction so as to build a new and progressive Afghan society for the benefit of the whole people."[76] Daoud warmly thanked the Soviet Union for its "disinterested aid given before and after the proclamation of the republican system" and especially aid extended for the realization of the republic's first Seven Year Development Plan.[77]

Daoud had not been entirely happy with the Colombo nonaligned summit, notably objecting to its tacit acceptance of Havana as the venue for the next summit, which would enhance the role of Cuba in the movement. As a nonaligned leader delivering a major foreign policy statement, he did, however, express in his speech a few words of praise about the achievements of the summit. He had included those remarks in his speech on the insistence of Waheed Abdullah, who had concluded that the choice of Havana as the venue for the next summit was a fait accompli, and, therefore, it was better politics to accept gracefully what had happened in Colombo.

The next day it was the host country's turn to make its presentation. Brezhnev, as the head of the Soviet delegation, took the floor. Although seemingly less tired than the previous day, he still spoke with difficulty and perspired profusely. Brezhnev repeated a few words of welcome to President Daoud. He expressed his happiness that the Helsinki Accords on security and cooperation in Europe had been signed. He characterized that as a great step in the process of détente, which, in his view, was making progress in spite of difficulties. He cited the "militarist circles" in the United States and Europe and the "hegemonists" in the People's Republic of China as the main obstacles to the relaxation of international tensions and the consolidation of peace. He said that the Soviet Union wished to improve its relations with China, but it was the latter's fault if this had not yet been realized. He expressed his country's desire to see Afghanistan prosper and, to that end, promised increased economic and technical help. Brezhnev described Afghanistan's non-alignment as important to the Soviet Union and essential to the promotion of peace in Asia and hoped that the nonaligned movement would not fall victim to imperialist machinations and intrigue.

At this point, Brezhnev looked straight at Daoud and said something that seemingly made Gavrilov, the interpreter, quite uncomfortable. But, after a brief pause, he hesitatingly translated Brezhnev's words, and what we heard was both crude and unexpected: Brezhnev complained that the number of experts from NATO countries working in Afghanistan in bilateral ventures, as well as in the UN and other multilateral aid projects, had considerably increased. In the past, he said, the Afghan government at least did not allow experts from NATO countries to be stationed in the northern parts of the country, but this practice was no longer strictly followed. The Soviet Union, he continued, took a grim view of these developments and wanted the Afghan government to get rid of those experts, who were nothing more than spies bent on promoting the cause of imperialism.

A chill fell on the room. Some of the Russians seemed visibly embarrassed, and the Afghans appeared greatly displeased. I looked at Daoud, whose face had grown hard and dark. Brezhnev had stopped talking, as if he were waiting for an answer from the Afghan president. In a cold, unemotional voice Daoud gave Brezhnev his reply, which apparently was as unexpected to the Russians as Brezhnev's words had been to us. He told Brezhnev that what was just said by the Russian leader could never be accepted by the Afghans, who viewed his statement as a flagrant interference in the internal affairs of Afghanistan. He went on to say that Afghanistan greatly appreciated its ties with the Soviet Union, but this partnership must remain the partnership of equals. Daoud added, and I remember clearly his exact words,

we will never allow you to dictate to us how to run our country and whom to employ in Afghanistan. How and where we employ the foreign experts will remain the exclusive prerogative of the Afghan state. Afghanistan shall remain poor, if necessary, but free in its acts and decisions.

After saying this, Daoud abruptly stood up. All the Afghans did the same. Daoud nodded slightly to the Russians and started walking toward the exit of the huge conference room. At this point, Brezhnev, as if emerging from a state of shock, rose from his chair with some difficulty. Accompanied by his two colleagues, Podgorny and Kosygin, and followed by the Russian interpreter, he took hurried steps toward Daoud. It was clear that he intended to repair the damage done. Waheed Abdullah and I, who were walking close to the president, saw the Russians coming. Waheed Abdullah whispered to Daoud that, for the sake of diplomatic niceties, it was advisable to take leave of the Russians properly, otherwise the visit to Moscow would be a total fiasco. He pleaded with him more than once before Daoud paused and turned back. The anger had gone from his face. He advanced towards the Russians and shook Brezhnev's extended hand. Sporting a big smile, Brezhnev said "I am told that Your Excellency wishes to have a private meeting with me; I am at your disposal. We shall meet whenever it is convenient for you." Daoud replied in a clear, loud voice for all to hear, "I wish to inform Your Excellency that there is no longer any need for that meeting." Having said that, he shook Podgorny's and Kosygin's hands and quickly walked out of the room. That was the last time that Daoud met Brezhnev. The interrupted meeting between the two delegations was never resumed, and the Russians' presentation remained unfinished.

Nothing like Brezhnev's words to Daoud had ever been heard before in any high-level Russo–Afghan meeting. It was obviously an intentional outburst by which Brezhnev had wanted to demonstrate the Soviet annoyance with the new trends in Daoud's domestic and external policies. He did it in a manner that he knew would be most displeasing to Daoud, by telling him to deal with an internal matter according to Russian wishes. But if he had wanted at the same time to chide and embarrass Daoud, his ploy had backfired pitifully, for he had received a formidable dressing down from the Afghan president in front of his peers and most of his close associates.

It has been speculated by some commentators that the Moscow incident marked the beginning of the end for Daoud. Undoubtedly Russo–Afghan ties were qualitatively impaired by it. That brusque exchange between the two leaders dramatically brought into the open the frustration that lay under the seemingly serene relations between the two countries and highlighted the fundamental differences that existed in their conceptions of friendship and cooperative assistance.

The next day, contacts between the two delegations continued as if nothing had happened. The treaty on the development of economic cooperation between Afghanistan and the USSR, which extended Russian economic and technical assistance to Afghanistan in various fields for another twelve years and enlarged the scope of that assistance, was signed by Ali Khurram and S. A. Skachkov.[78] Specific projects in these fields were to be identified and agreed upon by both sides. Agreement was also easily reached on the text of the joint communiqué. It was essentially the same as the 1974 Moscow communiqué and the one adopted in Kabul in 1975, particularly those parts pertaining to the Asian collective security scheme and Afghanistan's dispute with Pakistan. The standard statements with regard to the positive state of Russo–Afghan relations sounded hollow after what had happened between Daoud and Brezhnev, but no outsider was supposed to know about that dramatic incident.

One new point in the communiqué was the endorsement by the parties of "the idea that all countries who signed the final act of the European Conference [the Helsinki Accords] should conclude a treaty on abstaining from dealing the first nuclear strike against each other."[79] The "idea," of course, belonged to the Russians, who insisted that it should be included in the communiqué. Although the matter did not concern the Afghans directly and its controversial nature was known to them, they heeded Russian insistence and reluctantly agreed to a reference to it in the communiqué.

After Daoud's return from Moscow, Russo–Afghan relations continued as before. Although those of us who were associated on a daily basis with Daoud knew that he was extremely hurt by Brezhnev's offensive remarks, he neverthe-less counseled his associates to try to keep relations with the Soviet Union as friendly as possible. He told me more than once that, for the sake of Afghanistan's survival, the preservation of good relations with the Soviet Union was essential "even if now and then the Russians make it difficult for us to do so." He often said that Afghanistan, in its foreign relations, would never give cause for alarm to the Russians, but if Afghanistan's friendly intentions and its legitimate freedom of action were interpreted by them as contrary to their interests, there was really not much that Afghanistan could do about it. Daoud mentioned privately on many occasions, even to some foreign visitors, that it was his hope that the Russians, after so many years of association with the Afghans, understood the importance that Afghanistan attached to Russia's friendship. Daoud used to say that, if the Russians had correctly assessed this fact, they would never have had anxieties with regard to Afghanistan's actions. I remember that, in a meeting attended by several of his ministers, Daoud mentioned that the Russians were obsessed with the fear of encirclement, but it was high time they realized that Afghanistan would never be a link in the chain they feared would eventually be drawn around them. In his characteristically forceful manner, he added that the Afghan republic's nonalignment would always be genuine and that an unbiased analyst would never find Afghan policy to be in contradiction with any of the fundamental norms of nonalignment. Daoud continued by saying, "If the Russians wish to have a genuinely nonaligned Afghanistan at their borders, they must know that they have it. If they wish to have something else, we cannot provide that for them."

Although the Russians were conducting polite official business with the Afghans, it was known that they had stepped up their subversive activities, especially so far as the strengthening of the Communist organization in Afghanistan was concerned. In July 1977 the fusion between Parcham and Khalq took place, and it appeared that the Russians were inclined to keep the present leadership of the two factions as leaders of the united PDPA, at least for the moment.

It was a couple of months after his return from Moscow that President Daoud told me that the government should seriously consider asking the Russians to reduce the number of their diplomatic and nondiplomatic personnel at their embassy in Kabul. The unlawful activities in which some of these personnel were involved, he said, had gone far beyond the tolerable level. I told him that a decision to request the Russians to reduce the number of their embassy's personnel would be a very important political one, a decision that would certainly adversely affect Russo–Afghan friendship, which he always maintained should be safeguarded. I asked him whether Afghanistan was ready for such an eventuality. Daoud replied that he was well aware of the consequences that a request for a reduction of the embassy's personnel might entail, but cutting down the size of the embassy was important enough to be given serious thought. I told Daoud that certain people in the Russian embassy might be targeted for expulsion as persona non grata and that that approach might be considered less injurious by the Soviets than requesting them to cut down sharply the size of their embassy. He said that this was also a way of getting rid of the undesirable elements, but the size of the embassy's staff was really too big. I told him that the Ministry of Foreign Affairs would prepare a paper on the practice of states in such matters for his consideration. After a few days I informed him that the paper was ready. He told me to give it to him at some future date. In the months to come, several times I mentioned the issue to Daoud, but, while he had not changed his basic position, he seemingly had become more concerned about the implications of such a demand. Consequently, Daoud never read the paper prepared by the foreign minister, and no decision was made on that matter.

In October 1977 frequent overflights of Afghan airspace by Russian transport aircraft, Tupolev and Antonev 22, were reported. It was later confirmed by other sources that these overflights were part of a massive weapon airlift to Ethiopia to prop up that country's armed forces in its war with Somalia. The Russian transport aircraft were avoiding Iranian airspace, where radar surveillance was intense, by overflying Afghanistan and Pakistan. From Pakistan, the transports flew over the Arabian Sea to Aden, where they refueled and continued to Ethiopia. On several occasions Russian aircraft even landed in Karachi for refueling. These landings were authorized by the Pakistani authorities, who were led to believe that the aircrafts' cargo consisted of farm machinery. It was said that, on one occasion while a plane was being refueled in Karachi, the real nature of the cargo was discovered, to the great embarrassment of both the Russians and the Pakistanis. The landings were henceforth discontinued, but the Pakistanis, probably for political reasons, thought it wise not to publicize the incident.

Daoud wanted the Soviets to be given a stiff note of protest for these violations of Afghan airspace. He changed his mind, however, and instructed the Foreign Ministry to refrain from giving the note to the Russians, probably wishing to avoid irritating or embarrassing them at a time of mounting tension in Russo–Afghan relations.

Meanwhile, in contrast, he continued to refuse relatively minor Russian requests. One such matter, for example, was the transfer of the Soviet Union's permanent industrial exhibition from an annex in its embassy, situated in the suburbs, to downtown Kabul. The relocation of that exhibition would have afforded the Russian presence in Afghanistan a higher degree of visibility, which Daoud apparently wished to prevent.

During the fall of 1977 some officials of the Ministry of Planning were complaining of a slowdown in Soviet participation in the development plan. There were also allegations that the Soviets had become evasive in negotiating contracts and agreements with some of the technical ministries. Usually the Russians were less forthcoming when negotiations got down to specifics; it was therefore not easily discernible whether their reported reluctance was part of a new directive or conformed to their customary practice. We in the Ministry of Foreign Affairs, however, enjoyed excellent relations with Puzanov and his colleagues. Under the supervision of the Afghan and Russian foreign ministries, the work of the joint Soviet–Afghan frontier commission, entrusted with the task of assessing the extent of erosion of the banks of the Murghab River and recommending means of correcting the damage and permanently strengthening the river banks at the frontier between the two countries, was progressing very well.[80] In fact, the Russians were showing themselves surprisingly accommodating in the talks that were alternatively being held in Afghanistan and the Soviet Union. Likewise, when a Russian frontier patrol was discovered on a small island on the Oxus River (Amu Darya) claimed by the Afghans, the matter was settled amicably by the Afghan and Russian frontier authorities, and the Russian patrol was withdrawn forthwith without the Ministry of Foreign Affairs having to use diplomatic channels. It was also in the fall of 1977 that the Russians informed the Afghans of their long-awaited agreement with regard to a substantial rise in the price of Afghan natural gas. According to Assifi, "they agreed to raise the price of gas by about 30 percent—from $16.10 to $21."[81]

Nonetheless, these instances of Soviet amicability did not provide any cause for satisfaction when viewed against the background of Russian subversive activities. Soon conditions would be deemed reasonably favorable for the Russians to do away with Daoud and bring Afghanistan under their direct control. On April 27, 1978, they launched the Communist coup and the republican regime fell to Soviet ambitions.

Notes

1. *Anis* (a Kabul newspaper), 18 July 1973. Translation from Dari by the author.
2. Ibid.
3. *The Times* (London), 27 July 1973.
4. Official Records of the Plenary Meetings of the UN General Assembly, Twenty-Third Session 1690 Plenary Meeting, 10 October 1968.
5. Quoted by Hyman, *Afghanistan Under Soviet Occupation*, 68.
6. Asian *Recorder*, Regd. No. D 727, vol. XX, No. 2, January 1974, 11785.
7. *Pakistan Affairs* (Washington, D.C.: Embassy of Pakistan, 1 December 1973). Khan Abdul Ghafar Khan, the prominent Pashtun leader, the founder of Khudai Khidmatgaran and an advocate of self-determination for the Pashtuns, had been in and out of British and Pakistani jails for years and had lived in exile in Afghanistan. Ghafar Khan was the father of Khan Abdul Wali Khan, then president of the National Awami Party (see note 10).
8. Ibid.
9. *Le Monde*, 3–4 February 1974.
10. The NAP had gained an absolute majority in Baluchistan in the Pakistan-wide elections of 1970 and was thus allowed to constitute the provincial government of Baluchistan in 1972. A coalition of the NAP and *Jamiat-i-Ulama-i-Islam* (JUI), a religious party, had won a majority in the NWFP. That electoral success had enabled a coalition of NAP–JUI to form the NWFP provincial government. Bhutto's Pakistan People's Party (PPP) had fared extremely poorly in the two frontier provinces but had won the majority of votes in Punjab and Sind. In East Pakistan (which later became Bangladesh), Sheik Mijibur-Rahman's Awami League had won the absolute majority. The NAP was the national party of the Pashtuns and the Baluchis in Pakistan. It stood for the realization of Pashtun and Baluch aspirations. Afghanistan had become increasingly supportive of the NAP and of the position of its leadership on Pashtun and Baluch issues. The NAP advocated friendship and close relations with Afghanistan. The

Pakistani establishment viewed the NAP with extreme suspicion. It was considered by Pakistani ruling circles to be working for the secession of the NWFP and Baluchistan from Pakistan. The standard accusation leveled against NAP was that it had never accepted the "ideology of Pakistan."

11. *Asian Recorder*, Regd. No. D-(c)-82 vol. XXI, No. 18, 3–13 May 1975, 125–67.
12. *Kessing's Contemporary Archives*, 17–23 March 1975, 27018.
13. Ibid.
14. Ibid.
15. Ibid.
16. Ibid.
17. *Asian Recorder*, 23–29 April 1975, 12557.
18. *Kessing's Contemporary Archives*, 17–23 March, 27018.
19. *Asian Recorder*, 5–11 February 1975, 12423.
20. Ibid.
21. *Asian Recorder*, 23–29 April 1975, 12557.
22. *Kessing's Contemporary Archives*, 19–25 December 1975, 27851.
23. Ibid.
24. Ibid.
25. Bhutto was accompanied by Aziz Ahmad, minister for defense and external affairs; Yusef Buch, special assistant to the prime minister; Agha Shahi, foreign secretary; and Shah Nawaz, additional foreign secretary.
26. This passage and others that follow have been recreated from memory. Although they are not perfect quotes, I am confident they are accurate accounts of what was said and what transpired during this critical phase of Afghan foreign relations. This confidence stems from the fact that my memory of the events, statements, exchanges, and conversations is extremely acute as a result of my close involvement and my awareness at the time of their historical significance.
27. For the full text of the communiqué, see the *Kabul Times*, 12 June 1976.
28. Members of the Afghan delegation in the talks with the Pakistanis were Waheed Abdullah; Dr. Rahim Sherzoy, Afghan chargé d'affaires in Islamabad; Mohammad Gul Jahangiri, director of the first political bureau; Abdul Ahad Nasser Ziayee, deputy chief of the foreign minister's secretariat; and me.
29. All quotations from the Shalimar speech are from the *Kabul Times*, 23 August 1976.
30. *Kabul Times*, 23 August 1976.
31. The remnants of the outlawed NAP that had not been jailed, had taken part, along with some elements of other opposition parties, in the 1977 March elections under the banner of the National Democratic Party. They were overwhelmed by the PPP, which was victorious in all the provinces. Later all opposition parties gathered together in the Pakistan National Alliance.
32. Etemadi was arrested in Kabul by the Communists after their takeover of Afghanistan and subsequently "disappeared" from his prison when he was apparently killed.
33. General Zia-ul-Haq was not the head of state of Pakistan but the head of its government. Choudhry was still the president of Pakistan.
34. The members of Daoud's official delegation were Waheed Abdullah; Ambassador Noor Ahmad Etemadi; Mohammed Gul Jahangiri, director of the first political bureau, Ministry of Foreign Affairs; Abdul Ahad Nasser Ziayee, deputy chief of the foreign minister's secretariat; and I.
35. *Asian Recorder*, 26 March–1 April 1978, 14237.
36. Translation from Dari by a learned friend who wished to remain unnamed.
37. *Asian Recorder*, 26 March–1 April 1978, 14237.
38. Ibid.
39. Ibid.
40. Ibid.
41. Selig S. Harrison, *In Afghanistan's Shadow* (New York: Carnegie Endowment for International Peace, 1981), 81. (Emphasis added.)
42. See, for example, speeches by Waheed Abdullah, *Official Records of the Plenary Meetings of the UN General Assembly*, Thirty-first Session (1976) and Thirty-second Session (1977).
43. Conversations with Mohammad Naim in late 1973.
44. *Kabul Times*, 2 November 1974.
45. Bradsher, *Afghanistan and the Soviet Union*, 24. Presumably the sum mentioned was spent since the inception of U.S. aid in the 1950s.

46. *Kabul Times*, 9 August 1976.
47. *Pravda*, 31 July 1973.
48. *Life Magazine*, 9 April 1956. By "supply and communications facilities" the Russian probably meant grain silos, gasoline storage tanks, and all-weather roads.
49. Bradsher, *Afghanistan and the Soviet Union*, 64.
50. *Kabul Times*, 6 June 1974.
51. Ibid.
52. Ibid.
53. For an interesting account of Afghan natural gas and its export to the USSR, see Abdul Tawab Assifi, "The Russian Rope: Soviet Economic Motive and the Subversion of Afghanistan," *World Affairs* 145 (Winter 1983): 253–64.
54. The Afghans had a pretty clear idea of what the price of their natural gas should be. They had studied the matter intently and had collected data by sending technical missions to nonaligned gas-producing countries, notably Algeria.
55. Quoted in Alvin Z. Rubinstein, *Soviet Policy Toward Turkey, Iran and Afghanistan* (New York: Praeger, 1982), 140.
56. Quoted in Ibid., 144.
57. *Kabul Times*, 9 June 1974.
58. Ibid.
59. Ibid.
60. Assifi, *"The Russian Rope,"* 264.
61. Ibid., 263.
62. Ibid.
63. The advance of Russian power in Africa, spearheaded in 1975 by the deployment of 20,000 Cuban troops in Angola, airlifted and seaborne by the Soviet Union, and the rapid expansion of this power to the strategically important region of the Horn of Africa had been of concern to the Afghan leadership. This concern was caused not only by reconfirmation of Russia's expansionist policies but also by U.S. inaction and lack of resolve to effectively oppose aggressive Russian moves. It was understandable that such a situation could be disturbing for a country like Afghanistan, living under the unavoidable shadow of a northern neighbor bent on expanding its influence even to regions situated thousands of miles away from its recognized frontiers. Waheed Abdullah and I on several occasions pointed out the gravity of the matter to U.S. ambassador Eliot and shared with him our concern about the spread of Soviet influence in Africa.
64. *FBIS/USSR International Affairs, South Asia III* J 1, 17 December 1975.
65. Bradsher, *Afghanistan and the Soviet Union*, 64 (emphasis added). It should be noted that the joint communiqué issued at the end of Mohammad Daoud's visit to Moscow in April 1977 referred to the Afghan–Soviet talks during that visit as having taken place in an "atmosphere of trust, friendship and understanding." There was no mention of frankness, but the word *friendship* was prominent. However, at that stage, relations between Afghanistan and the Soviet Union were showing signs of stress, and as the reader will discover later in this chapter, those talks could in no way be described as having taken place in "an atmosphere of trust, friendship and understanding." It is, therefore, not prudent to rely only on the wording of a communiqué between two countries to assess the nature of their relations at a given moment or to attach too much importance to the purported meaning of certain words in "the Soviet diplomatic jargon."
66. Alfred L. Monks, *The Soviet Intervention in Afghanistan* (Washington, D.C. and London: American Enterprise Institute, 1981), 14.
67. The Soviet leaders were accompanied by Andrei Gromyko, minister of foreign affairs; Semen Skachbov, chairman of the state committee for foreign economic contacts; Alexander Puzanov, USSR ambassador to Afghanistan; and a few other Russian officials. Daoud was accompanied by Mohammad Khan Jalalar, minister of trade; Ali Ahmad Khurram, minister of planning; Jumah Mohammad Mohammadi, minister of water resources and power; Waheed Abdullah, minister in charge of foreign affairs; Ali Ahmad Popal, Afghan ambassador to Moscow; Mrs. Rafik, head of the foreign minister's secretariat; a few other members of the Foreign Ministry including one official who spoke fluent Russian; and me.
68. *FBIS/USSR International Affairs, South Asia III*, 13 April 1977, J4.
69. Ibid., J5.
70. Ibid.

71. Ibid., J6.
72. Ibid.
73. Ibid., J7.
74. Ibid.
75. Ibid., J8.
76. Ibid.
77. Ibid., J9.
78. Fields involving Russian economic and technical assistance included development of gas, oil, petrochemical, and chemical industries; irrigation; transport and communcation; public health; veterinary sciences; geological prospecting for oil, gas, and solid minerals, among others.
79. *FBIS/USSR International Affairs, South Asia, III*, 18 April 1977, J2.
80. The Murghab River has its source in Afghanistan and crosses into Soviet Uzbekistan.
81. Assifi, "The Russian Rope," 256. Assifi stated that, just a few days before the Soviet coup of April 1978, the Russians once again raised the price of gas to $37 per 1,000 cm^3, "making the price retroactive for three years."

8

The Downfall of the Republic

The 1978 Coup

Mohammad Daoud had seized power primarily with the help of Communist military officers. As part of the price for their help, he had to include them in the government apparatus. However, the number of leftists and their sympathizers appointed to sensitive jobs by their fellow Communists in positions of importance in the cabinet and the administration quickly reached alarming proportions. The Ministry of the Interior, for example, headed by Faiz Mohammad, a well-known Communist (Parchami) officer, who was intimately involved in Daoud's coup d'état, absorbed like a sponge almost all the unemployed Marxist–Leninists roaming the streets of Kabul. The Ministries of Education and of Information and Culture, important targets of infiltration, followed closely.

The army, of course, contained a core of Soviet-trained Communist officers. Contrary to widely held beliefs, their number was not more than around 800; the majority of the officer corps was patriotic and devoutly Muslim. But the Communists were politically motivated and extremely active. Emboldened by their participation in the successful military takeover, the Communist officers, in their contacts with military and civilian bureaucrats, systematically conveyed the impression that their political stance had received the sanction of Mohammad Daoud. They were openly boasting of being "king makers" and the "power behind the throne," capable of protecting and promoting their protégés. This led opportunists, particularly in the army, to jump on the bandwagon of the "heroes of the revolution."[1] Daoud realized the seriousness of the rapidly growing Communist influence in the military and in civilian administration, but his political acumen prevented him from taking immediate action. He knew in particular that weeding out and neutralizing the Communists in the army would be a lengthy and delicate undertaking, because it would have to be accomplished at a minimum risk to domestic stability and to Afghan–Soviet relations. Therefore, at the early and sensitive stage of the republic, a certain degree of accommodation, even of concurrence with

187

Communist excesses, was inevitable to allow for consolidation of the regime.

In reorganizing the government and its military and civilian cadres, Mohammad Daoud decided to dismiss some highly placed officials of the previous regime and not to bring in a few who, as his former associates, expected to be reinstated in important jobs. These disgruntled individuals, many of them corrupt and notorious bribe takers, became the most severe anti-Daoud critics.

In the early years of Daoud's republic, three anti-regime plots were discovered. The importance of those anti-government attempts was greatly exaggerated, however, by the newly appointed Communist functionaries in charge of the Ministry of the Interior and its police department, who were keen on settling old accounts with their personal and ideological foes. These zealots exploited events for their own benefit, arresting scores of people and committing every kind of excess, including murder. Of those foiled anti-government plots, the most talked about was the one in which former Prime Minister Mohammad Hashim Maiwandwal was involved.

On September 20, 1973, Maiwandwal, along with forty-four non-Communist army officers (generals and colonels), exmembers of parliament, and merchants, was arrested for plotting to overthrow the new regime.[2] One of the most important members of the group was General Khan Mohammad, a former chief of staff of the army and a close associate of Daoud who had been dropped from participation in the new republican regime. After the initial arrests, the police jailed scores of others and accused them of being part of Maiwandwal's plot. Most of them, however, were only guilty of long-standing feuds with the leftists. News of Maiwandwal's participation in the aborted coup was received with disbelief by all those who knew him. He was well liked by Daoud and his brother Mohammad Naim the former minister of foreign affairs, who Maiwandwal had considered his mentor when serving in that ministry. Maiwandwal had hailed the advent of the republic and was believed to be in line for an important assignment in Daoud's government.[3]

Maiwandwal had the reputation of being an anti-Communist. He had a long history of antagonism to the leftists dating back to the days of constitutionalism. The Communists considered Maiwandwal's Progressive Democratic Party (*Massawat*), although embryonic and unofficial, one of the obstacles to the spread of their ideology and the furtherance of their interests. The Communists of the Ministry of the Interior must have been delighted when they were allowed to arrest Maiwandwal and his colleagues.

It seems that originally Maiwandwal's coup d'état was planned against the previous Shafiq government. After Daoud's takeover, he had tried to persuade his fellow conspirators to call off their coup, but the frustration of some of his colleagues with the new regime and the apprehension of the others that Daoud's alliance with the Communists might bring about conditions detrimental to their interests caused them to strike before the republic took deeper roots. The ease with which Daoud's coup had succeeded may have also encouraged the plotters to test their luck. It seems that Maiwandwal, already deeply involved in the plot, had no alternative but to give, perhaps reluctantly, his agreement. From the documents and the tape recordings of conversations between Maiwandwal and the other conspirators, it could reasonably be assumed that, at the time of his arrest, he had been a full participant in the conspiracy. Several of these documents, as well as confessions made by some of the plotters, indicated that Pakistan was also involved in the plot.[4]

Officials of the Ministry of the Interior had undoubtedly sensed that Daoud held a degree of sympathy for Maiwandwal, leading them to believe that he could eventually be pardoned and even reinstated. This they had to prevent at all costs. The surest way was to do away with Maiwandwal. They decided to strangle him and try to make his death look like suicide. On the night of October 20, 1973, a Communist (Parchami) police officer by the name of Samad Azhar, who was one of those in charge of the investigation, and a couple of his henchmen strangled Maiwandwal. (After the Communist takeover, Azhar became the chief of security in the Ministry of the Interior.[5]) Daoud very soon discovered that Maiwandwal had been killed by the Communists. This wanton act of murder infuriated him, but he allowed the publication of the official cover-up story, informing the public that Maiwandwal had committed suicide. By the end of the year, the court that tried the conspirators sentenced Maiwandwal to death in absentia. General Khan Mohammad was among those sentenced to death and executed. Others were given jail terms, and quite a few were released.

In late 1973 unrest was fomented by local Muslim fundamentalists, the Ikhwan-al-Muslimin, in Darwaz, a small town in the northern part of Badakhshan on the Punj River, at the entrance to the Wakhan corridor. The Ikhwanis had never been fond of Daoud and his progressive reforms. Although a devout Muslim himself, Daoud had reservations about the religious fundamentalists and, like King Amanullah, considered the reactionary element of the Muslim clergy and their followers unsupportive of his reform and modernization programs. The Darwaz incident was probably quite insignificant, but the Communists of the Ministry of the Interior made a great fuss about it and persuaded the government to send in security forces. The rugged terrain did not make Darwaz easily accessible by land, and only small planes could land on its primitive airstrip. The government commandeered three Bakhtar Airlines (the domestic Afghan airline) Twin-Otter planes and dispatched them, loaded with troops, to Darwaz. When the planes landed, it was found that the unrest had already fizzled out. That incident, however, gave a good pretext to the Communists in the Ministry of the Interior to accelerate their witch-hunt for Muslim fundamentalists. By mid-1974 a number of Ikhwanis had been arrested, and quite a few had fled across the border to Pakistan.[6]

Deteriorating relations between Afghanistan and Pakistan helped the fugitives find ready refuge in Pakistan. "Although by themselves of little significance, the Afghan fundamentalists were welcomed not only by like-minded circles of Pakistani Muslims, but also by the Bhutto government, which was quick to sense potential political advantage."[7] Pakistani authorities, under the direct supervision of Bhutto himself, took on the training and arming of Afghan dissidents. These were regularly dispatched by the Pakistanis to attack localities within Afghanistan, with a view to creating difficulties for the government. The Pakistani connection made it easier for the Communists of the Ministry of the Interior to justify their crackdown on the fundamentalists. Profiting from the situation, the Communists also arrested some members of the Muslim clergy whom they disliked, but who were not in fact Pakistani agents.

As time passed and the republican regime became stronger, Mohammad Daoud began distancing himself from the leftists who had helped him seize power. In April 1975, after his return from an official visit to Tehran, Daoud proclaimed in a speech delivered in Herat that the Afghan nation would not tolerate the introduction into Afghanistan of any "imported ideology" and would resist its spread with all the strength at its command. That by imported ideology Daoud meant communism was clear to everyone. It has been said that the Herat speech angered the Russians and made them realize that it was impossible to influence Daoud to follow their political line.

By the end of 1975, Daoud had greatly curtailed Communist influence in the government and the administration. In the shake-up that took place, the Ministry of the Interior was the first to be systematically purged of its Communist elements. When their turn came, the Communists in the other ministries were either dismissed or shifted to unimportant jobs.

There were a few known Communists in the Ministry of Foreign Affairs like Shah Mohammad Dost, who was said to have been recruited by the Russians while serving as a second secretary in the Afghan embassy in Washington, and Abdul Hadi Mokamel, a long-time friend of Dost. At the inception of the republic, Dost was Afghanistan's consul in Peshawar, and Mokamel was serving as Afghan consul in Quetta. As part of the Foreign Ministry's cleaning up, these two individuals were fired from their respective jobs, although Mokamel was appointed for a brief period as deputy minister of frontier affairs. (After the Communist takeover, Dost became deputy foreign minister for political affairs and, under Babrak Karmal, foreign minister, Mokamel became the deputy foreign minister for administrative affairs and later ambassador to Iraq.) Sakhi Daneshjo, another Communist, was counselor of the Afghan Embassay in Moscow. Before the decision to dismiss him could be carried out, the Communist coup took place, and he was saved from dismissal. (Karmel appointed Daneshjo deputy foreign minister for political affairs, but, after a short while, he was demoted to an insignificant job.) Screening of new applicants fresh out of the university for jobs with the ministry was not an easy matter. It came to be known later that, from among the young men who had been accepted in 1974, three were Communists, although one of them, Mohammad Farid Zarif, was in all likelihood nothing more than a clever opportunist. (This individual, under Karmal, was appointed Afghanistan's permanent representative to the United Nations.) I personally had my moment of surprise when I arrived at the Ministry of Foreign Affairs on the morning of April 29, 1978, to confront my fate after the Communists had taken over the country. The person who received me there that morning in the name of the "Democratic Republic of Afghanistan," seemingly in charge of the ministry's administration and security, was a certain Mohammad Akbar Mehr, a young and well-thought-of member of the Protocol Department of the ministry, whom everybody, including myself, had always thought to be a staunch patriot! (Later that day I was arrested and taken to the Ministry of Defense, while our former colleague of the Protocol Department looked amusedly at the spectacle.)

One after another, Communist ministers were also ousted from the cabinet. The incompetents and the vocal militants were simply dropped; the other few were posted abroad as ambassadors. By late 1977, there were no known Communist ministers in the government.[8]

The cabinet, purged of its Communist elements, had become a more harmonious body, although not as closely knit as Daoud would have liked. Three ministers who were close confidants of the head of state were considered by the majority of the cabinet to be ambitious politicians interested only in power and prestige: Said Abdullellah, the minister of finance (who, after the election of Daoud to the presidency, was appointed vice president of the republic); Kadeer Nouristani, the minister of the interior (who had replaced Faiz Mohammed); and, to some extent, Haidar Rasooli, the minister of defense. The general view was that they were corrupt and grossly mismanaged their ministries. There was considerable pressure on Daoud from various quarters to drop Abdullellah, Kaddir, and even Rasooli, but he stood steadfast at their side and never agreed to their ouster. Both Abdullellah and Kadeer later proved their loyalty by remaining and dying with Daoud when the Communists took over the presidential palace in April 1978. (Rasooli was not in the palace at the time of its takeover by the Communists. He was caught later and executed.)

Daoud had also begun to contain the Communist influence in the army. He was aware of the difficulties of the task. Any heavy-handedness in the matter was bound to be construed by the Russians as a direct challenge and might upset the whole structure of Russian involvement in the training of the armed forces and the procurement of Russian military hardware by Afghanistan. Sanitizing the army necessitated fundamental changes not only in Afghanistan's military cooperation with the Soviet Union but also in basic Afghan policies. The time had not yet come for such drastic measures. To the extent possible, the well-known Communists in the army were placed under discreet surveillance. They quickly sensed their unpopularity with the regime and accordingly reduced their political activity. It was no longer fashionable in the armed forces to advocate world revolution and the army's role in bringing it about. It seemed that, on instructions from Moscow, its agents in the military had changed their tactics. They adopted a low profile, feigning acceptance of the regime's political philosophy, which, to their dismay, was developing contrary to their aspirations. New arrivals from the Soviet Union were carefully scrutinized. Those officers found to be too pro-Soviet were sent to remote and isolated garrisons, and efforts were made to keep them separated from one another. As additional measures for containing the Soviet influence in the army, Mohammad Daoud had endorsed plans to send a number of junior officers to Egypt and India to train on Soviet-made weapons, and to reduce the number of Russian military advisers by confining them to the levels of brigade and division. In spite of these measures, Daoud remained worried about the army and the loyalty of some of its elements, so vulnerable to Soviet influence.

To render the organ of state security, *Massoonyat-i-Milli*, more atuned to new challenges, efforts at reorganizing it had been under way since the beginning of 1975. Although, in all likelihood, its chief, General Ismail Firman, was loyal, there was evidence of some infiltration of the organization by leftist elements. While identification of the Communists in the army had been relatively easy, and, while the police (Ministry of the Interior) had been almost entirely purged of Communist elements, ferreting them out of the state security agency proved extremely difficult. Unfortunately, not much had been achieved in this regard when Daoud's republic ran out of time and fell to Communist subversion.

Since the very beginning of the republican regime, Daoud had focused his attention on improving Afghanistan's economic situation. He believed deeply that the survival of the country depended on rapid economic development. As in the 1950s, growth was his prime consideration, and he worked relentlessly to make it possible. A prosperous Afghanistan, he used to say, would block the spread of Communism, whereas a poor Afghanistan would fall prey to it. He was anxious to see a strong and progressive Afghanistan standing proudly among the nations of Asia. That reward, he believed, justified certain social and political deprivations that the nation had to temporarily endure.

The traditional sources of foreign aid were obviously not sufficient for the economic development of Afghanistan as envisaged by Daoud. Besides, a diversification of aid sources not only was economically necessary but had also become politically attractive to Daoud. Happily, the oil boom in Iran and some other Arab countries had provided new monetary sources for development assistance, and Daoud had moved cautiously to tap these new sources. The subsequent improvement of relations with Pakistan further cleared the atmosphere for Islamic–Arab financial assistance to Afghanistan. Over a period of three years, a Seven Year Development Plan was prepared on the basis of internal possibilities and foreign pledges. The plan was launched in September 1976 with high hopes and guarded optimism. Obviously these positive steps and developments and their perceived beneficial consequences displeased the Communists.

In 1977, which seems to have been a watershed year for Daoud, a couple of events took place inside Afghanistan that distressed him considerably. Some of his close associates even thought that the strain caused by these occurrences had adversely affected his stamina and had hampered his enthusiasm for work. The first was a split in the cabinet that surfaced when the composition of the Council of the new Party of National Revolution, founded by Daoud and the only legal party authorized by the new constitution, was made public. A number of ministers who were not included among the members of the council (and who had firmly believed that they would be) reacted angrily by tendering their resignations. Chief among the dissenters were Waheed Abdullah, the minister in charge for foreign affairs, and Azizullah Wassefi, the minister of agriculture, both close to Daoud. For the president, this was an unexpected development. He thought that he commanded the complete loyalty of his colleagues and that none of them would allow any of their disagreements with him to emerge into the open. He suddenly realized that this was not the case. Although, due to Mohammad Naim's efforts, the ministers eventually resumed their duties, Daoud's relationship with them was never the same again. It was as if a sacred trust had been broken.

Another disturbing occurrence was the horrendous discovery of seventy-seven cadavers in various stages of decomposition in the basement of an asylum for mentally disturbed prisoners. An investigation quickly pointed to the culpability of the commandant of that establishment. It came to be known that he was a sadistic and demented individual who satisfied his base penchant by choosing from among the prisoners those without family or friends and disposing of them in the most horrible manner. He had been at this dreadful task even before the advent of the republic, but most of the killings had been committed in later years. That such a terrible crime could have been perpetuated over a long period of time without the authorities uncovering it was inexcusable and demonstrated to what degree the Ministry of the Interior, under whose jurisdiction that infamous establishment functioned, had been lax in its duties. The ghastly fate of those wretched prisoners saddened Daoud immensely. He told me that nothing in his life had shocked him so much. Undoubtedly, to that feeling of sorrow, a sense of guilt was added; he knew that, as the last resort, he the president was ultimately responsible for what had happened.

In July 1977 the Soviet Union, exerting direct pressure and using the good offices of the Indian and Iraqi Communist parties and Ajmal Khattak, succeeded in reuniting the Parcham and Khalq factions of the PDPA in a shaky coalition.[9] Since late 1976 there had been signs that some lower-level elements in Parcham and Khalq, in reaction to Daoud's negative attitude toward them, were willing to close their ranks to prevent their complete annihilation. Government measures, subtle but effective, that had prevented the Communists from being selected as representatives to the Loya Jirga of February 1977 and the nature of that constituent assembly's decisions—the adoption of the

new constitution; consecrating traditional Afghan values; acceptance of a
one-party system establishing the Party of National Revolution as the only
lawful party, which consequently barred the Communists from legal political
activities; and election of Mohammad Daoud as president for a term of seven
years—probably contributed to, and also to some extent accelerated, the
reunification of Parcham and Khalq. This was an event of significance, at least
as a reflection of Soviet intentions toward Daoud's regime. After all, the split
between Parcham and Khalq had existed for some twenty years, and the Soviet
Union until now had exerted no serious effort to bring about their reunification.
That it chose that particular time to reunite them was disturbing. It could only
mean that Moscow had concluded that the time to render the Soviet presence
in Afghanistan more effective had arrived and that conditions were fast
becoming ripe for the seizure of power by pro-Moscow Communists.

Mohammad Daoud was annoyed by the reunification of Parcham and
Khalq, but Mohammad Naim saw it as an ominous sign. One day in September
1977, while commenting casually on internal and external policies of the
government, he abruptly stopped and told me, "You know the gamble is lost.
We played our hand but lost. Sooner or later a small minority will seize power
and, by the force of arms, will rule over the entire people. Of course
Communism will never be accepted willingly by the Muslim people of
Afghanistan. But, I see rivers of blood flowing. . . ." By referring to the
"gamble" he was alluding to the decision in the 1950s to accept massive military
and economic assistance from the Soviet Union and to seek to ensure Afghanistan's survival through friendship and closeness with its northern neighbor. I
confess that, when I left Mohammad Naim that day, I was shaken.

Although the merger of Parcham and Khalq had taken place, it was known
that a cutthroat contest for power existed within the PDPA. Some Khalqis,
like Hafizullah Amin and his band, did not believe that the Parchamis would
accept the predominance of Khalq, which had a larger following. Probably old
animosities, coupled with the necessity of securing control of the party by
Khalqi elements, inclined Amin, who by then had become the active leader of
the Khalqi faction and had established strong ties with the military, to resort to
a more radical and effective method of eliminating the recalcitrant Parchami
leadership. No Parchami of stature was to be allowed to challenge Amin's
authority in an eventual PDPA government.

In August 1977, Inam-ul-Haq Gran, a pilot with Ariana, was gunned down
late one evening in front of his apartment. He was not a Communist but bore a
striking resemblance to Babrak Karmal and was unfortunate enough to live
next door to him. On April 17, 1978, Mir Akbar Khyber, a prominent
Parchami theoretician, perhaps ranking even higher than Karmal himself in
the party hierarchy, was assassinated on a Kabul street. Although no arrests
were made in connection with these killings, the predominant belief in Kabul
was that both men had been assassinated (Gran mistakenly) on orders from
Hafizullah Amin by his henchmen, Siddiq Alamyar and the latter's brother

(Alamyar became Amin's minister of planning and his brother president of the general transportation authority). Between those two assassinations, a number of lesser Parchamis died under mysterious circumstances.

These events kindled speculation that something of importance was brewing in the Communist cauldron. Perhaps the Khalqis were clearing out their potential rivals in anticipation of a seizure of power. Intelligence reports indicated an increase in the level of activity of Soviet Committee for State Security (KGB) agents in Kabul. Shedding the customary Russian secrecy and caution, Novokreshchnikov, the Russian deputy chief of mission at the Soviet embassy, and one of the most important KGB operatives in Afghanistan, personally visited Khalqis and Parchamis at their homes. On one occasion several prominent Khalqis and Parchamis were present together at a meeting he attended. According to intelligence reports, a major part of this activity was directed toward holding together the rival factions of the PDPA. In retrospect it can be assumed that Novokreshchnikov's activity and those of his cronies were was not confined to cementing the uneasy alliance between Parcham and Khalq and that they devoted some of their time to devising ways of bringing about the PDPA's cherished dream, seizure of political power.

In mid-March of 1978, the Afghans were treated by a foreign source to a sensational piece of news about the future of their regime. The British Broadcasting Corporation, during one of its commentaries in its Persian language program, mentioned that a military coup d'état against Daoud's regime was imminent. The finality of tone with which that commentary had been delivered greatly perplexed us in the Ministry of Foreign Affairs. I showed the transcript to Daoud, who seemingly had already seen it. He read the paper again and gave it back to me, but he said nothing. The same day, at a social gathering, I raised the matter, off the record, with the British ambassador. He said that probably there was nothing to it and that the BBC sometimes spoke off the top of its head. I nevertheless remained disturbed and could not keep my mind off that bizarre commentary.

As April progressed, Kabul became increasingly alive with rumors of some kind of move by the Communists. I spoke of those rumors to Daoud, who said that all rumors should be taken seriously. I am convinced that he knew of the planning of a coup, but he certainly did not know that it was going to be launched so precipitously. In fact, if Noor Mohammad Taraki, the secretary general of PDPA, who, after the Communist coup d'état, became the first Communist ruler of Afghanistan, is to be believed, and there is every reason to believe him in this respect, the coup was originally planned for August.[10] The Russians were probably hopeful that by that time they would be able to deliver a truly united PDPA, which, in their view, was a prerequisite for taking the offensive and ultimately governing Afghanistan.

Immediately following Khyber's murder on April 17, the PDPA accused the government, through the distribution of "night letters," of assassinating him as part of its campaign of liquidating the left. An unusual delay of two days took place between Khyber's murder and burial. Undoubtedly this delay was spent assessing the situation and determining if Khyber's assassination could be used for something more than merely embarrassing the government with marches and protests. In all likelihood, the Parchami and Khalqi leadership reached the conclusion that the murder had stirred their followers and sympathizers so thoroughly that they could be mobilized at that particular time into a highly motivated anti-government force, compensating for their numerical inferiority. They probably also agreed that advantage should be taken of what had happened, as similar galvanizing occasions did not present themselves often. The Communist leadership decided to use the galvanizing factor of Khyber's murder to stage large-scale anti-government demonstrations that would weaken the government's vigilance and capabilities. Accordingly, they must have advised the Communist army officers already designated to launch the forthcoming military coup to be prepared to carry it out earlier than envisaged.

A massive march in downtown Kabul by PDPA members, sympathizers, and onlookers preceded Khyber's burial. Though it was more a funeral procession than a demonstration, "a focus of the marchers was the U.S. embassy, where slogans against the CIA and imperialism were enthusiastically shouted by the youthful mourners."[11] The vehemence of the slogans, the defiant attitude of the party workers, and the ferocity of the speeches by leading Parchamis and Khalqis at the burial ceremony bordered on deliberate provocation and reflected a degree of confidence hitherto unseen at such leftist gatherings.

With the exception of Hafizullah Amin, all the leading Parchamis and Khalqis, including Taraki and Karmal, spoke at the burial ceremony. In their speeches they openly accused the government of Khyber's murder and expressed their conviction that Daoud had decided to liquidate them collectively or assassinate them one by one and destroy the PDPA. They exhorted their followers to end their silence and inaction and unite to overthrow by force the "despotic" Daoud regime.

After Khyber's burial, the government banned all demonstrations. That ban was scrupulously enforced. Thus, contrary to many reports in the West, only this one demonstration took place.

Daoud instructed Minister of Justice and Attorney General Wafiullah Samiey to determine whether sufficient grounds existed for legally prosecuting those PDPA leaders who had spoken at Khyber's burial. He was anxious to avoid any steps that would be interpreted within or outside Afghanistan as arbitrary and unlawful. Samiey told me that the president was obsessed with this aspect of the matter. After a week of meticulous investigation, Daoud was informed that PDPA leaders had violated the law and that, accordingly, they were liable to arrest and prosecution. Daoud knew of the risks involved in taking this action but felt that it was politically inadvisable to leave the arrogant attitude of the PDPA unchallenged. The government, after listening to tape recordings of all the speeches and to the legal explanation furnished by the

Office of the Attorney General, decided that the PDPA leadership should stand trial for subversion. Immediately, warrants for their arrest were issued, and they were picked up one by one by the police on the night of April 26.

One exception was made: Hafizullah Amin was not arrested. A number of Western writers have been mystified by this apparent laxness of the security forces. But there was no case against him; he had not spoken at the funeral. Ironically, the same was true of the Communist army officers; no legal action could be brought against them at the time.

It seems in retrospect that the PDPA leaders, anticipating their wholesale incarceration, may have asked Amin, the inveterate speaker, to refrain from speaking at the funeral for tactical reasons, so he could remain free and contribute to the launching of the coup. He was, after all, the liaison and the strongest link with the group of Communist army officers who constituted the PDPA's pivotal asset. It can also be imagined that the cunning Amin, foreseeing the government's action against the PDPA leadership, deliberately abstained from showering vituperations and abuses on Daoud and his regime, hoping that all his hated rivals would be jailed and he would be left in total control of the party. Nevertheless, on the morning of April 27, as a result of reports of suspicious activities going on in and around his house, the government also decided to take Amin into protective custody. With his arrest, all male civilian members of the PDPA leadership were behind bars.

According to PDPA pamphlets published after the seizure of power by the Communists, Amin, while at liberty, had had time to contact the Communist army officers and launch the military takeover. However, it is doubtful whether his absence from the scene could have made much difference in the unfolding of events. Undoubtedly the perception of the PDPA leadership was that the whole lot was going to be executed. The perception of the Communist officers, and that of the Russians, could not have been different. The officers and their Russian mentors could not allow this to happen. With or without Amin, the group of officers, composed of professional coup makers like Abdul Kadder (a deputy chief of the Air Force) and Aslam Wattanjar (an officer of the Fourth Armored Force) would have started the coup with Soviet blessings.[12] This they did around 11:00 A.M. on April 27, with Amin still in jail.

Although Amin was portrayed, after the successful conclusion of the Communist takeover, as a military genius (among other things), it is doubtful whether, in the actual carrying out of the military operations of April 27 and 28, he was more helpful to the Communist officers than the Russian military advisers. According to eyewitness accounts, these advisers never left the sides of their local comrades, exhorting them to action and helping them in every way they could. It is well known that the advisers were instrumental in sabotaging the armed forces communication system, isolating and incapacitating contingents loyal to Daoud. The advisers may have even taken part in the fighting. One eyewitness swore to me that he saw a "blond stocky soldier, who was definitely not an Afghan, advancing with Afghan regulars behind the shield of a tank and shooting his machine gun toward a group of loyal gendarmes not far from the Kabul Hotel." So much has been said by various sources about Soviet MiGs flying in from Tashkent to provide air cover for the insurgents and to "precision bomb" the presidential palace, where Daoud, his family, and his cabinet members were besieged, that it is difficult not to take the allegations of direct Soviet military involvement seriously.

Aslam Wattanjar moved his tanks from Pul-i-Charkhi barracks, where the Fourth Armored Force was stationed, into the city before noon on April 27 and at around 12:00 occupied the Ministry of Defense. A tank fired one unnecessary shot at the beautiful marble building, which was undefended. Then Wattanjar's tanks positioned themselves in front of the presidential palace, on the other side of the street. It is reported that, when the duty officer at Pul-i-Charkhi barracks asked Wattanjar where his column was heading, he replied that, in anticipation of a Communist upheaval, the minister of defense had ordered him to position his tanks at important points in Kabul.

By then the day had grown unseasonably chilly. Dark gray clouds were crowding the sky; a fine drizzle had started to fall. Inside the palace a cabinet meeting was in progress. Daoud was informed of the emergence of a crisis situation in Kabul. For reasons of safety, he ordered his family and close relatives to be brought in to the palace from their homes in the city, and, in his typically calm way, he asked his ministers to please proceed with their work.[13] At about 3:00 P.M. the presidential palace was almost surrounded by the insurgents.

Meanwhile, Lieutenant Colonel Abdul Kadder had gained control of Bagram Air Force base with the help of Major Daoud Tarrum, who "machine-gunned thirty surrendered Air Force officers, by way of example."[14] This gave the insurgents an advantage that could in no way be matched by those loyal to Daoud. As soon as Bagram was secured, jets and helicopter gunships began overflying Kabul, and, toward the end of the afternoon, first the helicopters and then the MiGs started to attack the presidential palace with rockets. The concerted aircraft attacks were sometimes so fierce that, at one point, it was thought that the palace's arsenal had caught fire, which it had not. Helicopter fire was also used to knock out pockets of resistance in and around Kabul. By early evening all government buildings, with the exception of the presidential palace, which was valiantly defended by the Republican Guard, had been secured by the conspirators. Radio Kabul, a prime target, was one of the first to be occupied. Some elements of the police put up a courageous fight in the Ministry of the Interior and in Pashtunistan Square, but they were overwhelmed and slaughtered to the last man.

The people of Kabul, who had never witnessed the kind of battle that was going on around them, were literally stunned. At 7:00 P.M., Wattanjar, assuming the title of Chief of Staff of the Revolution, and Kadder made the following announcement over Radio Afghanistan (the former in Pashtu and the latter in Dari):

For the first time in the history of Afghanistan, the last remnants of monarchy, tyranny, despotism, and power of the dynasty of the tyrant Nadir Khan have ended and all powers of the state are in the hands of the people of Afghanistan. The power of the state rests fully with the Revolutionary Council of the Armed Forces. Dear Compatriots! Your popular state, which is in the hands of the Revolutionary Council, informs you that every anti-revolutionary element who would venture to defy orders and instructions of the Revolutionary Council will be delivered immediately to the revolutionary military centers.[15]

Although Wattanjar was not well known to the public at large, there was no doubt about Kadder's political affiliation. It was clear that the Communists had taken control of the government.

At 7:30 P.M. I called an unlisted telephone number in the palace from my house and got hold of Waheed Abdullah. Surprisingly enough the telephones were still working in some areas of Kabul, but the system went completely dead at about 10:00 P.M. Waheed Abdullah sounded calm and asked whether I had heard the announcement on the radio. When I replied in the affirmative, he said that the situation was very serious. He added that the besieged palace was drawing heavy tank fire from almost all sides, but the aerial bombardment had ceased, probably due to darkness. I inquired about the president. Waheed Abdullah said that he was all right and that he had retired with Mohammad Naim and the rest of his family to an adjacent room. Waheed added that communications between the palace and all military units and garrisons in and around Kabul and in the provinces were cut off and that there was no possibility of contacting them. He said that it was hoped in the palace that the Eighth Army Division in Qargha (near Kabul) and the Seventh Army Division in Rishkhor (also near Kabul) would take the initiative and move on the capital.

A little later I was informed by a highly placed intelligence officer with whom I was well acquainted that all the Parchami and Khalqi leaders had been freed from jail by the insurgents. I was told that at present they were gathered on the premises of Radio Afghanistan, where they were adopting measures for the purpose of administering the state and that Puzanov, the Russian ambassador, was with them.

The Communist coup had apparently succeeded. After a lull, at about 2:00 A.M. on April 28, all hell broke loose. It seemed that they were blowing up the presidential palace. Flares lighted up the sky as bright as day. Wave after wave of MiGs and helicopters was attacking the palace as if the insurgents were administering the coup de grâce. Heavy aerial bombardment was also taking place in the direction of Karteh-Seh and Darulaman. It was learned later that the object of rebel air attacks there was the Seventh Division, which had succeeded in holding together and had begun its advance on Kabul from Rishkhor, in an attempt to reach the presidential palace. On the Darulaman Road, the Seventh came under the heaviest air attack and sustained a significant number of casualties. The Communists had complete mastery of the air and were using it effectively. After a while the Seventh reversed its course and dispersed into the countryside. It came to be known afterward that Minister of Defense Rasooli had succeeded in reaching the Eighth Division, stationed in

Qargha, but was unsuccessful in organizing its march on Kabul. From there he had gone to Rishkhor and stayed with the Seventh Division until its debacle. Rasooli was caught on the morning of April 29, brought to Kabul, and summarily executed. The pro-Daoud commanders of the air force and important military units like the Eighty-Eighth Anti-Aircraft Artillery Force, the Thirty-Second Brigade, and the Commandos had already been either incapacitated or killed by a handful of Communist officers in the early hours of the coup, in conformity with a well-coordinated plan.

It was a little before 4:00 A.M. on April 28 when the terrible noise suddenly stopped. An eerie silence fell over the city. We knew that the end had come. At the presidential palace the Republican Guard's resistance to the Communist onslaught had at last collapsed. Those valiant men, under continuous tank and air bombardment, had fought almost to the last man. The conspirators overran the survivors and entered the inner buildings. Mohammad Daoud had asked the ministers and the staff of the presidential secretariat to surrender and avoid unnecessary loss of lives. With the exception of Abdullellah and Kadeer Nouristani, who refused to leave the president, the others left him. It was around 6:00 A.M. that a throng entered the room where Daoud, his family, and the two ministers were staying. One of the insurgents shouted at Daoud to surrender. It is said that he replied, "I am not surrendering to a bunch of godless aliens." Whereupon the president, his brother Mohammad Naim, almost all of their families (including small children), and the two ministers were shot by the Communists. The same day the Democratic Republic of Afghanistan was proclaimed. All the ministers were arrested after the fall of the presidential palace. In the week following the Communist takeover, Wafiullah Samiey and Waheed Abdullah were put to death by the Communist government; the others were kept in prison.

Analysis of the Downfall of the Republic

Why did the Daoud regime, seemingly so well entrenched, collapse so easily and so quickly? To be sure, there is no ready answer. But one thing is certain. The sudden demise of Daoud's regime was not brought about or accelerated by street demonstrations or food shortages and student unrest, as implied by some Western writers. Any resident of Kabul in those days can testify that there were no street demonstrations (with the exception of Khyber's funeral procession, as described), or food shortages, or student unrest, either prior to the coup or on the day of its actual launching. One more thing is equally certain. What carried the day for the handful of Communist officers was their determination and, above all, Soviet planning and support. Very quickly the Communist officers took hold of the air force, in a meticulously prepared move, and made effective use of it. Once in possession of that devastating instrument of war (which was probably further strengthened by Soviet MiGs flying in from Tashkent), they were in a position to deny the loyalists, although far superior in number, any chance of reversing the course of the struggle. Recalling the events of that somber day in April, an old English verse comes to mind, making one ponder the vagaries of human fate.

In your straight path a thousand
May well be stopped by three.[16]

One often reads in Western writings about Daoud's authoritarian rule and his determination to gain total control over the political life of Afghanistan. It is suggested that his policies and style of government cost him the support of influential political groups, the right (probably referring to the religious fundamentalists) and the liberals, leaving him isolated and prone to leftist danger. In this connection it is necessary to be absolutely clear about one point. There were no organized political groups of rightists or liberals of any significance at that time that could have been made part of a political arrangement, although most of the cabinet and the high echelons of the bureaucracy were mildly conservative or of liberal leaning. Daoud's Party of National Revolution, the only legal party in Afghanistan at that time, was still embryonic and unorganized. It aimed at attracting all nationalist, reformist, and developmentalist forces and forging them into one single political unit. The Muslim fundamentalists had never been supportive of Afghan goverments. Their numbers were not large enough to have an impact on the political scene in Afghanistan, especially once they bore the stigma of collaboration with Pakistan.

Likewise, there had been no falling out between Daoud and "the traditionally important tribal and community leaders," as alleged by some analysts.[18] One hates to disappoint romantic "Afghanologists" for whom the vision of fiercely independent Afghan tribes in perpetual revolt against the central government will never die. But the dull truth is that, during Daoud's republic, apart from the brief unrest in Darwaz, no tribal uprising took place, and there was no hostility between Daoud and the "traditionally important" segments of the population to whom reference is made. Besides, we have to ask ourselves one basic question: Could the sympathetic attitudes of these segments of the population toward Daoud and their support for him, which, according to the analysts, was lacking, have prevented the success of the Soviet-backed coup d'état? I, for one, fail to see how that could have happened.

In spite of taking all the right steps, which should have brought about favorable conditions for Afghanistan's survival, the republic's policy failed in that respect. It is my belief that the policy failed for the simple reason that it could in no way cope with Russian expansionist ambitions toward the Indian Ocean and the Persian Gulf in the absence of a countervailing force in the region, such as the British in the nineteenth and twentieth centuries. In the late 1970s the Soviet empire had undoubtedly determined that the time was ripe for it to resume its southward move. No more cogent proof exists of this Russian determination than the absorption of Afghanistan itself, which, as a country, was of no great value to the Soviets except that it lay on its southern flank and was considered the key to the Indian subcontinent. Moreover, Afghanistan posed no threat to Soviet security, and Russian leaders knew that Afghanistan's nonalignment was totally genuine. The acquisition of Afghanistan was important, even if the southward drive beyond the Afghan frontiers was to be accomplished not by naked military aggression but by more surreptitious and contemporary methods of subversion and intrigue. In this context Russia's direct control of Afghanistan acquired greater significance and urgency when Afghan irredentism appeared to wane under Daoud and could no longer be used as a means of bringing about the eventual disintegration of Pakistan. Short of declaring its complete allegiance to the Soviet Union and becoming an extension of Soviet central Asia, which would have terminated its independent existence anyway, no matter what attitude and policies Afghanistan adopted, it would have fallen when the Soviets began to move. Afghan rulers have been blamed for opening their country to Russian takeover by accepting massive economic, technical and military assistance from the Soviet Union. However, Soviet assistance had only the effect of softening the ground for that inevitable takeover. Without that penetration Russia would have taken Afghanistan in a few days perhaps instead of in a few hours. This would have been the only difference.

Through long association with the Russians, Afghan leadership in general had come to know that Soviet power was expansionist, and, when it was time for it to move again in Asia, Afghanistan would be the first to get crushed, because of its geopolitical situation. The history of the Russian conquest of central Asia had also taught them that the Russian power advanced in bursts and, thus, the present pause was only temporary. They, therefore, entertained no illusions as to Russian aims, but, meanwhile, assiduously continued their work of developing the country, hoping that the international situation would change in such a way as to forestall, hopefully indefinitely, the materialization of Russian designs.

But that hoped-for change did not come. On the contrary, the situation developed in a way that seemed to favor the Soviet Union. After withdrawal of the British countervailing force from the Indian subcontinent and east of the Suez, the United States was perceived as destined to fill the vacuum. However, after a series of flawed experiments with military pacts, it seemed that, for a variety of reasons, the United States could not replace British influence in Asia. After the tragedy of Vietnam, the United States, handicapped by inhibitions unfitting a superpower of global responsibilities, became even more introverted. In addition, the complacency brought about by détente further weakened U.S. influence. China was encouraged now and then by the United States to assume a more assertive role in the containment of the Soviet Union. But, in fact, China even today appears to pursue only the fulfillment of its own particular interests, balancing one superpower against the other.

The U.S. attitude toward Afghanistan, an avenue through which the Indian subcontinent could eventually be overrun and the Persian Gulf's maritime routes threatened by Russia, had been one of remarkable disinterest. American policymakers had apparently concluded that Western interests could best be defended beyond the eastern borders of Afghanistan. Other considerations came to be added to this disinterest. Chief among them was the U.S. assumption that a more active U.S. involvement with Afghanistan would prove fatal for the latter, because Russia would feel threatened by a greater U.S. role there. Therefore, lack of U.S. involvement would increase the chances of Afghanistan's survival. This would have been true if Russia's posture were accepted as defensive, but, if it were agreed that the Soviets were bent on fulfilling their manifest destiny, that argument lost all its validity. Besides, when U.S. aid and its presence substantially increased in Afghanistan during the latter part of the cold war years, the latter's nonalignment did not suffer nor did Russia make any assertive move to terminate this state of affairs. On the contrary, a healthy competition set in between the two superpowers from which the development of Afghanistan benefited immensely. The irony of this American assumption has been well noted by a keen observer of U.S.–Afghan relations: "For unknown reasons, this fear of provoking the Soviets did not extend to other sensitive borderlands such as Turkey, Iran, and Pakistan."[18]

What the Afghans wanted was an effective and meaningful American presence in their country, which, coupled with Afghanistan's positive nonalignment, would offset Russia's predominance and discourage its eventual southward move. If British steadfastness had barred the way of the Russian advance in Asia, why could not American determination accomplish the same end? Granted, this was a rather simplistic view when one took into account the hard facts of contemporary international life, the corresponding responsibilities of the United States as a superpower, and its global interests. But the Afghans, imbued with a sense of history, believed in the correctness of their opinions and shared them freely with their American friends. In the last two years of the republic, it was clear that the Americans were acquiring a better understanding of Afghanistan's position in Asia, its problems, and the need for a sizable increase in American aid, which would have necessarily enhanced the American presence. But there was a long way to go for that presence to become effective and meaningful.

The impossibility of expanding at the time in Europe being well understood by the Soviets, they had determined that conditions were favorable for a cautious, expansionist move in Asia. In this new phase of Asian expansion, after a pause of almost a century, the incorporation of Afghanistan was to be the logical first step. One of the important factors that must have helped the Russians decide to resume their southward move was the state of readiness of their armed forces. Since the Cuban missile crisis of 1962, the Soviet Union had been methodically developing its military might, and by the early 1970s, Moscow appeared to be satisfied with what had been achieved. In 1975, Podgorny told Mohammad Daoud that Soviet military forces were now capable of pushing back any aggression by the combined forces of the West. Other incentives that gave definite shape to the Soviets' determination to move at that time were directly connected with Afghanistan itself, a country once described by Khrushchev to Mohammad Daoud as "the only window still open in the south through which the Soviet Union can breathe." The Russians had endeavored to assert themselves in Afghanistan as advantageously as possible, and by the early 1970s, they believed they had achieved their immediate aims. However, by 1975 they were disillusioned. Mohammad Daoud's crackdown on the local Communists, Afghanistan's success in diversifying its sources of aid, the eventual lessening of Afghan dependence on the Soviet Union, the betterment of relations with Pakistan, the consequent denial to Russia of permission to manipulate those relations whenever it wished, and the possibility that a Tehran–Kabul–Islamabad axis might emerge with a pro-Western inclination prompted the Soviets to perceive Afghanistan as rapidly distancing itself from them. All this obviously militated in favor of a more speedy takeover of Afghanistan.

After the confrontation between Daoud and Brezhnev in the spring of 1977, the Russians must have realized for certain that Daoud was not a man who would reverse policies in order to please the Russians. Probably it was after that meeting that the Soviets decided to do away with Daoud and the Afghan republic as soon as possible. The implementation of their decision to incorporate Afghanistan into the Soviet realm through a Communist takeover, however, was hastened by Soviet perception of a favorable international environment and the pace of events in Iran, and it was undoubtedly precipitated by the murder of Mir Akbar Khyber.

Among international conditions perceived by the Russians as favorable for taking a first step in the resumption of their southward advance was undoubtedly the lack of American response to their moves into Africa, which began in 1975 with their intervention in Angola. Soon much of the geopolitically sensitive area of the Horn of Africa fell under Soviet influence. Aden, at the western tip of the Arabian Peninsula and at the entrance to the Red Sea, had already become a Russian satellite. The surprising American inaction with regard to these important Russian gains undoubtedly emboldened Moscow and prompted it to entertain cautious optimism about the attainment of its broader objectives. If, at the same time, these actions by the Russians were meant to test American resolve, they must have been encouraged by the U.S. lack thereof. The Russians must have also determined that the United States no longer possessed any pressing interests to protect in southwest Asia and that, in any case, in the wake of the Vietnam war, the mood of the American public was such that it would not allow the government to get involved again in a conflict abroad, especially in Asia.

Relations between the United States and Pakistan were cooling also, especially as a result of their disagreement over Pakistan's nuclear policies. The gradual U.S. disengagement from Pakistan and the latter's evolution toward nonalignment must also have been construed as a welcome development in Moscow. A few months before the April Communist coup, Puzanov, who I am certain never spoke even privately without Moscow's permission, told me that the decrease in the American presence in Pakistan and the demise of the U.S.-inspired military pacts to which Pakistan belonged would certainly render Pakistan more receptive to the special and legitimate interests of the Soviet Union in the region. He suggested that the Soviet Union was also an Asiatic state, and, as such, was entitled to some specific and undeniable considerations. He added that he hoped Pakistan would now adopt a more accommodating stand toward Russia's "close friend," India. Obviously an increase in the vulnerability of Pakistan delighted the Russians, who saw it, among other things, as a contraction of American power and interest in Asia. On the basis of these considerations, Moscow must have assumed that the Americans would not react in any meaningful manner to a Russian move into Afghanistan.

For astute observers of the Asian scene, as the Russians were, the rumblings in Iran too were undoubtedly serious enough to prompt them to act, in order to position themselves more advantageously in the region by assuming direct control of Afghanistan in anticipation of important developments in Iran, especially after President Carter's visit to Tehran in January 1978 (which they no doubt interpreted as an expression of complete U.S. support for the shah) and the massive riots in the city of Qum later that month.

It is more than probable that the assassination of Mir Akbar Khyber precipitated the Russian move into Afghanistan, a move that had already been decided upon by the Kremlin. Local Communist leadership impressed upon the Russians that Khyber's murder had galvanized the rank and file and that it was doubtful that such emotionally favorable conditions for launching the Communist takeover could emerge again in the near future. More important, it is said that Hafizullah Amin had told the Russians that Daoud had decided to liquidate the entire Communist organization in Afghanistan.[19] This was something that Moscow could hardly allow to happen. Even an open and impartial trial of the Communist leadership, as Daoud was known to advocate, had to be stopped, lest at the trial the scope and magnitude of subversive Soviet actions in Afghanistan become publicly known.

There is, nevertheless, evidence that the Russians were hesitant to move forward the timing of the coup, principally because they were not certain about the strength of the recent union between Parcham and Khalq.[20] The Russians considered a complete fusion of Parcham and Khalq into a really effective PDPA a prerequisite for ordering the toppling of the Daoud regime and replacing it with a Communist government. They had no misgivings about the ability of the Communist officers in the army to carry out a military coup with their advisers' help. But that was not enough. For the purpose of controlling and administering the country, they needed the civilian cadres of the PDPA and a Communist government constituted of loyal elements closely linked to the Soviet Union. Besides, the Soviet Union believed that the continuation of the Parcham–Khalq rift not only would render the Communists ineffective in the task of carrying out Soviet directives but could also involve the Soviet Union, the patron, and mentor of the leaders of both of the factions, in an unwanted and costly rivalry.

However, it seems that the Communist leadership succeeded in persuading the Soviets to agree to launch the coup earlier than planned. It is said that the pathologically ambitious Amin, more than anybody else, was instrumental in getting the Russians to change their minds. He is purported to have told them that the unity between Parcham and Khalq was real and lasting and not a mere patchup that would disintegrate under the pressures of office. He further told them that the Communist leadership, having sprung from among the people, was completely attuned to their problems and aspirations. He reassured the Russians that he knew for certain that the people would welcome the Communists with open arms because they considered them the true representatives of the poor and downtrodden. Amin said that the Communists, having emerged from among the people, knew how to handle them and comfort the masses. He suggested to the Russians that they need not worry about the administration of the country, because the Communist leadership, having spent years observing and assessing the inadequacies, and also the successes, of the monarchy and of the Daoud regime, was now totally familiar with all aspects of the goverment.[21] The Russians were probably rushed into accepting Amin's solicitations after hearing of the mass arrest of the Communist leadership by the security forces. The Soviets agreed that the Daoud regime should be disposed of by lauching the coup on the morning of April 27, 1978.

There is no need to speculate whether the Soviets were aware of the planned coup. Without equivocation it can be said that the Soviets, for a variety of reasons had decided on Daoud's elimination. In the absence of Soviet complicity, no proxy of theirs would have dared undertake his overthrow and murder. There is no doubt not only that the Soviets were the originators of the plot, but also that they had assumed responsibility for various stages of its implementation.

The Communist coup and its denouement have been described earlier in this book. But it is appropriate to mention that, a few short weeks after the fall of Afghanistan to Communist subversion, all that Amin had presumably told the Russians proved to be no more than grotesque lies. The precarious Parcham–Khalq unity quickly fell apart, and their rift became open hostility, each trying to annihilate the other. Although Amin had boasted that the Communist leadership had emerged from among the people of Afghanistan, it quickly became apparent that the Communists knew nothing of the Afghan people's traditions, hopes, and problems, and, hence, they alienated them entirely. So far as governing and administering the country were concerned, the Khalqis and Parchamis proved to be extraordinarily ineffective, so much so that the Soviets had to import thousands of advisers to shoulder those responsibilities.

The Communist takeover, coupled with the ruthlessness of Taraki and Amin and their lack of awareness of Afghan customs and aspirations, prompted people in all parts of Afghanistan to rise in arms against the new rulers. The uprising of the Afghan nationalists against alien rule began almost immediately after the seizure of power by the Communists, as did the flow of Afghan refugees to Pakistan and Iran, fleeing persecution and hardship. Amin, who had replaced Taraki at the head of the Communist regime after having had him murdered, handled the insurgency lamentably inefficiently, in spite of massive Russian assistance. The Communist regime was falling apart under the onslaught of Afghan resistance.

The Russians, sensing that their easy gain in Asia through subversion might soon become an embarrassing loss, intervened militarily to save the situation. At that stage of Russia's southward move, the Soviet aim was the securing of Afghanistan by the establishment of a Communist regime there and not the introduction of their military force in that country. There is no doubt that the Soviet military occupation of Afghanistan in December 1979 was largely the result of the Russian desire to shore up the Communist regime. Consequently, the horrors of the Russian military "pacification" of Afghanistan were added to the excesses and atrocities of the Afghan Communists. (Very soon after the Russian troops invaded Kabul and installed Babrak Karmal as the head of the Afghan Communist regime, they executed Amin, perhaps partly because of the lies he had told and the bad advice he had given.)

Perhaps another motivation for the Soviet military occupation of Afghanistan was the heightening of the U.S.–Iranian crisis in the wake of the seizure of American hostages by Iranian radicals. The Russians were probably surprised that the United States did nothing to save Mohammad Reza Shah and his dynasty, and they may have assumed that Iranian intransigence about freeing the hostages could push the United States to act militarily against Iran. The Russians may have wanted to be better prepared by moving their armed forces into Afghanistan for any eventuality that such an American action could have brought about.

The Communist coup of April 1978 in Afghanistan had been generally perceived, particularly in the West, as an event of less significance than the occupation of that country by the Soviet army in December of 1979. The psychological impact of military aggression was far greater than that of the coup, which was viewed at the time by most observers as an internal Afghan matter, not directly affecting Western interests. There was also an element of shock involved: The West suddenly woke up to the dangers of the Soviet physical presence in Afghanistan when it saw the Red Army poised at the Khyber Pass. It was at that point that the West scrambled a semblance of opposition to Russia's move into Afghanistan, but it was already too late.

Almost unnoticed by the West, the Communist coup that toppled Daoud was the critical step in the new phase of Russian expansion in Asia. After the decision to seize Afghanistan had been reached, the only measure necessary for the Russians was to eliminate Daoud and replace him with a pro-Moscow Communist regime. Once that was achieved, the country was theirs, and, whenever their plans warranted the introduction of their armed forces into Afghanistan, they would do that comfortably "by invitation." And the Russians knew that any strategic point on the western, southern, and eastern borders of Afghanistan could be reached by their forces within a few short hours.

Notes

1. A favorite expression used by the press to designate the officers who had helped Daoud in his coup.
2. Hyman, *Afghanistan Under Soviet Domination*, 65.
3. I learned from Mohammad Naim in early 1974 that Maiwandwal was to be posted to Washington as ambassador.
4. I have seen written statements by at least one conspirator, a certain Zanghoon Shah, who had confessed to receiving large sums of money from Pakistani sources. The ambassador of Pakistan to Kabul, when invited by the Foreign Ministry to review and assess the documents and confessions tying his country to the coup, declined to do so.
5. This episode was narrated to me by Waheed Abdullah in late 1973.
6. Gulbudin Hekmatyar, who, after the fall of Afghanistan to Communism in 1978, became leader of one of the resistance organizations in Peshawar, was one of those who had fled across the border.
7. Hyman, *Soviet Domination*, 67.
8. Minister of Commerce Mohammad Khan Jalalar, who was retained in the cabinet, was suspected in some quarters of being a Soviet agent. Some time after the Communist takeover of Afghanistan, he was posted by Taraki to an important economic job. Babrak Karmal reappointed Jalalar minister of commerce.
9. Ajmal Khattak was the former secretary general of NAP, living in exile in Kabul. After the rapprochement between Afghanistan and Pakistan, Khattak had grown disenchanted with Mohammad Daoud, his benefactor.
10. Hyman, *Soviet Domination*, 75, and *Kabul Times*, 3 May 1978.
11. Hyman, *Soviet Domination*, 76.
12. Abdul Kadder and Aslam Wattanjar had participated in Mohammad Daoud's coup in 1973.
13. Neither Mohammad Daoud nor members of his family lived in the presidential palace, the former royal palace. Part of the palace was used as presidential offices, and its other buildings and living quarters were closed.
14. Hyman, *Soviet Domination*, 76.
15. The text in Hyman, *Soviet Domination*, 77, was helpful for translation from a Communist publication in Dari.
16. Quoted in Colonel H. D. Hutchinson, *The Campaign on Tirah* (London: Macmillan and Co., 1898), 187.
17. Nancy and Richard S. Newell, *The Struggle for Afghanistan* (Ithaca, N.Y.: Cornell University Press, 1981), 48.
18. Leon B. Poullada, "Afghanistan and the United States," 183.
19. Conservations with jailed Khalqis during my imprisonment in Pul-i-Charkhee prison near Kabul in 1980.
20. Ibid.
21. Ibid.

Epilogue

The Russians brought Afghanistan's independent existence to an end. In April of 1978, the tenuous game of survival was at last over for the Afghan rulers. The essential component of survival for Afghanistan had been the maintenance of a certain balance by the Afghans between their strong but conflicting neighbors. With the departure of Britain from Asia, that balance was upset. No other outside powers ventured meaningfully to replace Britain. In the absence of a balancing power and the necessity for speedy economic development, creation of a modern army, and attraction of political support for Pashtunistan, the balance was inevitably tilting northward. Consequently, the Afghan rulers had to make certain adjustments in their traditional policies. They chose to ensure Afghanistan's independence by seeking friendship and close cooperation with the Soviets. The Afghans wished to give Russia a stake in the preservation of Afghanistan's independence. But all this proved to be of no avail once the Soviets decided to resume their southward move. At times staunch nonalignment was thought to render Afghanistan immune to aggression from the north. But this also proved to be mere illusion. An elder had told me, on the day that the Salang Tunnel was being inaugurated, that the Afghans were living on borrowed time.[1] I had smiled, I remember. In retrospect, I think that he could not have been more accurate.

Unless a fundamental change occurs in the Kremlin's policy, the Russians will not relinquish control of Afghanistan. They may withdraw their armed forces from that country, if an advantageous deal is offered to them in a superpower settlement or if the West and, especially, Pakistan recognize a pro-Moscow government in Kabul (though not necessarily headed by the present leadership). Obviously, the evacuation of Afghanistan by the Soviet army would represent an immediate short-term strategic gain for the West and would certainly be hailed as if the long awaited "political settlement" of the Afghan problem had at last been attained. In the euphoria of Soviet military withdrawal, the other components of the political solution would be conveniently forgotten, and the Soviets would continue to control Afghanistan through a pro-Moscow government. The USSR would insist that the pro-Moscow Afghan government is nonaligned, Islamic, and representative, and probably others, because of their own selfish interests, would acquiesce in this, with the exception of the people of Afghanistan, who, shortchanged at every step, would have to endure this farce. This situation would enable the Russians to return their armed forces to Afghanistan at any time, at the "invitation" of the Kabul government, international "guarantees" notwithstanding. The existence of such a strong possibility, or should it be said threat, would also act as a deterrent to the outside world's moral and material support for the Afghan freedom fighters, because it seems that the outside world's sole preoccupation is to keep Russian soldiers out of Afghanistan and the matter of who is governing the country is of no great importance. This kind of Soviet predominance would in fact mean the integration of Afghanistan into the Soviet system.

The Russians will not relinquish control of Afghanistan because Afghanistan is another irreversible step in the fulfillment of their manifest destiny. Their advance in Afghanistan has also considerably strengthened their position vis-à-vis their Asian arch rival, the People's Republic of China, and has certainly given them an edge over the United States in the superpower competition. Furthermore, the immediate strategic gains evolving from Afghanistan's takeover are of such magnitude that, in themselves, they militate against the Soviets' relinquishing their control of Afghanistan. One analyst familiar with the region has described in the following terms these advantages acquired by the Soviet Union:

The conquest of Afghanistan represents, in one audacious but carefully planned act of rapine, an advance of the Soviet Union's strategic power to within 500 miles of the Persian Gulf and the Straits of Hormuz. If the Soviets succeed in pacifying Afghanistan and consolidate it as a forward base, they can intimidate the entire region and can choke off the oil supply to Europe and Japan. The Western alliance will not long survive in opposition to a power that controls its essential oil supplies.[2]

When the next step will be taken by the Soviet Union in its southward move depends on when conditions will be deemed favorable by the Kremlin leadership. But it is certain that, if the West is not more vigilant, it will come sooner than expected.

It is appropriate to close these pages of Afghan history with a few words about the founder of the Afghan republic, Mohammad Daoud, and the kind of man he was.

Mohammad Daoud was, and will always remain, a controversial figure. While part of the political public had strong objections to his autocratic rule and considered him an obstacle to acceleration of the democratic process in Afghanistan, there was no dissent regarding his patriotism and his dedication to the advancement of the Afghan nation. His methods of government were not always popular, but he could never be accused of selfishness or vanity. Daoud did not tolerate waste and corruption in public life. He was tough and demanding and an indefatigable worker, who expected the same from his associates. He listened to the opinions of others but made his own decisions. Generally, once those decisions were made, they were seldom changed, although there were instances when other counsel prevailed and Daoud amended his initial decisions. He did not delegate power easily. This trait, not uncharacteristic of Afghan gentlemen of the old school, was bound to bring an excessive centralization of government affairs, inconsistent with the speed of execution that he demanded and the requirements of the modern bureaucracy he wished to establish.

With regard to individuals, Daoud rarely modified his opinions. He was devoted to his loyal friends, but nothing in the world would alter his view about someone whom, for whatever reason, he disliked. His grasp of problems was quite remarkable. He had an erudite knowledge of Afghan history. He was a compassionate man. His concern for the poor and the underprivileged was sincere. When relaxed and in a good mood, Daoud enjoyed a hearty laugh. He was not at all the grim autocrat he has often been portrayed as being. But, undeniably, he exuded an air of authority that immediately prompted the respect of his interlocutor and, in all frankness, brought about a certain degree of tension.

Years of careful scrutiny of the leftist movement in Afghanistan had made Daoud extremely skeptical of the Afghan Communists' allegiance to the country. His old-fashioned nationalism was in flagrant conflict with Communist internationalism. Although he retained ties of friendship with a few of the leftist army officers who had assisted him in his coup, he could not bring himself to accept the hard-core Communists as patriotic Afghans. He was equally intolerant of those whom he suspected of allegiance to the interests of the right.

Daoud was obsessed with discipline. He detested chaos and anarchy. He often spoke of the unpleasantness of the "constitutional period" during the monarchy, when parliamentarians had behaved in a most irresponsible manner, damaging the credibility of the system and the effectiveness of the government. There was, certainly, no place for chaos in any system that he would establish. He wished it to be understood clearly that democracy was not synonymous with anarchy. Contrary to the impression conveyed by most of Daoud's publicists, he was not opposed to a pluralistic democratic system for Afghanistan. But he believed democracy to be a sacred trust and the people its custodian; it would flourish only if the people realized its value and acted accordingly. He thought that, to attain the goal of democracy in Afghanistan, certain prerequisites had to be fulfilled. In his opinion once illiteracy was overcome and economic progress had reached a certain satisfactory level, the proper environment for the evolution of democracy would have come into being. It would then be up to the people to let democracy take root and grow.

Under the prevailing circumstances, Daoud favored a mild form of socialism for Afghanistan that would take due consideration of Afghan traditional values and a mixed economy similar to the systems adhered to by most of the developing countries. Judging from Mohammad Daoud's past performance and keeping in mind the emergence of more favorable conditions such as the betterment of the situation with Pakistan and the availability of new funds for assistance from Islamic–Arab sources, one can reasonably assume that, had he been given time, he would have firmly established Afghanistan on the road to economic and social progress.

Likewise, the orientation of Mohammad Daoud's foreign policy apparently suited the needs and aspirations of the Afghan people. Had it been allowed to develop fully, this policy would have undoubtedly firmly asserted Afghanistan's Islamic and nonaligned stance.

For Mohammad Daoud, nonalignment was one of the safeguards of Afghanistan's survival. However, his concept of nonalignment was quite different from that of the Russians. Daoud adhered strictly to the criteria laid down in Belgrade in 1962, while the Russians considered a country nonaligned if it followed the Moscow line in foreign affairs and proclaimed that the Soviet Union was the "natural ally of the nonaligned world."

Daoud was keenly aware of the crushing weight of Afghanistan's northern neighbor. Undoubtedly that was an important consideration preventing him from taking early and decisive action against the left, in spite of the aggravation caused by its anti-national and subversive activities.

Mohammad Daoud recognized that the Soviet Union had to be afforded particular considerations but, beyond those, Afghanistan's conception of independence and nonalignment could not possibly be modified to suit the Russians. Daoud too often assumed that the Soviets understood the limits of Afghanistan's acquiescence to their policies and interests. In his view, the nonalignment and the friendship of Afghanistan were to be rewarded by such an understanding. Unfortunately, they were not.

With the murder of Mohammad Daoud, an era, a whole way of life, came to an end. More than two hundred years of tightrope walking by Afghan rulers to ensure the survival of their nation ceased, as did the existence of Afghanistan as an independent entity. The role of the country of the Hindu Kush as a buffer, first between two empires, later between two ideologies and ways of life, was abruptly terminated. The result is not only the enormous suffering of the people of Afghanistan but also a more dangerous world.

Notes

1. The Salang Tunnel, inaugurated in August 1964, crosses the Hindu Kush at an altitude of 11,000 feet on the main highway from Kabul to the Soviet border and is 1.7 miles long. The tunnel and the highway, built by the Russians, considerably shorten the distance between the ports on the Amu River and the Afghan hinterland.
2. Leon B. Poullada, "The Failure of American Diplomacy in Afghanistan," *World Affairs* (Winter 1982–1983); 230.

Index